T0306084

MANAGING COMMUNITY RESETTLEMENT

Each year millions of people are displaced from their homes and lands. While international environmental and social performance standards on land access and involuntary resettlement exist, no framework supporting livelihood restoration has been developed. This book provides a framework that will help improve practice for those who are involved in resettlement projects and, crucially, improve the outcomes for the resettlement-affected households and communities.

Evidence from the implementation of public- and private-sector-led resettlement projects indicates that livelihood restoration is a persistent shortcoming, if not failure, across these projects. This book addresses this issue by re-characterising the 'livelihood restoration' objective as 'livelihood re-establishment and development' and proposes a framework for the entire resettlement process that puts livelihood considerations first. The framework enables proactive identification of the potential livelihood challenges associated with each step of the resettlement process (design, planning, execution, monitoring and evaluation), as well as the opportunities that resettlement, project development and induced economic growth create.

This book is essential reading for experts in social impact assessment, resettlement specialists, planners, administrators, non-governmental and civil society organisations and students of development studies and social policy.

Robert Gerrits is a social development specialist with 30 years of experience in applied research in rural development, the design and delivery of aid programmes and the management of social risks and impacts of large-scale private sector projects. The development of rural household livelihoods has been a central focus throughout his career.

"Managing Community Resettlement: Putting Livelihoods First is essential reading for all those involved in land access, displacement and livelihood restoration, and who are concerned with working to improve the livelihood outcomes for communities impacted by projects."

Gerry Reddy and Mike Steyn, *Steyn Reddy Associates*

"Gerrits addresses two fundamental questions associated with livelihood development: What if? Why not? He audaciously shifts the paradigm of livelihood development for people affected by project-induced displacement. Rather than merely mitigating the impact of projects, he suggests an approach to livelihood programs that is integral for community development. He conveys an approach that creates value while ensuring long-lasting benefits associated with investments in rural communities. This is a guide for social development practitioners concerned with poor development outcomes associated with regional and local projects."

Rachi Picardo, *Social Development Expert*

"Rob Gerrits has written the book as one wearing the shoes of a displaced person. He provides a deeper look into the shortcomings of resettlement livelihood and introduces a shift from 'livelihood improvement/restoration' to 're-establishment and development of livelihoods' as the key to successful mitigation of impacts and avoidance of the typical outcomes that return the displaced populations to historical marginal livelihoods or leave them even worse off. The perspective provides refreshing hope for positive outcomes for displaced people."

Susan Muchiri, *Land Resource Management Expert*

"Livelihood re-establishment and development is an elusive but necessary objective. This book offers keys to unlocking some of its mysteries. It takes livelihood re-establishment and development seriously by analysing how livelihood perspectives can and should be integrated in land access and resettlement processes, including replacement village and house design, human resource organization and monitoring and evaluation. What frontline professionals will also find valuable is the author's framing, explanation and reflection, based on years of practice."

Ivo Lourenço Jr., *Land Access and Resettlement Professional*

"Here is an insightful and instrumental book for the development stakeholders who are preoccupied by the after-project life of the affected communities that have always suffered the shortcomings of the traditional resettlement approach. In questioning the model, Robert is urging us to take the complex but unavoidable path to increasing attention and resources for achieving the ultimate development goal which is to ensure sustainability, inclusiveness, and equity in sharing the benefits expected from development investments."

Prof. Maman-Sani Issa, *Director of the African Development Bank Group's Department of Environmental and Social Safeguards and Compliance*

"*Managing Community Resettlement: Putting Livelihoods First* conceptualises livelihoods within resettlement projects through a clear set of typologies and operational recommendations for 'livelihood re-establishment and development'. Robert Gerrit's well laid out text provides a practical and accessible guide for resettlement planners, practitioners, financiers, policy makers, and academics alike."

Prof. Deanna Kemp, *The University of Queensland*

"Putting livelihoods first requires time, money, and skills. Project pressure often leads to putting livelihoods last, with land acquisition and compensation taking priority. Consequences for affected people can be disastrous. Also, rural livelihoods are complex, particularly amongst the poorest layers of the affected population, who often combine different streams of income to make ends meet. Rob Gerrits' book will provide invaluable support to practitioners and other parties involved in resettlement in understanding what to do at the successive stages of livelihood re-establishment and development (framing, planning, implementing and monitoring)."

Frederic Giovanetti, *Resettlement Consultant*

"Current standards and guidelines on development-induced displacement set out *best practice* for resettlement but generally focus on land acquisition. There is relatively little exploration of sustainable livelihood development in the context of land acquisition and resettlement. *Managing Community Resettlement: Putting Livelihoods First* recognises that successful resettlement is defined by the successful re-establishment and development of the livelihoods of the resettlement-affected people. The book combines theory and practice to offer insightful considerations on this vexing issue."

Célio Panquene, *Head of RAP Planning for EACOP*

"Improving livelihoods is a fundamental goal of many resettlement, rural development and disaster response programs - and yet there is barely consensus amongst social professionals about what a 'livelihood' is, let alone what strategies one might best employ to restore one. In *Managing Community Resettlement: Putting Livelihoods First*, Rob Gerrits provides a clear framework for defining livelihoods together with practical steps for assessing, planning, implementing and monitoring livelihood development programs. This handbook is an important resource for those of us concerned with improving the effectiveness of livelihood program strategy, design and delivery."

Robert Barclay, *Resettlement Practitioner*

MANAGING COMMUNITY RESETTLEMENT

Putting Livelihoods First

Robert Gerrits

Routledge
Taylor & Francis Group

LONDON AND NEW YORK

Designed cover image: Maxger / Getty Images

First published 2023
by Routledge
4 Park Square, Milton Park, Abingdon, Oxon OX14 4RN

and by Routledge
605 Third Avenue, New York, NY 10158

Routledge is an imprint of the Taylor & Francis Group, an informa business

British Library Cataloguing-in-Publication Data
A catalogue record for this book is available from the British Library

ISBN: 978-1-032-39723-8 (hbk)
ISBN: 978-1-032-39721-4 (pbk)
ISBN: 978-1-003-35872-5 (ebk)

DOI: 10.4324/9781003358725

Typeset in Joanna
by Deanta Global Publishing Services, Chennai, India

CONTENTS

Assessment of the Rural Environment and Natural Resource-Based
Livelihoods   73

5   The Rural Environment and Livelihoods of Rural Households   75

6   Assessment of the Rural Environment and Rural Livelihoods   87

PART III
Application of a Livelihood Model to the Resettlement Process   127

7   Applying the Sustainable Livelihood Framework to the
    Assessment, Diagnosis and Design of Land Access and
    Resettlement   129

PART IV
Re-establishment and Development of Livelihood Activities   181

8   Re-establishment and Development of Livelihood Activities   183

PART V
Monitoring and Evaluation of Livelihood Re-establishment and
Development   233

9   Monitoring and Evaluation   235

PART VI
Conclusion   259

10 Towards an Integrated View of Livelihood Re-establishment
    and Development   261

    Bibliography   273
    Appendix 1   A Critique of RAP Approaches to Restoration
                 of Livelihoods and Livelihood Activities   283
    Appendix 2   Application of the IRR Framework to
                 Resettlement Associated with the Tangguh
                 Project, Papua, Indonesia   288
    Appendix 3   Resettlement Issues by Project Footprint   295
    Appendix 4   Livelihood Re-establishment and
                 Development Issues and Approaches by Primary
                 Livelihood Systems   302
    Index   309

PREFACE

This book is the product of work experience in applied research in rural development, in emergency and development assistance-sponsored livelihood programming and in managing project social performance delivery in the private sector, including land access and resettlement.

I started writing this book in 2009 but was subsequently absorbed by other work commitments, only managing to return to this work periodically and never for long enough to finalise the manuscript. Despite the long gestation period, I remain convinced of the need for a more systematic approach to livelihood re-establishment and development to support individuals, households and communities affected by project development, involuntary displacement and resettlement. In reflecting upon 20 years of working in social performance (and resettlement) associated with large-scale project development, I note that there does not appear to have been a consistent improvement in livelihood re-establishment and development outcomes for people affected by project land access requirements and involuntary displacement.

Looking forward, various authors point to an increased scale and frequency of involuntary displacement and resettlement, citing the ongoing need for projects involving hydroelectricity (dams), agribusiness, linear infrastructure (roads, power, pipelines), and site-based industrial activity (oil and gas, mining, manufacturing [such as steel, cement]) and conservation while also recognising the increasing requirements for investment in renewable energy (either through sourcing relevant minerals or capturing wind or solar energy) and mitigating the impacts of climate change. At the same time, it is clear that there are increasing levels of scrutiny on the environmental and social impacts of projects; human rights impacts; and community engagement, participation, ownership and consent, suggesting that improved practice remains relevant.

This book aims to promote improvement in livelihood outcomes for people affected by involuntary displacement and resettlement. It brings together livelihood development theory, guidance and practice from applied research in rural development; emergency and development assistance programming; and involuntary displacement and resettlement and, in so doing, provides the reader with a broad understanding of the livelihood development field. Ultimately the book proposes that we re-think our approach to resettlement, recommending the adoption of a livelihood framework to guide all aspects of resettlement. Underlying the narrative is a strong orientation to ensuring resettlement and development.

ACKNOWLEDGEMENTS

The author wishes to acknowledge the contribution of many stakeholders to this work. Specifically I would like to thank both project and industry colleagues for their willingness to indulge my questions, discussion of ideas and review of multiple drafts. I would like to thank my family for both encouraging and accommodating a singular obsession while writing the book and for the critical discussion and review of drafts. Needless to say responsibility for content remains with the author.

LIST OF ACRONYMS

ADB	Asian Development Bank
AfDB	African Development Bank
AIIB	Asian Infrastructure Investment Bank
CAPEX	Capital Expenditure
CBO	Community-Based Organisation
DFID	Department for International Development (UK)
DIDR	Development Induced Displacement and Resettlement
EBRD	European Bank for Reconstruction and Development
EIB	European Investment Bank
ESIA	Environmental and Social Impact Assessment
FAO	Food and Agriculture Organisation
HLS	Household Livelihood System
IBRD	International Bank for Reconstruction and Development
ICMM	International Council on Mining and Metals
IADB	Inter-American Development Bank
IFC	International Finance Corporation
IPIECA	International Petroleum Industry Environmental and Conservation Association

IRR	Impoverishment Risks and Reconstruction Model
LARAP	Land Acquisition and Resettlement Action Plan
LRP	Livelihood Restoration Plan
M&E	Monitoring and Evaluation
NGO	Non-Governmental Organisation
RAP	Resettlement Action Plan
SIA	Social Impact Assessment
SLA	Sustainable Livelihoods Approach
SLF	Sustainable Livelihoods Framework
UN	United Nations
WB	World Bank

1

INTRODUCTION

In this chapter

DOI: 10.4324/9781003358725-1

Introduction

Involuntary displacement involves change and there should be no illusion nor expectation that the pre- and post-resettlement situation will be the same. One cannot: lose one's history, knowledge of, and relation to, place and sense of belonging; experience loss of access to land and natural resources together with the loss of relevance of one's knowledge and experience of in-situ natural resource use; pack one's belongings and relocate; experience disruption of social networks; and finally, re-start, with the expectation of seamless continuity. It is the responsibility of resettlement to ease this transition, to promote continuity where possible and to facilitate new beginnings where necessary. Ultimately, it is the responsibility of resettlement to ensure that those impacted by involuntary displacement and resettlement attain a positive development trajectory.

Development- or project-induced displacement[1] generally occurs where project development involves securing land access through land acquisition or by affecting the local population's access to and use of land and natural resources. Such projects typically involve involuntary displacement[2] (an impact commonly described as comprising physical displacement (relocation or loss of shelter) and/or economic displacement (comprising the loss of assets or access to assets that leads to loss of income sources or other means of livelihood)) of the affected population.

De Wet (2005) characterises resettlement as involving accelerated socio-economic change, with several change processes occurring simultaneously including: imposed spatial change; re-alignment of social relationships; a change in patterns of access to resources; incorporation into larger, more heterogeneous settlements; and involvement in wider administrative and political structures. These processes have the potential to disrupt livelihoods through:

- losses associated with pre-move restrictions on existing livelihood activities (e.g., house construction and improvement; agriculture; business)
- loss of personal, household and community history
- loss of connection to, and sense of, place/belonging (including spiritual attachment)
- disruption of traditional authority, community institutions and systems of governance

- loss of social status through loss of culturally important activities, assets, etc.
- loss of relevance of existing knowledge and expertise relevant to livelihoods and/or the need to learn, adopt and apply new knowledge and practices
- loss of or other changes (i.e., restrictions) in the population's access to, and use of, land and productive natural resources (including fisheries, forests and pastures)
- physical relocation of households and communities
- changes in housing, community infrastructure and access to services and utilities
- disruption and/or loss of social networks and relations
- increased and often unrecognised demand on resettlement-affected households, including human capacity and financial resources (e.g., new technologies in replacement housing, new livelihood activities, new natural resource management regimes). Project development often introduces inflationary pressures on food, housing and other goods and services, thus further stressing households
- loss of and/or changes in income sources and access to employment and markets
- uncertainty regarding intra- and inter-generational sustainability stemming from questions relating to how households and communities will be able to grow, particularly in relation to housing and settlements and access to land and resources within and between generations

Taken together these impacts describe the potential loss of or changes in the natural, physical, social, cultural and economic bases of existence.

Recognition of the impacts of involuntary displacement and resettlement on livelihoods has led to the inclusion of an objective to 'improve, or at least restore, the livelihoods and standards of living of displaced persons[3]' in international policies and standards for land acquisition and involuntary resettlement. Seen from the perspective of those who are displaced and whose lives are disrupted, the success in restoring and improving livelihoods might be considered to be the ultimate indicator of a successful resettlement programme. Yet, despite such recognition, the overwhelming evidence from projects involving land access, involuntary displacement and resettlement indicates that these impacts are typically not successfully mitigated, thus leading to the impoverishment of those who are displaced. As such, livelihood restoration (let alone improvement) remains an elusive goal for many resettlement programmes.[4] People rather than projects (that have secured the requisite land access) bear the consequences of this failure.

Understanding the Failure of Livelihood Restoration

Many reasons have been put forward to explain the shortcomings of resettlement livelihood restoration. Underlying many of the identified reasons is a failure to adequately conceptualise what constitutes a livelihood, the resettlement and recovery process for displaced households (Cernea in McDowell (1996)) and to apply a livelihoods framework to the entire resettlement process.

Scudder (2011) sets out a four-stage framework describing how individuals, households and communities can be expected to behave over two generations during a successful resettlement process that enables them to improve their livelihoods. The framework comprises:

Stage 1: planning for resettlement
Stage 2: coping (initial adaptation and recovery)
Stage 3: initiation of economic development and community formation
Stage 4: handover of sustainable resettlement process to the second generation of resettlers and non-project institutions

Stages 2 and 3 of the four-stage framework involve livelihood restoration. Scudder (idem) notes that most development-induced displacement fails to move beyond Stage 2, with resettlement, thus often being associated with impoverishment.

The failure to apply an understanding of the process through which displaced households are resettled and recover from displacement is associated with a failure to develop and apply a resettlement livelihoods framework that:

- informs comprehensive assessment of livelihoods
- adequately considers potential livelihood trajectories in an environment that is changing because of resettlement, project development and (its catalytic impacts on) area development

- articulates how livelihood re-establishment and development is to be achieved (as seen from the perspective of the displaced)

Levine (2014) states,

> A livelihoods approach is primarily concerned with understanding "how different people in different places live" (Scoones, 2009) and how and why people make the choices they do. As such, this approach rejects the idea that people's well-being can be based solely on a technical or financial analysis of the sectors in which people earn their living or that this would be an adequate basis for developing policy or interventions to support them.

This position stands in stark contrast to the approaches promulgated by most land acquisition and resettlement standards and associated guidance that indicate that the term livelihood refers to "the full range of means that individuals, families, and communities utilize to make a living, such as wage-based income, agriculture, fishing, foraging, other natural resource-based livelihoods, petty trade and bartering" (International Finance Corporation [IFC] PS 5 2012). Put differently, the standard's current conceptualisation of livelihoods inevitably leads one to focus on sectoral livelihood activities only.

Other reasons that help explain the shortcomings of resettlement livelihood restoration include:[5]

(i)   failure to link the resettlement-affected population and footprint with the broader context (institutions, infrastructure, markets and market linkages, etc.). Of relevance for mega-projects is the failure to understand and account for both project-induced area development and the political economy associated with project development and their potential impacts on resettlement and livelihoods.

(ii)   failure to adequately engage affected communities in all aspects of assessment, design and implementation of resettlement, especially re-establishment and development of livelihood activities. Relatedly, resettlement frameworks that involve the introduction, if not imposition, of external notions of what constitutes development and the processes to support development.

(iii) seeing strict compliance with policies, the legal framework and project plans as sufficient. Within this context, primary reference to country frameworks that primarily address resettlement as a sub-set of property and expropriation laws, i.e., focusing on facilitating access to land for development and compensation for the displaced (Cernea in McDowell [1996]).

(iv)　project finance resettlement compliance requirements and guidance that focus on land access, compensation and relocation and accept more generic livelihood restoration frameworks. A reliance on out-puts (programmes, number of people trained, number of inputs provided, pilot projects [e.g., demonstration farms]) deemed to be sufficient evidence of progress on livelihood restoration.

(v)　in the public sector, Multilateral Financial Institutions' require-ments for countries to prepare project E&S documentation (including Resettlement Action Plans [RAPs]) prior to Board's approval of pro-posed projects although recognising that many countries lack both the expertise and financial resources to implement the requisite stud-ies and develop such documents. Subsequent pressures for disburse-ment may compromise optimal E&S management.

(vi)　in the private sector, uncertainty in commitment to and implementa-tion of private sector projects may adversely impact the livelihoods of those to be displaced, as potentially affected households may exist in limbo for protracted periods of time ahead of actual resettlement. Once a commitment exists, the identification of land access, displace-ment and resettlement as capital expenditure (CAPEX), thereby link-ing, and indeed generally limiting, the programme to the project construction period. With this perspective comes the front-loading of Resettlement Action Plans to support project land access and the rela-tively short duration of livelihood programming commitments estab-lished in RAPs. Consequently livelihood development becomes tied to resettlement rather than being seen as an integral part of broader area development.

(vii)　failure to recognise the requisite skills and resources required to sup-port successful livelihood restoration programmes. In the public sec-tor, multi-agency assumption of responsibility for land access and resettlement with no specialist resettlement expertise and limitations in motivation, capacity, etc.

(viii)　a belief in the adequacy of compensation (for assets[6]) to support live-lihood restoration (i.e., compensation is enough).

(ix) assigning blame to the affected population suggesting they are not accessing and adopting the opportunities provided.

As noted, interpreting the term livelihood as 'the means of earning a living' rather than 'the means of supporting one's existence or the means of securing the basic necessities of life' has resulted in a focus on sectoral economic activities. Limited consideration of what constitutes livelihoods drives inadequate assessment, design and planning. Too often Environmental and Social Impact Assessment (ESIA) and resettlement baseline assessments fail to describe livelihoods instead providing generic descriptive analyses of settlement, demography, living conditions, access to services and livelihood activities, thus failing to (i) assess the influence of the broader environment on livelihoods and livelihood development trajectories; (ii) comprehensively describe the livelihood chain from goals/objectives, to strategies, to activities and ultimately outcomes; (iii) differentiate household livelihood strategies in designing tailored approaches to livelihood restoration; and (iv) assess the influence of project development, induced area development and the political economy on livelihoods and livelihood development trajectories.

Ultimately, the preceding leads one to conclude that the management of land access, involuntary displacement and resettlement should be approached first and foremost as a livelihood question. The primary question in assessment, design and execution should be how people affected by involuntary displacement and resettlement will re-establish and develop their livelihoods. This formulation implies it is the whole, rather than component activities (e.g., compensation, relocation, restoration of economic activities), of resettlement that constitute livelihoods and that together facilitate livelihood re-establishment and development.[7]

Potential Contributions from Humanitarian and Development Assistance Sector

Looking at other disciplinary areas, the recovery, restoration and development of livelihoods is a common theme in emergency and development assistance programming. Various terms including livelihood recovery, livelihood rehabilitation, livelihood restoration, livelihood re-establishment and development or livelihood development may be used, with different terms reflecting the nature of the disruption and the objective of the livelihood programme in the recovery–restoration (or rehabilitation)–development continuum. While specific terms have merit, it is important to recognise that they share the common objective of livelihood development and differ in the cause of displacement (natural or man-made disasters, development-induced displacement and resettlement or development assistance), the characterisation of the displaced population (refugees, internally displaced people, development-induced displacement, rural poor), the circumstances in which the target population find themselves (cross-border, national or local displacement or in-situ) and the stakeholders involved in assisting the target population. It is also useful to note that for involuntary displacement and resettlement, a livelihood programme may span the recovery–restoration–development continuum.

Livelihood Re-establishment and Development in Resettlement

For involuntary displacement and resettlement, this book recommends the use of the term 're-establishment and development (RED) of livelihoods' in preference to the more commonly used 'livelihood restoration.' Characterising the livelihood objective of resettlement in terms of 're-establishment and development of livelihoods' better reflects the reality experienced by those who are displaced. Specifically, the term 're-establishment and development' serves to emphasise that people are dealing with a new paradigm that reflects the reality of the changing circumstances associated with resettlement, project development and the broader (regional) development that project development often catalyses as well as the changing aspirations and objectives of resettlement- and project-affected people. Put differently, the term allows project development and the broader development associated with projects to be seen as relevant to both shaping resettlement objectives and achieving outcomes rather than resettlement being only seen as the consequence of project land access and displacement and the obligation to return the displaced population to a historical (probably increasingly out-dated) and often marginal livelihood baseline.

This book addresses the challenge of livelihood re-establishment and development for rural[8] households and communities who are affected by land access, involuntary displacement and resettlement. The fundamental premise of the book is that to achieve greater success in the re-establishment and development of livelihoods requires that livelihood considerations inform all aspects of the land access, involuntary displacement and resettlement process rather than being seen as one component step thereof. Hence the title, *Putting Livelihoods First*.

Finally, at the outset, it is as well to acknowledge that there is no blueprint for getting it right – the diversity of context, project and people ensures that the nature of land access, involuntary displacement and resettlement and the opportunities and challenges to achieving successful livelihood outcomes will vary in every case. Nonetheless, a more deliberate, informed, systematic and consistent application of the livelihood objective in involuntary displacement and resettlement will promote the increased recognition of these opportunities and challenges and thereby will allow improvement in livelihood outcomes.

About This Book

This book presents the theory, guidance and practice of livelihood re-establishment and development for people affected by development-induced displacement. It is informed by:

- emergency-, development assistance- and resettlement-sponsored approaches to livelihood development programming
- the on-going challenges of livelihood development within and across these approaches
- the belief that improvement in livelihood development outcomes will occur by promoting greater awareness, understanding and discourse about livelihood development generally, and in the case of resettlement, livelihood re-establishment and development

In turn it is anticipated that the preceding will inform improved assessment, design, planning, resourcing, implementation and monitoring and evaluation of livelihood development programming generally and specifically in the context of involuntary displacement and resettlement.

(i) **Scope of Project, Involuntary Displacement, Resettlement and Livelihood Impacts:** land access, involuntary displacement and resettlement requirements vary by context and project. This book has been written with reference to large-scale (private sector) projects that are transformational at a landscape level. Such projects – that are often developed in remote and marginalised areas – typically involve substantial land access requirements and thus involve significant involuntary physical and economic displacement and resettlement while also catalysing landscape-level transformation.

While a mega-project perspective informs the book, the relevance of the approach described in the book should be determined by three attributes:

- the potential of the project to transform the political–social–economic–cultural (or more simply, livelihood) context
- the scale of land access, involuntary displacement and resettlement requirements
- the significance of livelihood impacts associated with involuntary displacement

Assessment of these aspects differs for different projects and their land access requirements (e.g., linear, single or multiple large landholdings). Further, such assessment is more complex for natural resource-dependent livelihood systems involving the use of common property resources (e.g., pastoralism, fishing). Appendices 3 and 4 describe resettlement requirements by project footprint and primary livelihood systems.

(ii) **Theory, Practice and Experience:** the book brings together literature on livelihood concepts and livelihood development models; emergency and development assistance theory, guidance and practice of livelihood programming; resettlement literature addressing livelihood restoration (including standards and guidance); and experience of delivering livelihood programs in donor-sponsored aid projects as well as implementing land access and resettlement plans.[9]

(iii) **Overall Approach:** Figure 1.1 summarises the overall approach of this book. The figure demonstrates that the book attempts to position livelihood development in the broader regional and local context for livelihoods and, more generally, development. This broader context is relevant insofar that it helps frame the existing livelihood strategies and the opportunities for local economic development including commodity value chains, enterprise, workforce and supplier

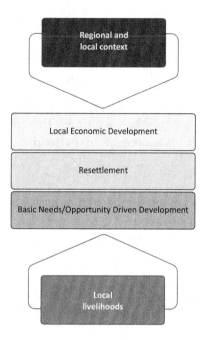

Figure 1.1 Overall Approach: Bridging Resettlement and the Local and Regional Context

development. At the same time, a bottom-up livelihood assessment, implemented with the participation of the affected population, provides the basis for understanding the existing livelihood strategies and activities, and the in-situ factors (e.g., human, social, natural, physical and financial resources and capacity) that define them.

(iv) **Emergency- and Development Assistance-Sponsored Livelihood Development Programming**: as noted, livelihood development is a common objective of emergency, development assistance and resettlement programming. Within these disciplines, there is a considerable body of literature and significant expertise and experience that has relevance to resettlement livelihood re-establishment and development. Specifically, the potential contribution of emergency- and development assistance-sponsored livelihood development programming to resettlement includes:

- a conceptual framework for livelihood development
- guidance and tools for the assessment of the rural environment and household livelihoods

- approaches to the development of livelihoods and livelihood activities
- approaches to monitoring and evaluation of the success (or failure) of livelihood development interventions

Emergency and development assistance experience in livelihood programming also demonstrates key challenges in rural development generally and livelihood development in particular. Key amongst these challenges are:

- the complexity of household and community livelihoods and the context in which they operate
- ensuring comprehensive livelihood assessment and its application in the design and implementation of component livelihood interventions
- the potential need to simultaneously address aspects of the enabling environment (i.e., access, infrastructure and services, access to finance, resource governance), basic needs, subsistence production and market-driven development
- the need for extended, continuous investment in the development of the rural environment and rural livelihoods to achieve success

That livelihood development remains challenging for emergency and development assistance programming (despite decades of work in this field) is indicative of the challenge that faces resettlement in achieving livelihood re-establishment and development in time frames aligned with project construction.

(v)   **Livelihood Models:** the book presents a number of livelihood models and applies one such model to the resettlement process. These models capture the complexity and dynamic nature of livelihoods. The purpose of presenting these models includes:

- to help improve awareness and understanding of how household and community livelihood strategies might be framed
- to promote the adoption and application of a livelihood model to the resettlement process, thereby encouraging a more deliberate, consistent and structured systems-based approach to livelihood development and livelihood outcomes

- to encourage a more integrated and holistic approach to livelihood development for resettlement- and, more generally, project-affected households

While this book advocates for the early adoption and application of a systems approach to livelihood development (as described by these models) and its application to the entire resettlement process, it does not prescribe a specific model. Rather the RAP design and implementation team is left with the task of selecting and adapting a livelihood model or indeed developing a new model to suit context and resettlement project requirements.

The Content of This Book

This book comprises six sections:

I. **Framing**

- an overview of strategic considerations for livelihood re-establishment and development in resettlement (Chapter 2)
- a summary of international standards and guidance on land access, involuntary displacement, resettlement and livelihood restoration (Chapter 3)
- the conceptual basis of livelihoods and livelihood (development) models (Chapter 4)

II. **Assessment of the Rural Environment and Natural Resource-Based Livelihoods**

- an overview of the rural environment and rural natural resource-based livelihoods (Chapter 5)
- guidance for the assessment of the rural environment and rural livelihoods (Chapter 6)

III. **Application of a Livelihood Model to the Resettlement Process**

- an example of the application of a livelihood model (namely the Sustainable Livelihoods Framework) to the entire resettlement process, including the assessment and design, planning, execution and monitoring and evaluation of resettlement (Chapter 7)

IV. **Re-establishment and Development of Livelihood Activities**

- a chapter addressing re-establishment and development of livelihood activities including the categorisation of potential interventions, good practice guidance for defining a strategy, the development and evaluation of a livelihood re-establishment and development strategy, developing scopes of work, contracting and procurement, project management, etc. (Chapter 8)

V. **Monitoring and Evaluation of Livelihood Re-establishment and Development**

- a chapter on monitoring and evaluation focused on the monitoring of livelihood re-establishment and development and evaluation of livelihood outcomes (Chapter 9)

VI. **Conclusion**
- a concluding chapter that draws together the key operational and technical recommendations stemming from the adoption and application of a livelihoods approach (Chapter 10)

The Intended Audience

By bringing together theory, practice and experience in livelihood development, the content of the book has relevance to various stakeholders including:

(i)   stakeholders involved in the design, planning and development of large-scale projects requiring involuntary displacement and resettlement to support project land access

(ii)   social development practitioners involved in the more detailed assessment, design, planning, resourcing, implementation and monitoring and evaluation of resettlement and, within this context, livelihood re-establishment and development. Given the importance of a whole-of-project life cycle perspective on livelihoods, this includes stakeholders responsible for Environmental and Social Impact Assessment (ESIA); the design, planning and development of Resettlement Action Plans (RAPs); the resettlement team responsible for the execution of resettlement plans; external expertise responsible for providing assurance, reviews and audits; and project socio-economic development functions that llok to develp livelihood programs separate from RAPs for the more broadly defined Project-Affected population.

(iii) non-government and civil society organisations that may either participate in the delivery of livelihood re-establishment and development

programmes or that may actively monitor the delivery of such programmes in resettlement
(iv) component chapters are of relevance to various stakeholders including International Financial Institutions and project management
involved in the development and management of public and private
sector projects

Beyond resettlement, the book has relevance to promoting the private sector project's contribution to livelihood development in the broader project
area of influence and to emergency- and development assistance-sponsored
livelihood programmes.

How to Use This Book

The book is written to allow reference to individual sections and chapters
or to be read as a whole. Where relevant and appropriate the contents of the
chapters are elucidated with case studies and tools.

Notes

1 Also described as development-forced displacement.
2 IFC PS 5 (2012) Resettlement is considered involuntary when affected persons or communities do not have the right to refuse land acquisition or
restrictions on land use that result in physical or economic displacement.
3 IFC Performance Standard 5.
4 Appendix 1 presents a critique of RAP approaches to livelihood restoration
and restoration of livelihood activities.
5 This list includes fallacies identified by Downing and Garcia-Downing, in
Oliver-Smith (2009).
6 In addition to compensation for lost assets (i.e., physical and natural capital)
other potential bases for compensation include the costs of arrested development, protracted transition costs and lost income, often associated with
longer than planned relocation, failure to recognise that re-establishment
and development of livelihood activities occurs over multiple years/seasons,
etc.
7 There is some basis for arguing that current standards and guidance focus
on the management of the land access process (i.e., the mechanics of land
access, compensation and relocation) rather than the mitigation of the

(livelihood) impacts of involuntary displacement. This might be addressed with new nomenclature – for example, *land and resource access, involuntary displacement and livelihood re-establishment and development* or more simply *involuntary displacement and livelihood re-establishment and development* – and standards and guidance that better reflect the affected population's anticipated recovery process and requirements for impact mitigation. Refer to Box 3.1 'What's in a Name? The Name of the Standard and Guidance.'

8 This book focuses on the rural environment and rural livelihoods and does not address the urban environment and urban livelihoods. While the systems approach advocated in this book is applicable to displacement and resettlement in urban contexts, the nature of the urban environment, urban populations and urban livelihoods is significantly different from the natural resource-dependent livelihoods of rural populations and warrants separate consideration.

9 The author has worked directly on large-scale resettlement projects associated with the extractive industry and on projects involving smaller-scale involuntary displacement while working with IFC.

Bibliography

Bebbington, A., and Humphreys Bebbington, D. (2018). Mining, Movements and Sustainable Development: Concepts for a Framework. *Sustainable Development*, 26(5), 441–449. https://doi.org/10.1002/sd.1888.

Bennett, O., and McDowell, C. (2012). *Displaced: The Human Cost of Development and Resettlement. Studies in Oral History.* Palgrave MacMillan, New York.

Cernea, M. M. and Guggenheim, S.E. (1993). *Anthropological Approaches to Resettlement: Policy, Practice and Theory.* Routledge, New York.

Cernea, M. M., and Maldonaldo, J. K. (2018). *Challenging the Prevailing Paradigm of Displacement and Resettlement: Risks, Impoverishment, Legacies, Solutions.* Routledge, London.

Cernea, M. M., and Mathur, H. M. (2008). *Can Compensation Prevent Impoverishment? Reforming Resettlement through Investments and Benefit Sharing.* Oxford University Press, New Delhi.

Cernea, M. M., and McDowell, C. (2000). *Risks and Reconstruction, Experiences of Resettlers and Refugees.* International Bank for Reconstruction and Development/World Bank, Washington, DC.

De Wet, C. (2005). *Development-Induced Displacement: Problems, Policies and People* (Studies in Forced Migration, Vol. 18). 1st edition. Berghahn Books, New York & Oxford.

IFC (2012). *Performance Standard 5 Land Acquisition and Involuntary Resettlement, IFC Environmental and Social Sustainability Policy.* International Finance Corporation, Washington, DC.

Intersocial Consulting (2013). *Land Acquisition and Resettlement Benchmarking Report.* Intersocial Consulting, Mauritius.

Levine, S. (2014). How to Study Livelihoods: Bringing a Sustainable Livelihoods Framework to Life. Working Paper No 22 Secure Livelihoods Research Consortium Overseas Development Institute, London.

Lillywhite, S., Kemp, D., and Sturman, K. (2015). *Mining, Resettlement and Lost Livelihoods: Listening to the Voices of Resettled Communities in Mualadzi, Mozambique.* Oxfam, Melbourne.

McDowell, C. (1996). *Understanding Impoverishment: The Consequences of Development-Induced Development* (Refugee and Forced Migration Studies, Vol. 2). 1st edition, Berghahn Books. Providence & Oxford.

Nakayama, M., and Fujikura, R. (2014). *Restoring Communities Resettled After Dam Construction in Asia.* Routledge, Abingdon, Oxfordshire/New York.

Oliver-Smith, A. (2009). *Development and Dispossession, the Crisis of Forced Displacement and Resettlement.* School for Advanced Research Press, Santa Fe, New Mexico.

Partridge, W. L., and Halmo, D. B. (2021). *Resettling Displaced Communities: Applying the International Standard for Involuntary Resettlement.* Lexington Books, MD, Lanham, Maryland/London.

Price, S. (2017). Chapter 17, Livelihoods in Development Displacement – A Reality Check from the Evaluation Record in Asia. In van den Berg, R., Naidoo, I., and Tamondong, S. D. (Eds.), *Evaluation for Agenda 2030, Providing Evidence on Progress and Sustainability.* International Development Evaluation Association (IDEAS), 273–289, Exeter/UK.

Reddy, G., Smyth, E., and Steyn, M. (2015). *Land Access and Resettlement, A Guide to Best Practice.* Greenleaf Publishing, Stafford/UK.

Satiroglu, I., and Choi, N. (2017). Development-Induced Displacement and Resettlement. In *New Perspectives on Persisting Problems.* Routledge, Abingdon/Oxfordshire and New York.

Scoones, I. (2009). Livelihoods perspectives and rural development. *Journal of Peasant Studies*, 36 (1). www.essentialcellbiology.com/journals/pdf/papers/FJPS_36_1_2009.pdf

Scudder, T. (2011). Development-Induced Community Resettlement. In Vanclay, F., and Esteves, A. M. (Eds.), *New Directions in Social Impact Assessment,*

Conceptual and Methodological Advances. Edward Elgar, Northampton, Massachusetts and Cheltenham, 186–201.

Smyth, E., Steyn, M., Esteves, A., Franks, D. M., and Vaz, K. (2015). Five 'Big' Issues for Land Access, Resettlement and Livelihood Restoration Practice: Findings of an International Symposium. *Impact Assessment and Project Appraisal*, 33(3), 220–225. https://doi.org/10.1080/14615517.2015.1037665.

Sonneburg, D., and Munster, F. (2001). *Involuntary Resettlement, Research Topic 3: Mining and Society. Mining Minerals Sustainable Development Southern Africa*. African Institute of Corporate Citizenship, South Africa.

UNHCR (2011). *UNHCR Resettlement Handbook*. UNHCR, Switzerland.

Vanclay, F. (2017). Project Induced Displacement and Resettlement: From Impoverishment Risks to an Opportunity for Development? *Impact Assessment and Project Appraisal*, 35(1), 2–21. http://doi.org/10.1080/14615517.2017.1278671.

Part I

FRAMING

2

STRATEGIC CONSIDERATIONS FRAMING RESETTLEMENT AND LIVELIHOOD RE-ESTABLISHMENT AND DEVELOPMENT

Introduction

Most of this book is technical in nature and focuses on the deliberate adoption and application of a livelihood model to the assessment, design, planning, resourcing and execution of land access, involuntary displacement and resettlement. Yet it is important to recognise and, where possible, address the reality that improved livelihood outcomes are not necessarily only dependent on improvements in project-level practice. This chapter

DOI: 10.4324/9781003358725-3

provides an overview of strategic considerations that frame the ease of achieving livelihood re-establishment and development (i.e., by creating enabling conditions) and in this way may require early recognition and intervention by the project.

Strategic Considerations: Enabling Conditions for Resettlement and Livelihood Re-establishment and Development

Eight enabling conditions that frame the ease of achieving livelihood re-establishment and development have been identified.

- Project Development and the Evolving Political Economy
- Linking Resettlement and Area Development
- Adopting a 'Resettlement with Development' Paradigm
- Adopting a Development vs Compliance Paradigm
- De-linking Resettlement Livelihood Commitments from the Project Cycle
- Continuous Resettlement and Livelihood Specialist Participation
- Assessment of Livelihood Needs and Opportunities
- Adequacy of Livelihood Specialist Resourcing During RAP Implementation

(1) **Project Development and the Evolving Political Economy**: project development has the potential to catalyse broad-based local and regional development. Various actors – including the State and private sector investors – are empowered, in various ways, to establish a framework for benefit capture early in the project development cycle (especially in relation to land) and thereby impact upon resettlement, the project and local and regional development and, ultimately, benefit distribution and capture. Specifically, the political economy associated with projects, land and people has the potential to define key aspects of resettlement including site selection, the design of replacement settlements and housing, and the availability and location of replacement land.

In this way the early steps of a resettlement process can be seen to be subject (if not vulnerable) to such processes, thereby influencing the basis (or lack thereof) for successful resettlement. Further, derivative (state-supported) development – for example, land allocation to support industrialisation – may occur, leading to a more significant cumulative impact on the natural resource base and the ability of the population to sustain themselves through natural resource-based livelihood activities alone. More generally the political economy may also lead to changes in the allocation of state resources to host communities (including resettlement-affected villages) often with the implicit assumption that these communities' needs are being addressed by the project.

To safeguard the resettlement-affected population and promote the sustainability of livelihoods post-resettlement, there is a need to incorporate the consideration of:

- how project development will catalyse on-going local and regional development
- the political economy of development and specifically how State and private sector investors influence development and benefit capture and distribution
- the role of the project in requiring enabling conditions for resettlement and livelihood development. For example, for private sector project proponents, requiring a government-sponsored local and regional development plan that serves as a counterpart to the project plan of development may be useful
- anticipated on-going area development (including industrialisation) and the need to prepare the resettlement-affected population to secure their livelihoods in an environment defined by the reasonably anticipated cumulative impacts of development

While stakeholder engagement and inclusive, participatory processes are necessary for successful resettlement, these are only useful where stakeholders and the project-affected population have a common awareness and understanding of the nature and scale of the project – and induced – development; are empowered to speak; and where the opinions, preferences and livelihoods of project-affected people will be meaningfully considered and factored into project and resettlement design. These elements entail aspects of respect, ownership, empowerment and inclusion throughout resettlement assessment, planning, design and implementation.

(2) **Linking Resettlement and Area Development:** the resettlement-affected population is a subset of the broader project-affected population, defined by the project's requirement for land, its impacts on availability, access to and use of common property resources or the need for the project to mitigate project impacts on health and safety that make continued in situ residence and use of land and resources impossible. Achieving development outcomes for the resettlement-affected population requires recognition that:

(i)   project development may lead to broader-based social–cultural–economic change

(ii)   the displaced population will be required to adapt to the impacts of displacement as well as the accelerated change brought about by project development

(iii) the project should consider the relationship between resettlement and area development

(iv)   with reference to the RAP, interventions that fall outside or beyond the resettlement footprint and resettlement-affected population may be required (refer (3) below)

(3) **Adopting a 'Resettlement with Development' Paradigm:** this book advocates for the adoption of a 'resettlement with development' paradigm where resettlement is both seen and used as an opportunity to promote broader-based development. Such development outcomes may be achieved through various means. Examples include – the development of commodity value chains; facilitating the entry and operation of entrepreneurs and promotion of market linkages; construction and operation of specific infrastructure, e.g., agricultural training centres, vocational training centres; agriculture/livestock/fisheries input supply infrastructure and services (e.g., veterinary services, ice making and cold storage facilities) to support the broader population, including the resettlement-affected population; development of appropriate modular low-cost housing that is accessible to, affordable and in this way replicable, across the broader population, etc. When framed as 'resettlement with development,' resettlement can be used as the basis for contributing to broader socio-economic development beyond the resettlement footprint and resettlement-affected population, thereby helping mitigate against the delivery of

disproportionate front-end benefits to the resettlement-affected communities (relative to the rest of the project-affected population).

(4) **Adopting a Development vs Compliance Paradigm:** the plethora of project finance E&S policies, standards and guidance demonstrates recognition of the risk that project-induced involuntary displacement and resettlement poses to projects and people. The standards and guidance tend to frame resettlement from the (project) land access and relocation perspective rather than a livelihood development perspective. In this way displacement and resettlement is seen as a derivative project necessary to allow a project to progress. Consequently, often the resettlement-affected population and footprint are treated as being unique and separate from the broader environment in which they live. Further the reference point for restoration is usually a pre-project (and increasingly outdated) baseline.

Progressive development of the standards and associated guidance has unquestionably contributed to improvement in resettlement practice (particularly in areas of land acquisition, compensation, recognition of impacts on availability, access to and use of common property resources, stakeholder engagement and grievance management). However, the standards and guidance continue to be less developed in other aspects of resettlement including the design of public infrastructure, services and utilities; the design of replacement housing; the handover of new settlements and public infrastructure, services and utilities to government; and re-establishment and development of livelihood activities, including defining standards for acceptable outcomes. Current practice in these areas suggests that effort rather than outcome is sufficient for compliance purposes.

Finally, the MFI E&S standards and guidance have encouraged the development of a compliance paradigm (compared with a development paradigm) focused on securing project finance. Standards should be seen as a necessary but insufficient condition for achieving development outcomes.

(5) **De-linking Resettlement Livelihood Commitments from the Project Cycle:** development-assistance livelihood programming demonstrates that longer implementation periods are required to deliver livelihood development. Accordingly, projects should commit to and

plan for longer livelihood re-establishment and development cycles, separating the mechanics of land access, displacement and relocation from the challenge of livelihood re-establishment and development. This outcome can be achieved by establishing mechanisms to de-link resettlement livelihood development from the project construction phase capital expenditure and creating functional structures that facilitate continuity (e.g., establishing a stand-alone area livelihood development function that supports resettlement and area development; early and deliberate decisions regarding the transition from resettlement livelihood re-establishment and development to area socio-economic development programs).

Further, innovative alternative approaches to benefit distribution that look to provide longer-term benefit streams to resettlement-affected people are being debated and indeed implemented. These approaches serve to support on-going area development; ensure that community, household and/or individuals receive direct benefits from project operations/activity; and/or provide safety nets for the most vulnerable individuals and households for extended periods.

(6) **Continuous Resettlement and Livelihood Specialist Participation:** there is a need to ensure early and continuous participation and influence of resettlement and livelihood specialists in all aspects of, and throughout, the entire resettlement process. Such participation and influence will ensure resettlement and livelihood considerations receive both timely and due representation and consideration within the project as well as with key external stakeholders (e.g., government). The later their involvement, the more likely that greater effort and resources will be required to execute resettlement and/or mitigate the impacts of sub-optimal early decisions rather than being devoted to improving resettlement and livelihood outcomes.

(7) **Assessment of Livelihood Needs and Opportunities**: assessment of the impacts of displacement and identification of livelihood re-establishment and development pathways relies on an early and comprehensive livelihood assessment in the project area of influence (at both the local and regional levels) and of the resettlement-affected population combined with an understanding of the anticipated development trajectories of the area where the project is being developed.

Experience demonstrates that assessment and analysis of livelihoods may be perfunctory and high level, often failing to:

(i)   comprehensively describe the livelihood chain from goals/objectives, to strategies, to activities and ultimately outcomes

(ii)   assess the influence of the political economy on livelihoods and livelihood development trajectories

(iii)   assess the needs and opportunities presented by the project and induced area development and the ability of the local population to provide for these needs and/or respond to opportunities

(iv)   differentiate between household livelihood strategies in designing tailored approaches to livelihood re-establishment and development. Often outsiders express the opinion that rural households' (subsistence) livelihood activities are under-developed, if not backward, and thus the potential for improvement is taken as a given with outsider views of preferred (sustainable) livelihood development pathways defining interventions. The lack of consultation with, and involvement of, the affected population and the failure to analyse why specific livelihood strategies have been adopted, what it is that needs to be improved, possible opportunities for livelihood development and the challenges of pursuing livelihood development are notable.

(v)   acknowledge that livelihood development may require broader-based change – for example, for market-driven livelihood opportunities, there may be a requirement for new infrastructure, the introduction of commodity value chains and new market actors as well as ensuring that potential primary production justifies market entry. Similarly, resettlement plans often only allude to potential project-related employment and provision of goods and services without adequate assessment of project needs and internal processes, local capacity to meet demand, and the type and duration of training required to meaningfully close identified gaps.

(8)   **Adequacy of Livelihood Specialist Resourcing During RAP Implementation:** to support livelihood re-establishment and development, resettlement projects need to engage livelihood development expertise on a timely and continuous basis. Experience indicates that resettlement projects tend to recruit technical sectoral specialists (e.g., agronomists, livestock experts, fisheries experts, micro- and small-business development, technical and vocational training) rather than

livelihood development expertise. Technical sectoral specialists often fail to consider livelihoods in their entirety and can be seen to:

(i)   fail to develop a holistic framework and roadmap through which livelihoods will be re-established and developed

(ii) focus on their technical area of expertise (without due consideration of other sectors)

(iii) place less emphasis on assessment, design and outcome of programmes and greater emphasis on programme management

Conclusion

The existence and/or creation of an enabling environment for resettlement and livelihood re-establishment and development requires an understanding of the political economy of resettlement, project construction and operations and induced development that may be associated with the project. In this way it will be recognised that key aspects of resettlement may be unduly influenced by the political economy, potentially raising concerns regarding the existence and nature of the enabling environment and how this affects the feasibility and, ultimately the sustainability, of resettlement.

Beyond the political economy, the approach to resettlement – specifically, if resettlement is framed as a development opportunity; the focus on compliance- vs development-driven practice; the timely engagement and empowerment of appropriate resettlement and livelihood re-establishment and development expertise – will determine if resettlement is managed as an exercise primarily concerned with securing project land access or one that seeks to manage the impacts of involuntary displacement on the displaced population.

Bibliography

Bennett, O., and McDowell, C. (2012). *Displaced: The Human Cost of Development and Resettlement. Studies in Oral History.* Palgrave MacMillan, New York.

De Wet, C. (2005). *Development-Induced Displacement: Problems, Policies and People* (Studies in Forced Migration, Vol. 18). 1st edition, Berghahn Books, New York and Oxford.

McDowell, C. (1996). *Understanding Impoverishment: The Consequences of Development-Induced Development* (Refugee and Forced Migration Studies, Vol. 2). 1st edition, Berghahn Books, Providence and Oxford.

Oliver-Smith, A. (2009). *Development and Dispossession, the Crisis of Forced Displacement and Resettlement*. School for Advanced Research Press, Santa Fe, New Mexico.

Price, S. (2017). Chapter 17, Livelihoods in Development Displacement – A Reality Check from the Evaluation Record in Asia. In van den Berg, R., Naidoo, I., and Tamondong, S. D. (Eds.), *Evaluation for Agenda 2030, Providing Evidence on Progress and Sustainability*. International Development Evaluation Association (IDEAS), Exeter/UK, 273–289.

3

LIVELIHOOD DEVELOPMENT IN RESETTLEMENT: THE REQUIREMENTS OF INTERNATIONAL STANDARDS AND GUIDANCE FOR LAND ACQUISITION, INVOLUNTARY DISPLACEMENT AND RESETTLEMENT

In this chapter

DOI: 10.4324/9781003358725-4

Introduction

International environmental and social (sustainability) policies, standards and guidance that define requirements (and to some extent aspirations) for project environmental and social performance have been established and applied by various actors including:

- Multilateral Financial Institutions (MFIs) including The International Bank for Reconstruction and Development (IBRD)/World Bank Group (more commonly referred to as the World Bank [WB]); International Finance Corporation (IFC)/World Bank Group; Asian Development Bank (ADB); Asian Infrastructure and Investment Bank (AIIB); African Development Bank (AfDB); European Bank for Reconstruction and Development (EBRD); European Investment Bank (EIB); and the Inter-American Development Bank (IADB). These MFIs (with the exception of IBRD and IFC) provide finance for both public sector- and private sector-led projects.
- the Equator Principles: the Equator Principles represent a risk management framework (based on the IFC E&S risk management framework) adopted by financial institutions, for identifying, assessing and managing project environmental and social risk in relation to the provision of project finance.
- industry bodies including the extractive industry, agricultural commodities.
- private sector entities with significant environmental and social impacts. For example, mining companies such as Anglo American and Rio Tinto.

Overview of Standards and Guidance for Land Acquisition, Involuntary Displacement and Resettlement

Typically, the set of environmental and social standards include a standard (and accompanying guidance notes) addressing land acquisition, involuntary displacement and resettlement (Table 3.1). The continuous evolution, revision and efforts to ensure harmonisation of the standards by each institution ensures that there is a considerable commonality in the objectives

Table 3.1 International MFI and Industry Bodies Standards and Guidance on Land Acquisition, Involuntary Displacement and Resettlement

No.	Institution	Standard	Land Access, Involuntary Displacement and Resettlement	Guidance Note	Good Practice Guidance
1	European Bank for Reconstruction and Development (EBRD)	Environmental and Social Policy (2014)	Performance Requirement 5, Land Acquisition, Involuntary Resettlement and Economic Displacement (2014)		EBRD (2017) Resettlement Guidance and Good Practice
2	European Investment Bank (EIB)	Environmental and Social Standards (2022)	6. Involuntary Resettlement		EIB Environmental and Social Handbook (2013)
3	World Bank, International Bank for Reconstruction and Development (IBRD)	Environmental and Social Framework (2017)	ESS5 Land Acquisition, Restrictions on Land Use, and involuntary Resettlement	ESS5 Guidance Note Land Acquisition, Restrictions on Land Use, and involuntary Resettlement	IBRD/World Bank (2004) Involuntary Resettlement Sourcebook, Planning and Implementation in Development Projects. The World Bank, Washington DC, USA Inspection Panel/World Bank Group (2019) Involuntary Resettlement Emerging Lessons Series No. 1. The World Bank, Washington DC, USA

Table 3.1 (Continued)

No.	Institution	Standard	Land Access, Involuntary Displacement and Resettlement	Guidance Note	Good Practice Guidance
4	International Finance Corporation (IFC)	Environmental and Social Sustainability Policy (2012)	PS 5 Land Acquisition and Involuntary Resettlement (2012)	Guidance Note 5 Land Acquisition and Involuntary Resettlement (2012)	IFC (2002) Handbook for Developing a Resettlement Action Plan. The World Bank, Washington DC, USA
5	Asian Development Bank (ADB)	Safeguard Policy Statement (2010)	Safeguard Requirements 2: Involuntary Resettlement		ADB (1998) A Handbook on Resettlement, A Guide to Good Practice ADB (2003) Gender Checklist Resettlement ADB (2012) Involuntary Resettlement Safeguards, A Planning, and Implementation Good Practice Sourcebook (Draft Working Document)
6	Asian Infrastructure Investment Bank (AIIB)	Environmental and Social Framework (2021)	ESS 2: Land Acquisition and Involuntary Resettlement		
8	African Development Bank (AfDB)	Integrated Safeguards System – Policy Statement and Operational Safeguards (2013)	Involuntary Resettlement Policy	Operational Safeguard 2 – Involuntary resettlement: land acquisition, population displacement and compensation	African Development Bank Group (2015) The African Development Bank's involuntary resettlement policy: Review of implementation, Cote D'Ivoire

(Continued)

Table 3.1 (Continued)

No.	Institution	Standard	Land Access, Involuntary Displacement and Resettlement	Guidance Note	Good Practice Guidance
9	Inter-American Development Bank (IADB)	Environmental and Social Policy Framework (ESPF) (2021)	Land Acquisition and Involuntary Resettlement (ESPF 5)	Guidelines For Environmental and Social Performance Standard 5: Land Acquisition and Involuntary Resettlement 2021	Private Sector Department, Guidelines for Resettlement Plans IDB (2019) Involuntary Resettlement in IDB Projects. Principles and Guidelines
10	Equator Principles	Equator Principles EP4 (2020)	IFC PS 5 Land Acquisition and Involuntary Resettlement (2012)	IFC Guidance Note PS 5 Land Acquisition and Involuntary Resettlement (2012)	IFC (2002) Handbook for Developing a Resettlement Action Plan
11	International Council on Mining and Metals (ICMM)	Mining Principles	NA	NA	ICMM (2015) Land Acquisition and Resettlement: Lessons Learned

and requirements of the land acquisition, involuntary displacement and resettlement standards and guidance across institutions.

For example, the objectives of IFC 2012 Performance Standard 5 Land Acquisition and Involuntary Resettlement standard are:

- To avoid, and when avoidance is not possible, minimize displacement by exploring alternative project designs
- To avoid forced eviction
- To anticipate and avoid, or where avoidance is not possible, minimize adverse social and economic impacts from land acquisition or restrictions on land use by: (i) providing compensation for loss of assets at replacement cost and (ii) ensuring that resettlement activities are implemented with appropriate disclosure of information, consultation, and the informed participation of those affected
- To improve, or at least restore, the livelihoods and standards of living of displaced persons
- To improve living conditions among physically displaced persons through the provision of adequate housing with security of tenure at resettlement sites

(IFC Performance Standard 5 Land Acquisition and
Involuntary Resettlement 2012)

Projects requiring land acquisition may involve both physical and economic displacement[1] or only economic displacement. In the case of the former, projects are required to develop a Resettlement Action Plan (RAP), while in the case of the latter, a Livelihood Restoration Plan (LRP) is required. Both the standard and the associated guidance elucidates the meaning and application of these requirements in different contexts.

The IFC Performance Standard 5 Land Acquisition and Involuntary Resettlement articulates the principle of improving or, at the minimum, restoring livelihoods and standards of living to pre-displacement levels. PS 5 Footnote 1 states that the term livelihood refers to "the full range of means that individuals, families, and communities utilize to make a living, such as wage-based income, agriculture, fishing, foraging, other natural resource-based livelihoods, petty trade and bartering," reflecting an all-too-common focus on viewing livelihoods in terms of only economic activities. In contrast the AfDB (2013) indicates that the term livelihood refers to the full range of economic, social and cultural capabilities, assets and other means that individuals, families and communities use to satisfy their needs, while the EIB (2022) indicates that the term livelihood refers to the full range of means that individuals, families and communities utilise to secure their living conditions, such as housing, food, clothing and others.

Both the standards and guidance use several different terms – which are aggregate measures of livelihood restoration including productivity (of primary production for natural resource-based activities or of labour), income-earning capacity and standards of living – to define the objective of livelihood restoration.

In addition to standards and guidance notes, most MFIs have also developed documents providing reviews of implementation experience, best practices, challenges, etc.

Finally various international bodies have defined positions, policies, standards and guidelines that include specific requirements regarding project development, land access, resettlement and livelihoods. Table 3.2 provides a summary of some of these documents.

BOX 3.1 WHAT'S IN A NAME? THE NAME OF THE STANDARDS AND GUIDANCE

The majority of institutional standards and guidance are framed in terms of land acquisition and involuntary resettlement. Increasingly the content of the standards and guidance recognises that project land access may involve land and/or common property resources (e.g., forest, grazing lands, lacustrine, riverine and marine shoreline, nearshore and offshore resources). While the broader formulation of land access is welcome, the name of the standards and guidance continues to place emphasis on land acquisition and the process of securing land access (i.e., eligibility, compensation, relocation) rather than mitigating the impacts of involuntary displacement.

Based on the above, and in acknowledgement of the evolution of the content of the standards and guidance, consideration should be given to re-naming the standards and guidance, evolving from the current notional emphasis on *land acquisition* to a more broadly framed *land (and resource) access and involuntary displacement*. Further, as the current

Table 3.2 Institutional E&S Standards and Guidance Addressing Aspects of Land Acquisition, Involuntary Displacement and Resettlement

No.	Institution	Agency	Document
1	United Nations	UN	Declaration on the Rights of Indigenous People (UNDRIP) (2005)
		OCHA	Guiding Principles on Internal Displacement (2004)
		OHCHR	UN Basic Principles and Guidelines on Development-based Displacement and Evictions. http://www.ohchr.org/Documents/Issues/Housing/Guidelines_en.pdf
		OHCHR	Basic Principles and Guidelines on Development-Based Evictions and Displacement/Anr ex 1 of the report of the Special Rapporteur on adequate housing as a component of the right to an adequate standard of living
		UN/HRC	Guidelines for the Implementation of the Right to Adequate Housing. Report of the Special Rapporteur on adequate housing as a component of the right to an adequate standard of living, and on the right to non-discrimination in this context (2020)
		OHCHR and UN-Habitat	The Right to Adequate Housing Fact Sheet No. 21 (rev 1)
		OHCHR and UN-Habitat (2005)	Indigenous peoples' right to adequate housing, A global overview. United Nations Housing Rights Programme Report No. 7
		OHCHR	Guiding Principles on Business and Human Rights (2011)
		FAO	Environmental and Social Management Guidelines (2015). ESS 6 Involuntary Resettlement and Displacement
2	OECD		OECD Guidelines for Multinational Enterprises (2011)
3	African Union		African Union Convention for The Protection and Assistance of Internally Displaced Persons in Africa (Kampala Convention) (2009)

standards and guidance focus on the management of the land acquisition, compensation and relocation process rather than on the mitigation of the impacts of involuntary displacement, consideration should
be given to adding the requirement for livelihood re-establishment and
development to the name, for example, *land (and resource) access, involuntary displacement and livelihood re-establishment and development.*
Ultimately it may be possible to exclude reference to the question of land
and resource access entirely and focus solely on impacts – for example,
*involuntary displacement, resettlement and livelihood re-establishment and
development* – thus reflecting the reality that there may be many drivers
of involuntary displacement and resettlement.

   To complement the focus on impacts associated with securing
project land and resource access, the standards and guidance should
better reflect the affected population's anticipated recovery and development process and requirements for livelihood re-establishment and
development.

Guidance for Livelihood Restoration

As noted, most MFIs elucidate the standard for land acquisition, involuntary
displacement and resettlement by providing accompanying guidance notes.
Many have also produced separate documents reviewing implementation
experience (Table 3.1). The majority of guidance is reflective and general in
nature with IFC providing the most detailed guidance on livelihood restoration. As noted in the previous section, generally livelihood restoration is
characterised in terms of livelihood activities only.

   With reference to IFC PS 5, while most of the guidance on livelihood
restoration and improvement is set out in the PS 5 Guidance Note (rather
than the standard), IFC PS 5 Para 28 states that:

   In addition to compensation for lost assets, if any, as required under
   paragraph 27, economically displaced persons whose livelihoods or
   income levels are adversely affected will also be provided opportunities to improve, or at least restore, their means of income-earning
   capacity, production levels, and standards of living:

- For persons whose livelihoods are land-based, replacement land that has a combination of productive potential, locational advantages, and other factors at least equivalent to that being lost should be offered as a matter of priority.
- For persons whose livelihoods are natural resource-based and where project-related restrictions on access envisaged in paragraph 5 apply, implementation of measures will be made to either allow continued access to affected resources or provide access to alternative resources with equivalent livelihood-earning potential and accessibility. Where appropriate, benefits and compensation associated with natural resource usage may be collective in nature rather than directly oriented towards individuals or households.
- If circumstances prevent the client from providing land or similar resources as described above, alternative income earning opportunities may be provided, such as credit facilities, training, cash, or employment opportunities. Cash compensation alone, however, is frequently insufficient to restore livelihoods.

IFC GN5 Para 12 provides summary recommendations for the design of measures to improve and or restore livelihoods that are land based, wage based and enterprise based as follows:

- **Land-based livelihoods:** Depending on the type of economic displacement and/or the site to which affected women and men are relocated, they may benefit from: (i) assistance in acquiring or accessing replacement land, including access to grazing land, fallow land, forest, fuel and water resources; (ii) physical preparation of farm land (e.g., clearing, levelling, access routes and soil stabilization); (iii) fencing for pasture or cropland; (iv) agricultural inputs (e.g., seeds, seedlings, fertilizer, irrigation); (v) veterinary care; (vi) small-scale credit, including rice banks, cattle banks and cash loans; and (vii) access to markets (e.g., through transportation means and improved access to information about market opportunities).
- **Wage-based livelihoods:** Wage earners in the affected households and communities may benefit from skills training and job placement, provisions made in contracts with project sub-contractors for temporary or longer-term employment of local workers, and small-scale credit to finance start-up enterprises. Wage

earners whose income is interrupted during physical displacement should receive a resettlement allowance that covers these and other hidden costs. Affected women and men should be given equal opportunities to benefit from such provisions. The location of resettlement housing, in the case of physically displaced persons, can be a significant contributing factor toward socio-economic stability. Careful consideration must be given to the ability of wage earners to continue to access their place(s) of work during and after resettlement; if this ability is impaired then mitigation measures need to be implemented to ensure continuity and avoid a net loss in welfare for affected households and communities.

- **Enterprise-based livelihoods:** Established and start-up entrepreneurs and artisans may benefit from credit or training (e.g., business planning, marketing, inventory, and quality control) to expand their business and generate local employment. Clients can promote local enterprise by procuring goods and services for their projects from local suppliers.

Table 3.3 provides a summary of the more detailed IFC guidance for mitigation of economic displacement by assets or type of livelihood activity (i.e., means of achieving livelihood).

While useful, there are limitations to the guidance. Most importantly the guidance is framed by individual and household assets and economic activities rather than presenting an integrated household and community livelihood framework that recognises the reality of diversified livelihoods within which sectoral activities may be implemented. Put differently – and as further described in Chapters 5 and 6 – typically a rural household will practice diversified livelihoods that may include:

- various forms of agriculture (house gardening, short fallow crop cultivation, shifting cultivation, commercial vegetable production, annual cropping, cultivation of perennial cash crops, etc.)
- livestock production
- various forms of collection of aquatic produce and fishing
- collection of resources from common property resources (including food plants, medicinal plants, fuelwood, timber, grazing or forage harvesting, etc.) for both subsistence and sale

Table 3.3 Mitigation of Economic Displacement by Livelihood Assets and Activities, IFC Guidance Note 5 Land Acquisition and Involuntary Resettlement (2012)

No.	Means of Achieving Livelihood	Assessment	IFC Recommended Mitigation/Compensation
1	Land	Households with recognised land rights	Replacement land that has a combination of productive potential, locational advantages, and other factors at least equivalent to that being lost.
		Households without recognised land rights	GN65. In cases where project-related land acquisition results in loss of livelihoods or income of those without any legal title or legally recognized or recognizable claim to land, they are normally entitled to a range of assistance, including compensation for lost assets and any structures on land, as well as targeted assistance and transitional support. The nature and extent of such assistance will in part depend on whether the livelihood of those affected is land-based, wage-based, or enterprise-based. Land-based compensation in these circumstances does not necessarily mean title to land but may include continued access to land under similar tenure arrangements to enable the affected people to maintain their land-based livelihoods. It will be necessary to tailor compensation and entitlement options to the needs of the displaced.
2	Access to resources	Households and communities utilising common property resources	GN60. In addition, land acquisition may restrict a community's access to commonly held natural resource assets such as rangeland, pasture, fallow land, and non-timber forest resources (e.g., medicinal plants, construction, and handicraft materials), woodlots for timber and fuelwood, or riverine fishing grounds. The client will provide either land-based compensation in the form of suitable replacement land, or access to other areas of natural resources that will offset the loss of such resources to a community. Such assistance could take the form of initiatives that enhance the productivity of the remaining resources to which the community has access (e.g., improved resource management practices or inputs to boost the productivity of the resource base), in-kind or cash compensation for loss of access, or provide access to alternative sources of the lost resource.

(Continued)

Table 3.3 (Continued)

No.	Means of Achieving Livelihood	Assessment	IFC Recommended Mitigation/Compensation
3	Other means of livelihood	Employment	GN12. Wage earners whose income is interrupted during physical displacement should receive a resettlement allowance that covers these and other hidden costs. Affected women and men should be given equal opportunities to benefit from such provisions. The location of resettlement housing, in the case of physically displaced persons, can be a significant contributing factor toward socio-economic stability. Careful consideration must be given to the ability of wage earners to continue to access their place(s) of work during and after resettlement; if this ability is impaired then mitigation measures need to be implemented to ensure continuity and avoid a net loss in welfare for affected households and communities.
		Business	GN59. In cases where land acquisition affects commercial structures, the affected business owner is entitled to compensation for the cost of re-establishing commercial activities elsewhere, for lost net income during the period of transition, and for the costs of the transfer and reinstallation of the plant, machinery, or other equipment. Assistance should also be made available to the employees of the business to compensate for their temporary loss of employment.

They may also operate small businesses and, where opportunity exists, have household members who are engaged in wage employment. Finally, households may also receive remittances from household members who have migrated to secure employment opportunities.

An approach based on identified economic activities and a checklist of technical opportunities for sectoral activity development that does not include consideration of the rationale for why livelihoods are constructed the way they are (based on pre-project context and household objectives) gives the impression that technical solutions alone are sufficient. If that were the case, livelihood re-establishment and development should demonstrate more success.

Clearly what is first required is a fulsome account of diversified livelihoods, an analysis of the who, what, when, where, why and how of livelihoods, and an understanding of how the broader environmental–political–social–economic–cultural reality influences the expression of livelihoods. Further, as intensification is often proposed as a solution to a diminished resource base (i.e., smaller landholdings, reduced common property areas for grazing, fishing or collection of forest products) more deliberate requirements for assessing the feasibility of such intensification and possible consequences (e.g., need for agricultural inputs (fertiliser, weedicide, pesticide) or conservation farming, resource depletion, resource use conflict) is required. In many contexts, inputs are not available or their cost is excessive compared to household cash income, while practices such as conservation farming involve changing traditional agricultural systems with significant increases in the demand for household labour.

Finally, IFC GN5 also provides specific guidance regarding marginal and vulnerable groups and the requisite mitigation and compensation.

> GN 5 Para 66 Special attention should be paid to economically displaced people who are vulnerable and/or marginalized as these groups are typically less resilient to change and may be made more vulnerable by project impacts. These groups may include households headed by women or children, people with disabilities, the extremely poor, the elderly and groups that suffer social and economic discrimination, including Indigenous Peoples and minorities. Members of vulnerable groups may require special or supplementary resettlement assistance because they are less able to cope with the displacement than the general population.

Vulnerability may be primarily thought of in terms of economic vulnerability. However other dimensions including access to decision-makers (i.e., power and influence) and social vulnerability should also be considered.

Aggregate Measures of Livelihoods

With reference to livelihood restoration, the standards and guidance commonly refer to aggregate measures of livelihoods including productivity (of natural resource-based activities), household income and household welfare. These aggregate indicators – which are focused on economic well-being – are reductionist in nature and risk simplifying the complexity of livelihoods, encourage a focus and allocation of resources towards addressing productivity and income and may ultimately fail to address key issues that drive sustainable livelihood development.

The Impoverishment Risk and Reconstruction Model

With specific reference to resettlement, the WB Involuntary Resettlement Sourcebook (2004) considers income improvement. While this focus implicitly equates livelihood restoration and standards of living with income, Box 8.1 (pg. 163) also presents the Impoverishment Risk and Reconstruction (IRR) framework (Cernea, 1997). IFC Guidance Note 5 (2012) makes reference to the IRR and provides PS 5 paragraph references for identified risks.

The IRR framework identifies eight categories of impoverishment risk in resettlement, with commentary on significance as set out below:

- *landlessness* – loss of land by displaced persons (DPs).
- *joblessness* – loss of employment affects many DPs and creating new employment is one of the greatest challenges in resettlement.
- *homelessness* – replacement of housing is only one aspect of relocation. Relocation may also disrupt family and neighbourhood relationships that are vital to the restoration of living standards.
- *marginalisation* – loss of economic power and social status pushes families closer to the poverty line or even further beneath it. Resettlement may similarly result in social marginalisation.

- *increased morbidity and mortality* – relocation tends to expose resettlers to new or more intensive sources of illness or debilitation or it may deprive them of access to health services or traditional remedies.
- *food insecurity* – diminished self-sufficiency and disrupted food production and supply can cause or exacerbate chronic under-nutrition.
- *loss of access to common property* – reduced access or loss of common property resources such as forests, water bodies, grazing areas and fuelwood is often associated with resettlement.
- *social disarticulation* – social capital can be lost through the dismantling or debilitation of community-level networks and associations, kinship systems and mutual help arrangements.

The IRR framework may be used as a diagnostic, design, planning and monitoring tool. As a diagnostic tool, it can be used to identify relevant risks and adverse impacts and to estimate their scope and intensity. As a design and planning tool, the IRR framework (which also shows how to mitigate the identified risks) helps direct project resources to risk management. As a monitoring tool, the IRR can be used to convert the relevant impoverishment risks into key performance indicators. In practice project application of the IRR appears to have been limited in extent. An example of the application of the IRR framework in the BP Tangguh Project Land Access and Resettlement Action Plan (LARAP) is provided in Appendix 2.

The IRR model is useful in promoting awareness and understanding of impoverishment risk and driving improvement in design. However, as demonstrated in Chapter 4, the IRR model is not a livelihood model and as such, does not drive improved framing or practice of livelihood development per se.

Conclusion

The standards and guidance for land acquisition and involuntary resettlement emphasise the management of the mechanics of securing land access (i.e., land acquisition, compensation and relocation processes) rather than the mitigation of the impacts of involuntary displacement. Further with reference to livelihoods, the standards and guidance for livelihood restoration focus on economic aspects of sectoral livelihood activities, emphasising improvement of productivity (of natural resource-based activities) and income. With this economic emphasis, they fail to recognise the complexity of livelihoods, including individual, household and community livelihood systems, the interface and dependency of livelihoods with the broader environment and the potential impacts of project development and area-wide socio-economic change on livelihood trajectories.

In summary while the standards and guidance have led to improved practice and outcomes in managing the mechanics of land acquisition, compensation and relocation, it remains that the standards and guidance for the restoration and/or improvement of the resettlement-affected population's livelihoods remain inadequate. Further an important dimension – specifically how external stakeholders view the resettlement programme and the benefits received by the resettlement-affected population (compensation, housing) and how this view influences the political–social–economic status of resettlement-affected communities vis-à-vis the project-affected population – is generally not addressed.

Subsequent chapters provide the basis for improved conceptualisation of livelihoods and the definition of livelihood frameworks (Chapter 4) aimed at promoting improved livelihood assessment (Chapters 5 and 6) and ensuring that livelihood re-establishment and development informs diagnosis, design, planning and implementation of resettlement (Chapter 7) and livelihood re-establishment and development (Chapter 8).

Note

1   Physical displacement comprises relocation or loss of shelter; economic displacement comprises the loss of assets or access to assets that leads to loss of income sources or other means of livelihood.

Bibliography

ADB (1998). *A Handbook on Resettlement, A Guide to Good Practice*. Asian Development Bank, Manila, Philippines.

ADB (2003). *Gender Checklist Resettlement*. Asian Development Bank, Manila, Philippines.

ADB (2010). *Safeguard Requirements 2: Involuntary Resettlement. Safeguard Policy Statement*. Asian Development Bank, Manila, Philippines.

ADB (2012). *Involuntary Resettlement Safeguards, A Planning and Implementation Good Practice Sourcebook* (Draft Working Document). Asian Development Bank, Manila, Philippines.

African Development Bank (2013). *Operational Safeguard 2 – Involuntary Resettlement: Land Acquisition, Population Displacement and Compensation, Integrated Safeguards System – Policy Statement and Operational Safeguards.* African Development Bank, Abidjan, Cote D'Ivoire.

African Development Bank Group (2015). *The African Development Bank's Involuntary Resettlement Policy; Review of Implementation.* African Development Bank, Abidjan, Cote D'Ivoire.

AIIB (2021). ESS2: Land Acquisition and Involuntary Resettlement, Environmental and Social Framework, Asian Infrastructure Investment Bank, Beijing.

African Union (2009). Convention for the Protection and Assistance of Internally Displaced Persons in Africa (Kampala Convention).

BP Tangguh Project (2005). *Land Access and Resettlement Action Plan.* BP Tangguh LARAP. BP Tangguh Project, BP Berau, Ltd.

Cernea, M. M. (1988). Involuntary Resettlement in Development Projects, Policy Guidelines in World Bank-Financed Projects, World Bank Technical Paper No 80. The International Bank for Reconstruction and Development, The World Bank, 1818 H Street, N.W., Washington, DC.

Cernea, M. M. (1997). The Risks and Reconstruction Model for Resettling Displaced Populations. *World Development*, 25(10), 1569–1587.

EBRD (2014). *Performance Requirement 5, Land Acquisition, Involuntary Resettlement and Economic Displacement*, EBRD, London, UK.

EBRD (2017). *Resettlement Guidance and Good Practice*, EBRD, London, UK.

EIB (2022). *Environmental and Social Standards, 6. Involuntary Resettlement*, EIB, Luxembourg.

EIB (2013). *Environmental and Social Handbook*, EIB, Luxembourg.

Equator Principles (2020). *Equator Principles EP4.*

FAO (2015). Environmental and Social Management Guidelines. ESS 6 Involuntary Resettlement and Displacement, FAO, Rome/Italy.

ICMM (2015). *Land Acquisition and Resettlement: Lessons Learned.* ICMM, London.

IDB (2021a). *ESPF 5 Land Acquisition and Involuntary Resettlement, Environmental and Social Policy Framework*, IDB, Washington DC.

IDB (2021b). *Guidelines for Environmental and Social Performance Standard 5: Land Acquisition and Involuntary Resettlement*, IDB, Washington DC.

IDB (2019). *Involuntary Resettlement in IDB Projects. Principles and Guidelines*, IDB, Washington DC.

IFC (2002). *Handbook for Developing a Resettlement Action Plan*. International Finance Corporation, Washington, DC.

IFC (2012). PS5 Land Acquisition and Involuntary Resettlement, Environmental and Social Sustainability Policy, IFC, Washington, DC.

HRC (2019). *Guidelines for the Implementation of the Right to Adequate Housing.* Report of the Special Rapporteur on Adequate Housing as a Component of the Right to an Adequate Standard of Living, and on the Right to Non-Discrimination in This Context. United Nations.

Inspection Panel/World Bank Group (2016) *Involuntary Resettlement Emerging Lessons Series No. 1*. International Bank for Reconstruction and Development/The World Bank, Washington, DC.

OCHA (2001). *Guiding Principles on Internal Displacement.* United Nations. https://www.unhcr.org/en-us/protection/idps/43ce1cff2/guiding-principles-internal-displacement.html.

OCHCR (2011). *Guiding Principles on Business and Human Rights*, United Nations. New York and Geneva.

OHCHR and UN-Habitat (2005). Indigenous Peoples' Right to Adequate Housing, A Global Overview. United Nations Housing Rights Programme Report No. 7.

Robinson, W. C. (2003). *Risks and Rights: The Causes, Consequences, and Challenges of Development-Induced Displacement*. The Brookings Institution-SAIS Project on Internal Displacement.

UHCHR (2009). Basic Principles and Guidelines on Development-Based Evictions and Displacement, Annex 1 of the Report of the Special Rapporteur on Adequate Housing as a Component of the Right to an Adequate Standard of Living. A/HRC/4/18. United Nations.

UNHCR (2011). *UNHCR Resettlement Handbook*. UNHCR, Switzerland.

Vivoda, V., Owen, J., and Kemp, D. (2017). Applying the Impoverishment Risks and Reconstruction Model to Involuntary Resettlement in the Global; Mining Sector/Mining, Resettlement and Livelihoods: Research and Practice Consortium, Centre for Social Responsibility in Mining (CSRM), Which is Part of the Sustainable Minerals Institute (SMI). University of Queensland, Australia.

World Bank (2004). *Involuntary Resettlement Sourcebook, Planning and Implementation in Development Projects.* The World Bank, Washington, DC.

World Bank (2017). *ESS5 Land Acquisition, Restrictions on Land Use and Involuntary Resettlement, Environmental and Social Framework.* The World Bank, Washington, DC.

4

UNDERSTANDING LIVELIHOODS: BASIC CONCEPTS AND LIVELIHOOD (DEVELOPMENT) MODELS

In this chapter

DOI: 10.4324/9781003358725-5

Introduction

The term 'livelihood' is commonly used in development circles, but within development-induced displacement and resettlement (DIDR) literature, it is rarely defined. With reference to Development-Induced Displacement and Resettlement (DIDR), the most common interpretation is that the term **livelihood** refers to the **means of earning a living**, and in this way, it is generally assumed it refers **only** to **sectoral livelihood activities**.

This chapter draws on development literature to present key livelihood concepts and models. An understanding of these concepts and models represents the building block for livelihood assessment and subsequent efforts to re-establish and develop livelihoods, including sectoral livelihood activities.

Livelihood concepts are usually applied at a household level, reflecting the fact that the household unit (however constituted) is typically the means through which livelihoods are achieved. However, this by no means excludes application at an individual, group or community level in certain circumstances.[1] As will be demonstrated, typically livelihoods are secured by involving individual, the household, the group and the community as a whole.

Key Livelihood Concepts and Definitions

A **livelihood** is defined as the means of supporting one's existence, the means of securing a living or the means of securing the basic necessities of life although it is often interpreted more narrowly as the means of earning a living (with a focus on occupation). Chambers and Conway (1992) describe livelihoods as comprising the capabilities, assets (stores, resources, claims and access) and activities required by an individual or household (or community) to provide for a means of living[2] (Figure 4.1). (Vanclay et al (2015) indicate that a livelihood refers to the way of life of a person or household and how they make a living, in particular, how they secure the basic necessities of life, e.g., their food, water, shelter and clothing, and live in the community. Livelihoods are interdependent on each other and on the biophysical environment.

Sustainable Livelihoods refers to a way of thinking about people and communities in terms of their capabilities, the livelihood resources (assets

Livelihood Capabilities describe the possession of human capabilities including education, skills, health, psychological orientation

Livelihood Assets include physical, natural and social resources (alternatively both tangible assets such as stores and resources, and intangible assets such as claims and access)

Capabilities

Assets

Livelihood

Activities

Livelihood activities include existing (and new) activities practiced by an individual and/or household (or other relevant social unit) to secure their livelihoods. Typically this may include subsistence and commercial/market activities reliant on use of private and common property natural resources, commercial enterprises including primary, secondary and tertiary production, provision of services, employment, remittances from non-local employment, etc. The suite of livelihood activities may be defined by several factors including the political environment, the natural resource endowment of the affected population,[1] and integration with and linkages to the mainstream economy.

Figure 4.1 Elements of Livelihoods – Capabilities, Assets and Activities

or capitals) and the livelihood strategies (activities) they undertake to make their living and conduct their way of life (Vanclay et al. 2015).

A **livelihood strategy** is a way in which an individual, household, group and/or community combines its capabilities, assets and activities to ensure viable (and perhaps sustainable) livelihoods. Livelihoods typically comprise multiple goals that may be defined at the individual, household, group and/or community level. These goals might include risk mitigation; physical security; shelter; food security; income levels and income security; preferred labour allocation between productive, domestic, social and leisure activities; maintenance of social networks, etc. 'Strategies' may never be articulated (by the individual or household), but they nevertheless influence people's choice of which activities to combine, which outcomes to pursue and which assets to invest in (Ashley and Hussein, 2000).

The **vulnerability of livelihoods** describes the ability of the existing livelihood to cope with the impacts of stresses (in population, resources, health problems, economy or governance) and seasonality (cyclic fluctuations in prices, production, health and employment) and shocks (sudden onset of natural disasters, conflicts, economic traumas, health problems, and crop or livestock distress).

At a household level, various approaches have been used to assess the economic vulnerability of a household:

- the number and diversity of household livelihood activities may be used as a proxy indicator of household vulnerability, with a larger number and diversity of livelihood activities being positively correlated with reduced vulnerability, particularly where activity risk is factored into the analysis. On this basis a reduction in both the number and diversity of livelihood activities and/or the stability of existing activities (e.g., as might be experienced by physical displacement onto the land of poorer quality than at the origin) is associated with increased household vulnerability.
- poverty – relative to established national poverty lines – is often used as an indicator of the vulnerability of an individual or household, i.e., the household's ability to cope.

As noted in Chapter 3, other dimensions of vulnerability – including power and social relations – should also be considered.

The **sustainability of a livelihood** is ascertained by the ability of the chosen livelihood strategy and component activities to maintain the individual, household or community in both the short- and long-term during normal conditions and in the face of challenges (e.g., stresses, shocks), to maintain or enhance individual and household capabilities and assets both now and in the future, and to provide sustainable livelihood opportunities for the next generation (Chambers and Conway. 1992). Within this framework Chambers and Conway (1992) consider environmental sustainability (whether livelihood activities maintain and enhance or deplete and degrade the local natural resource base) and social sustainability (whether the human unit can not only gain but maintain an adequate and decent livelihood, including ability to cope with stress and shocks and capabilities in adapting to, exploiting and creating change and assuring continuity). In relation to environmental sustainability the ecological concepts of stability and resilience should be considered in analysing the vulnerability of livelihoods. Stability is defined as the ability of a system to return to an equilibrium state after a temporary disturbance; resilience is defined as the persistence of a system and its capacity to absorb change and still maintain the same relationships within the system (Holling, 1973:17). Project development and project's direct and induced impacts (such as local and regional development, project-induced in-migration) may be considered as challenges to the sustainability of existing livelihoods because they may fundamentally change pre-project conditions and the affected population may be ill-equipped to recognise, withstand (resilience) and/or adapt to the evolving context, e.g., mitigate newly introduced challenges and risks and/or participate in new opportunities.

Livelihood re-establishment and/or development describes a proactive and planned series of interventions that aim to promote (sustainable) livelihoods by ensuring the re-establishment, improvement and/or introduction of (sustainable) livelihood strategies (after displacement) by maintaining or improving the capabilities, assets and/or activities of the affected population and/or addressing parameters that frame the current livelihood context (e.g., institutional, infrastructure, basic needs, markets – value chains, market actors). Improvement may be incremental or transformational in nature. Improvements in one element of livelihoods may introduce additional demands on other elements of livelihoods and, as such, may be dependent on changes in the livelihood system or context.

Aggregate measures of livelihood restoration and/or livelihood re-establishment and development (including production levels, income-earning capacity, standards of living and livelihoods) are typically used to define the objective (and outcome) of livelihood re-establishment and development and inform the identification of suitable monitoring and evaluation indicators.

BOX 4.1 AGGREGATE MEASURES OF LIVELIHOOD RESTORATION

Productivity: unit of assessment applied to primary production including agriculture, fisheries, etc. Productivity may be assessed in terms of production/unit area or production/unit of effort expended. In general, processes of intensification aim to secure higher levels of production from smaller areas and as such are associated with higher productivity per unit area and lower productivity per unit of effort expanded. Intensification involving increased complexity and management are often associated with higher labour requirements and in this way while production per unit area may increase, productivity per unit of effort expended is lower.

Intensification is often associated with greater labour and production inputs, although the former may be reduced through mechanisation.

Income: typically includes both in-kind and actual income streams. In-kind income streams include primary production activities for household subsistence, the harvest and collection of products from common property resources (e.g., fuelwood, timber and non-timber forest products, fisheries). Sources of income may include the sale of primary produce, business activities, employment, etc.

Standard of Living: level of material well-being enjoyed or aspired to by individuals and/or groups. Where physical displacement occurs, the provision of replacement housing is typically associated with increases in the standard of living (i.e., housing, water and sanitation, electricity). Where whole communities are displaced, the development of new settlements also often allows for increased access to and quality of services (i.e., health and education) and utilities (electricity, water, sanitation). While these improvements are typically cited as contributors to increased standards of living, a degree of caution is appropriate. Improvements must be culturally appropriate and must reflect local capabilities and local inputs; the resettlement-affected population must have the ability to operate, maintain, repair and replicate houses and utilities; and the resettlement-affected population and/or public services must have the ability to pay for utilities and services.

Livelihoods: describes the means to support existence

Livelihood Models

Beyond basic livelihood concepts and definitions, various (rural) livelihood models[3] have been developed through applied research in agriculture and rural development, to support emergency and development programming and for environmental and social impact assessment and management including resettlement (refer Sections 'Sustainable Rural Livelihoods Framework,' 'Sustainable Livelihoods Approach (SLA),' 'DFID Sustainable Livelihoods Framework (SLF),' 'CARE Household Livelihood Security (HLS) Approach' and 'Resource Framework for Projects'). These models have wide-ranging potential applications including:

- to provide a basis for the conceptualisation of livelihoods
- to inform description and assessment of livelihoods
- to provide a framework for, and help identify potential areas of, interventions to support livelihood development
- to help design and deliver livelihood programmes aimed at re-establishment and development of sectoral livelihood activities, and;
- to design a livelihood-centred monitoring and evaluation system

The first three sections describe the 'Sustainable Rural Livelihoods Framework,' 'Sustainable Livelihoods Approach (SLA)' and 'DFID Sustainable Livelihoods Framework (SLF)' which together describe the development of the Sustainable Livelihoods Approach and its evolution to the Sustainable Livelihoods Framework. This evolution traces the development of the model from a tool to support applied agricultural research and development in rural landscapes to its adoption by DFID to guide development assistance programmes.[4] The next section presents the 'CARE Household Livelihood Security (HLS) Approach'. The final section presents the Resource Framework developed by Reddy et al. (2015) and promoted as a tool to inform the description and assessment of livelihoods in Environmental and Social Impact Assessment (ESIA) and resettlement.

Sustainable Rural Livelihoods Framework

The Sustainable Rural Livelihoods Framework derives from applied research in agricultural and rural development (Figure 4.2).

The framework argues that three elements, namely context, livelihood resources (also referred to as capitals or assets) and institutions and organisations, and the relationship between them form the basis for selected livelihood strategies and livelihood outcomes. By implication, an essential first step in understanding current livelihoods is to ensure a comprehensive awareness and understanding of these factors and the relationships between them. The development of livelihoods may occur through interventions in context (e.g., markets), livelihood resources (e.g., building capacity, introducing new technology and practices, improving access to finance) and/or institutional processes and organisational structures (e.g., land tenure systems, provision of land titles, control of access to common property resources). However, it should be recognised that interventions

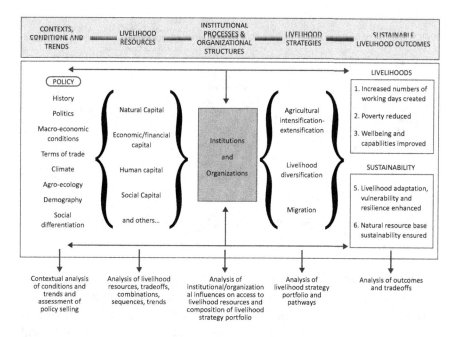

CONTEXTS, CONDITIONS AND TRENDS	LIVELIHOOD RESOURCES	INSTITUTIONAL PROCESSES & ORGANIZATIONAL STRUCTURES	LIVELIHOOD STRATEGIES	SUSTAINABLE LIVELIHOOD OUTCOMES

LIVELIHOODS

POLICY

History
Politics
Macro-economic conditions
Terms of trade
Climate
Agro-ecology
Demography
Social differentiation

Natural Capital
Economic/financial capital
Human capital
Social Capital
and others...

Institutions
and
Organizations

Agricultural intensification-extensification
Livelihood diversification
Migration

1. Increased numbers of working days created
2. Poverty reduced
3. Wellbeing and capabilities improved

SUSTAINABILITY

5. Livelihood adaptation, vulnerability and resilience enhanced
6. Natural resource base sustainability ensured

Contextual analysis of conditions and trends and assessment of policy selling	Analysis of livelihood resources, tradeoffs, combinations, sequences, trends	Analysis of institutional/organization al influences on access to livelihood resources and composition of livelihood strategy portfolio	Analysis of livelihood strategy portfolio and pathways	Analysis of outcomes and tradeoffs

Figure 4.2 Sustainable Rural Livelihood Framework (Scoones, 1998)

in one area may fail to deliver improved livelihoods if aspects of the other two factors constrain or limit their potential. For example, addressing primary production capacity for the sale of produce may not yield results if the market, enabling conditions (infrastructure) and value chain actors are not present.

From a resettlement-livelihood re-establishment and development perspective, it is important to recognise that the livelihood resources element directly involves the resettlement-affected population, while interventions in context and institutional processes and organisation may involve interventions beyond the resettlement-affected population and resettlement footprint. In this way a resettlement-sponsored livelihood intervention may well bring development benefits to a broader population.

Sustainable Livelihoods Approach (SLA)

The Sustainable Livelihoods Approach (SLA) uses the same building blocks as the Sustainable Rural Livelihoods Framework but formalises the approach, both in narrative and schematic form (Figure 4.3).

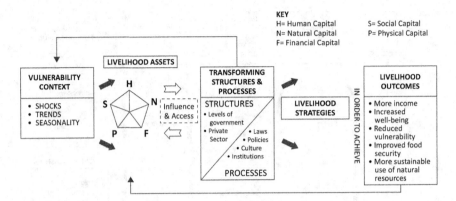

Figure 4.3 Sustainable Livelihoods Approach (Ashley and Carney, 1999). Permission: FCDO

The Sustainable Livelihoods Approach (SLA) characterises livelihoods by considering the relationship between capital assets (human, natural, financial, physical and social[5]) and the broader policy and institutional environment in determining livelihood strategies and achieving livelihood outcomes (e.g., well-being, income, food security, vulnerability/risk management, sustainable use of natural resources). Table 4.1 provides a description of identified livelihood assets (also referred to as capitals or resources).

Transforming structures and processes gives meaning and value to livelihood assets. In this context 'structures' are all levels of government and the private sector that have a role in shaping livelihoods. 'Processes' include policies, laws and institutions that frame the way in which structures and individuals operate and interact. Structures and processes determine access to public and private resources and the terms of trade between different types of livelihood assets. They also influence the returns to livelihood strategies.

The Sustainable Livelihoods Approach (SLA) captures the multiple dimensions of livelihoods. Specifically, the Sustainable Livelihoods Approach recognises that:

(i) well-being is not only about increased income. Other dimensions of livelihoods that must be addressed include ownership and/or access to physical assets, food insecurity, social inferiority, exclusion and vulnerability.

Table 4.1 Description of Livelihood Assets

No.	Livelihood Assets	Description
1	Human	Health, nutrition, education, knowledge and skills, capacity to work, capacity to adapt
2	Social	Settlement patterns, representation and leadership, mechanisms for participation in decision-making and leadership, networks and connections (patronage, neighbourhoods, kinship), relations of trust and mutual understanding and support, formal and informal groups, shared values and behaviours/customs, common rules and sanctions (e.g., land tenure systems)
3	Natural	Land and produce, water and aquatic resources, trees and forest products, wildlife, wild foods and fibres, biodiversity and environmental services
4	Physical	Infrastructure (transport, roads, vehicles, secure shelter and buildings, water supply and sanitation, energy, communication), tools and technology (tools and equipment for production, seed, fertiliser, pesticides, traditional technology)
5	Financial	Access to regular income (in-kind or wages, remittances, pensions), savings, credit and debt (formal and informal)

(ii) livelihood objectives/priorities vary; outsiders cannot assume knowledge of the objectives of a given household or group.

(iii) livelihoods are determined by many factors, particularly access to assets and the influence of policies and institutions.

The SLA promotes a comprehensive, holistic consideration of the definition of the objectives, scope and priorities for development interventions by requiring a systematic analysis of factors that constrain or enhance livelihood opportunities and their relationship to one another.

DFID Sustainable Livelihoods Framework (SLF)[6]

The Sustainable Livelihoods Approach (SLA) gained traction in the development sector in the early 2000s, this being exemplified by DFID's development and adoption of the Sustainable Livelihoods Framework (SLF) to increase the agency's effectiveness in poverty reduction.[7] The SLF is essentially the same as the SLA. Both the narrative and figure are included here to convey the extent to which the model gained traction in the assessment, design and delivery of development programming.

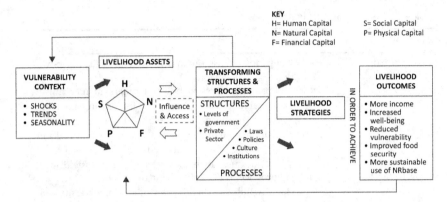

H represents human capital: the skills, knowledge, ability to labour and good health important to the ability to pursue different livelihood strategies;

P represents physical capital: the basic infrastructure (transport, shelter, water, energy and communications) and the production equipment and means that enable people to pursue livelihoods;

S represents social capital: the social resources (networks, membership of groups, relationships of trust, access to wider institutions of society) upon which people draw in pursuit of livelihoods;

F represents financial capital: the financial resources which are available to people (whether savings, supplies of credit or regular remittances or pensions) and which provide them with different livelihood options; and

N represents natural capital: the natural resource stocks from which resource flows useful for livelihoods are derived (e.g. land, water, wildlife, biodiversity, environmental resources)

Figure 4.4 DFID Sustainable Livelihoods Framework (Carney et al., 1999). Permission: FCDO

The SLF is centred upon the following definition of sustainable livelihoods: *a livelihood comprises the capabilities, assets (including both material and social resources) and activities required for a means of living. A livelihood is sustainable when it can cope with and recover from stresses and shocks and maintain or enhance its capabilities and assets both now and in the future while not undermining the natural resource base.* Figure 4.4 illustrates the Sustainable Livelihoods Framework providing the conceptual basis for the approach.

DFID notes that the value of using a Sustainable Livelihoods Framework is that it

> encourages users to take a broad and systematic view of the factors that cause poverty – whether these are shocks and adverse trends, poorly functioning institutions and policies, or a basic lack of assets – and to investigate the relations between them. It does not take a sectoral view of poverty but tries to reconcile the contribution made by all the sectors to building up the stocks of assets upon which people draw to sustain their livelihoods. The aim is to do

away with pre-conceptions about what exactly people seek and how they are most likely to achieve their goals, and to develop an accurate and dynamic picture of how different groups of people operate within their environment.

(Carney et al. 1999)

Application of the Sustainable Livelihoods Framework in support of addressing poverty is also guided by key principles as follows:

- **people-centred:** sustainable poverty elimination will be achieved only if external support focuses on what matters to people, understands the difference between groups of people and works with them in a way that is congruent with their current livelihood strategies, social environment and ability to adapt.
- **responsive and participatory:** poor people themselves must be key actors in identifying and addressing livelihood priorities. Outsiders need processes that enable them to listen and respond to the poor.
- **multi-level:** poverty elimination is an enormous challenge that will only be overcome by working at multiple levels, ensuring that micro-level activity informs the development of policy and an effective enabling environment and that macro-level structures and processes support people to build upon their own strengths.
- **conducted in partnership:** with both the public and the private sector.
- **sustainable:** there are four key dimensions to sustainability – economic, institutional, social and environmental sustainability. All are important – a balance must be found among them.
- **dynamic:** external support must recognise the dynamic nature of livelihood strategies, respond flexibly to changes in people's situations and develop longer-term commitments.

CARE Household Livelihood Security (HLS) Approach[8]

CARE is an international humanitarian aid organisation delivering emergency relief and development projects. CARE developed the Household Livelihood Security (HLS) approach as a framework for programme analysis, design, monitoring and evaluation (Figure 4.5).

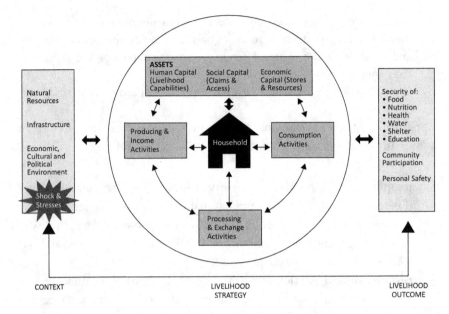

Figure 4.5 CARE Household Livelihood Security Approach (Kranz, 2001).
        Permission: SIDA

The HLS approach is based upon the Chambers and Conway definition of livelihoods and the consequent identification of three fundamental
attributes of livelihoods, namely:

(i)   the possession of human capabilities (such as education, skills, health,
       psychological orientation)
(ii)   access to tangible and intangible assets
(iii) the existence of economic activities

The interaction between these attributes defines what livelihood strategy a
household will pursue.

CARE has used the Household Livelihood Security approach in both
rural and urban contexts. It identifies three, not mutually exclusive, categories of livelihood activity development, relevant to, and appropriate for,
different points in the relief-development spectrum. These are:

• **livelihood promotion** – activities aimed at improving the resilience
  of households (e.g., through programmes which focus on savings and

credit; crop diversification and marketing; reproductive health; institutional development; personal empowerment or community involvement in service delivery activities). Most livelihood promotion activities are longer-term development projects that increasingly involve participatory methodologies and an empowerment philosophy.

- **livelihood protection** – activities helping prevent a decline in Household Livelihood Security (e.g., programmes that focus on early warning systems; cash or food for work; seeds and tools; health education; flood prevention).
- **livelihood provisioning** – activities that involve direct provision of food, water, shelter and other essential needs, most often in emergency situations.

These activity categories recognise the multiple objectives of livelihood strategies balancing issues associated with vulnerability and resilience with growth and development. Further these activity categories are non-exclusive, implying that a good livelihood promotion strategy would also have a 'protection' element, which deals with existing areas of vulnerability and helps to ensure that any improvements in livelihood security are protected from re-erosion. Likewise, the aim is that elements of 'protection' and 'promotion' are built in as early as possible to 'traditional relief' (provisioning) activities. Cross-cutting with these categories of livelihood support activity are CARE's three focus areas of activity:

- **personal empowerment**: interventions focused on expanding human capacity, and hence the overall resource (asset) and income base of the poor
- **social empowerment**: interventions such as education, community mobilisation, political advocacy
- **Service delivery**: expanding access to basic services for the poor

Resource Framework for Projects

Reddy et al. (2015) present a Resource Framework that identifies eight components of the social context that help define household and community well-being (Figures 4.6 and 4.7). This has been adapted by Smyth and Vanclay (2017) who thus define a social framework that comprises eight

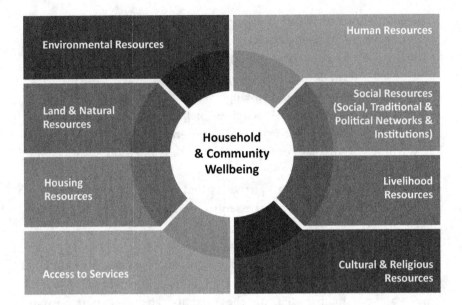

Figure 4.6 Resource Framework Defining Household and Community Well-Being. Copyright (2015) From Land Access and Resettlement: A guide to best practice by Gerry, G., Smyth, E and Steyn, M. Reproduced by permission of Taylor and Francis Group, LLC, a division of Informa plc

social categories that can be used to capture the social dimensions specific to the local context and thereby help assess the potential social impacts of a project.

The Resource Framework is not a livelihood model and is perhaps better suited to ensuring a comprehensive description and assessment of livelihoods (refer Chapters 5 and 6). From a resettlement perspective, the Resource Framework might be considered to be analogous to the World Bank Impoverishment Risk and Reconstruction (IRR) Framework, although it is recognised that the categories that comprise the Resource Framework are broader in nature and, as such, provide a comprehensive account of what together helps define livelihoods rather than focusing on key livelihood impacts and risks of resettlement (as exemplified by the IRR).

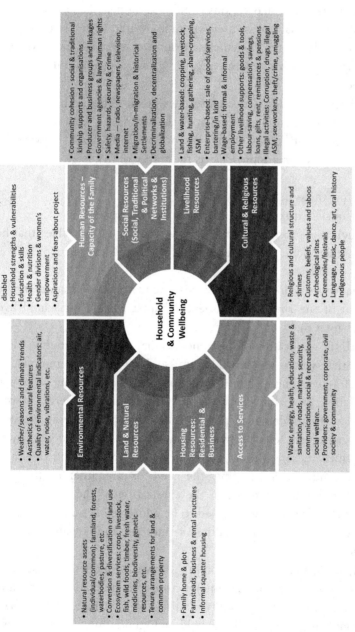

Figure 4.7 Elaboration of the Eight Dimensions of Resource Framework Defining Household and Community Well-Being. Copyright (2015) From Land Access and Resettlement: A guide to best practice by Gerry, G., Smyth, E and Steyn, M. Reproduced by permission of Taylor and Francis Group, LLC, a division of Informa plc

Challenges in the Application of Livelihood Models

This chapter has presented various livelihood models (i.e., essentially systems approaches) that can be used to guide livelihood description, assessment and development. Nonetheless from a conceptual and operational perspective, there is some debate regarding the scope and utility of livelihood models.

First, by definition systems approaches are holistic, and, in this way, livelihood models aim to ensure that all the factors that help shape a livelihood and its evolution in a changing world are considered. However, the challenge with systems approaches is the ability of the user:

- to define the system
- to adequately describe and analyse the whole system
- through this process, identify the parameters and variables that help define the system and present opportunities for its development

These challenges will be addressed in subsequent chapters addressing the assessment of the rural environment (Chapter 5) and household livelihoods (Chapter 6).

Second, the application of these models may fail to site households and communities within the broader local and regional system, including aspects of (government) administration, land use planning, access and transportation, provision of services and utilities and commerce and trade. In this way the models may result in undue emphasis being placed on capacity, assets and activities without understanding the broader system within which these attributes are expressed. In recognition of the preceding, Scoones (2015) identifies the need for strengthening the use of a political economy approach in the application of the SLF model and concludes that four core areas need to be addressed to bring politics back into livelihood analysis, namely the politics of interests, individuals, knowledge and ecology.

Third, although increasingly comprehensive, the models and use thereof provide a static (i.e., a point in time) picture of household and community livelihoods. Increasing their utility requires the introduction of a dynamic component – including the household and community and the enabling environment over time. In the context of project development, this would require consideration of the development trajectory catalysed by the project and any induced area development.

Considering the above and, as noted in the introduction, livelihood models should be seen to provide frameworks for the description, assessment and development of livelihoods. Their application should be adaptive and responsive to context and need, rather than being seen as prescriptive and/or definitive or as a panacea to the challenge of livelihood re-establishment and development.

Conclusion

The definition and broad characterisation of livelihood restoration in MFI land acquisition and involuntary resettlement standards and guidance indicate that livelihood restoration is a complex, multifaceted concept. In its broadest sense livelihood restoration can be interpreted as comprising all aspects of livelihoods and overall outcomes (i.e., well-being, welfare) rather than being restricted to livelihood activities and measures thereof (i.e., productivity, income-earning capacity). Defining livelihoods in terms of capabilities, assets and activities reflects this complexity.

The livelihood models presented in this chapter consistently identify the three elements of livelihoods – capabilities, assets and activities – and the context as the basis for the description, analysis and development of livelihoods. The models also identify that households may pursue multiple goals and develop livelihood strategies through which these goals are to be achieved.

The relationship between the three elements of livelihoods – capabilities, assets and activities – implies that decisions regarding one aspect of a livelihood will affect both the opportunities for and the requirements of other components. For example:

- where decisions regarding replacement land (i.e., an asset) are made, the characteristics of the land will (i) affect the potential livelihood activities and the capabilities and assets required to practice these activities (e.g., type of crop, requisite intensification of production, new management practices) and (ii) determine the requirement for other inputs (e.g., irrigation, fertiliser, pesticide), which may affect the cost

of practising selected livelihood activities and consequently increase the returns which that livelihood activity **has to** achieve.
- where replacement housing includes the provision of utilities (electricity, water, waste management, sanitation), the operation, maintenance repair of these assets may require cultural change, and different capabilities and may involve significant additional costs, and thereby significantly affect the targets needed to be achieved regarding capabilities on the one hand and the requisite (monetary) returns derived from livelihood activities.

With reference to the objectives outlined in the introduction, the models described in this chapter provide the basis for:[9]

(i)   conceptualisation of livelihoods
(ii)   description and assessment of livelihoods
(iii) providing a framework for and informing possible approaches and areas of intervention to support the improvement and development of livelihoods
(iv)   helping design and deliver livelihood programmes aimed at the re-establishment and development of livelihood activities, and the participation of affected households and communities
(v)   designing a livelihood-focused monitoring and evaluation system

From a resettlement-livelihood perspective, livelihood models have the potential to be used as a means to systematically apply the livelihood criterion to involuntary displacement and resettlement. Such application should be to the entire resettlement process to ensure that livelihood considerations inform every step of the resettlement process (as would be the case with physical and economic displacement). Notwithstanding the preceding it is possible to limit the application of such models to the re-establishment and development of livelihood activities (as would be the case for projects involving only economic displacement).

This book applies the Sustainable Livelihoods Framework to the involuntary displacement and resettlement process.[10] Chapters 5 and 6 provide the basis for the description, assessment and analysis of the rural environment and rural livelihoods. Chapter 7 applies the SLF to the resettlement process. Chapter 8 considers the re-establishment and development of livelihood activities. Chapter 9 provides an example of the use of the SLF in the design and implementation of monitoring and evaluation.

Notes

1 In certain circumstances considering both household- and community-level livelihoods may be appropriate.
2 Adapted from Chambers, R., and G. Conway (1991) *Sustainable rural livelihoods: Practical concepts for the 21st century.* IDS Discussion Paper 296. Brighton: IDS (pp. 7–8).
3 Livelihood models are distinct from (economic) models of livelihood activities that can be developed to describe the economic basis for specific activities.
4 Scoones (2015) describes the instrumentalization of livelihoods analysis, through the appropriation of the livelihoods framework in aid agency debates and program delivery and the consequent loss of the political dimension of livelihood analysis.
5 Some descriptions of the SLA suggest that the institutional–political context should also be considered as an asset
6 From DFID (1999), Carney et al (1999) and Kranz (2001).
7 The UNDP also adopted the Sustainable Livelihoods Framework to guide development assistance programming.
8 From Carney et al (1999) and Kranz (2001).
9 For example, refer to Ashley and Hussein (2000).
10 It is important to recognise that the purpose of the book is to elucidate the approach (i.e., the consistent application of a livelihoods framework throughout the resettlement process) rather than recommend a particular model. While the SLF was selected as an example for use in this book, other models could be used in a similar way.

Bibliography

Ashley, C., and Carney, D. (1999). *Sustainable Livelihoods: Lessons from Early Experience.* Department for International Development, London/UK.

Ashley, C., and Hussein, K. (2000). Developing Methodologies for Livelihood Impact Assessment: Experience of the African Wildlife Foundation in East Africa. Working Paper 129. ODI.

Bebbington, A. (1999). Capitals and Capabilities: A Framework for Analyzing Peasant Viability, Rural Livelihoods and Poverty. *World Development*, 27(2), 2021–2044. https://doi.org/10.1016/S0305-750X(99)00104-7.

Bebbington, A. (2000). Re-encountering Development: Livelihood Transitions and Place Transformations in the Andes. *Annals of the Association of American Geographers*, 90(3), 495–520. https://doi.org/10.1111/0004-5608.00206.

Bury, J. (2004). Livelihoods in Transition: Transnational Gold Mining Operations and Local Change in Cajamarca, Peru. *The Geographical Journal*, 170(1), 78–91. https://doi.org/10.1111/j.0016-7398.2004.05042.x.

CARE (2002). *Household Livelihood Security Assessments: A Toolkit for Practitioners*. Prepared for the PHLS Unit by: TANGO International Inc., Tucson, AZ.

Carney, D. (2002). *Sustainable Livelihoods Approaches: Progress and Possibilities for Change*. DFID, London.

Carney, D., Drinkwater, M., Rusinow, T., Neefjes, K., Wanmali, S., and Singh, N. (1999). *Sustainable Livelihoods Approaches Compared, A Brief Comparison of the Livelihoods Approaches of the UK Department for International Development (DFID), CARE, Oxfam and the United Nations Development Program (UNDP)*. DFID, London.

Chambers, R., and Conway, G. (1992). Sustainable Rural Livelihoods: Practical Concepts for the 21st Century. IDS Discussion Paper 296. IDS, Brighton.

De Haan, L. J. (2012). The Livelihood Approach: A Critical Exploration. *Erdkunde*, 66(4), 345–357.

De Haan, L.J. (2017). *Livelihoods and Development, New Perspectives, Koninkjlijke*. Brill, Leiden, The Netherlands.

Department for International Development (1999). Sustainable Livelihoods Guidance Sheets. https://www.livelihoodscentre.org/documents/114097690/114438878/Sustainable+livelihoods+guidance+sheets.pdf/594e5ea6-99a9-2a4e-f288-cbb4ae4bea8b?t=1569512091877.

Emery, M., Gutierrez-Montes, I., and Fernandez-Baca, E. (2013). *Sustainable Rural Development, Sustainable Livelihoods, and the Community Capitals Framework*. Routledge, New York.

Haidar, M. (2009). *Sustainable Livelihood Approaches, the Framework, Lessons Learnt from Practice and Policy Recommendations*. UNDP.

Holling, C. S. (1973). Resilience and Stability of Ecological Systems. *Annual Review of Ecological Systems*, 4(1), 1–23.

IFRC. https://www.livelihoodscentre.org.

Krantz, L. (2001). *The Sustainable Livelihoods Approach to Poverty Reduction, an Introduction*. SIDA.

Levine, S. (2014). How to Study Livelihoods: Bringing a Sustainable Livelihoods Framework to Life. Working Paper No 22 Secure Livelihoods Research Consortium Overseas Development Institute, London.

McDowell, C. (2002). Involuntary Resettlement, Impoverishment Risks and Sustainable Livelihoods. *Australian Journal of Disaster and Trauma Studies*, 6(2), 1–10.

Reddy, G., Smyth, E., and Steyn, M. (2015). *Land Access and Resettlement, A Guide to Best Practice*. Greenleaf Publishing, Sheffield/UK.

Scoones, I. (1998). Sustainable Rural Livelihoods; A Framework for Analysis. IDS Working Paper 72.

Scoones, I. (2015). *Sustainable Livelihoods and Rural Development*. Practical Action Publishing.

Smyth, E., and Vanclay, F. (2017). The Social Framework for Projects: A Conceptual but Practical Model to Assist in Assessing, Planning and Managing the Social Impacts of Big Projects. *Impact Assessment and Project Appraisal*, 35(1), 65–80. http://doi.org/10.1080/14615517.2016.1271539.

Vanclay, F., Esteves, A. M., Aucamp, I., and Franks, D. M. (2015). *Social Impact Assessment: Guidance for Assessing and Managing the Social Impacts of Projects*. International Association for Impact Assessment.

Part II

ASSESSMENT OF THE RURAL ENVIRONMENT AND NATURAL RESOURCE-BASED LIVELIHOODS

5

THE RURAL ENVIRONMENT AND LIVELIHOODS OF RURAL HOUSEHOLDS

Introduction

As outlined in Chapter 4, livelihoods can be described in terms of the capabilities, assets and activities of individuals, households and communities. Further, the livelihood models demonstrate that the broader environment frames current livelihoods and their potential development pathways. This chapter identifies and describes key attributes of the rural environment and rural household livelihoods that together should inform the design and

DOI: 10.4324/9781003358725-7

conduct of an assessment of rural livelihoods (Chapter 6) and the identification of opportunities for livelihood development.

Rural Environment

The term rural can be used to describe matters relating to, or characteristic of, the countryside, country people and country life (in contrast to the term urban describing matters relating to, or characteristic of, built-up areas [e.g., towns, cities]).[1] Beyond the preceding, the nature of a specific rural environment can be described with reference to the attributes identified below. These attributes are inter-related and, as such, not mutually exclusive:

Geographical Location: the rural environment refers to all areas that fall outside of the urban and peri-urban environments. This includes areas relatively close to built-up urban areas and extends to remote and isolated areas existing at the margins of a country's borders, the mainstream economy and associated infrastructure, services and utilities.

Accessibility: a rural environment can be described in terms of its physical accessibility, through land (road) networks; lacustrine, riverine or marine shipping routes; and by air.

Connectedness: beyond physical accessibility, connectedness can be understood with reference to centre–periphery relations (i.e., politics) and market integration (i.e., economics). With regard to centre–periphery relations, both the historical and current local, regional and national political economy play a key role in defining the integration and development of rural environments within the region and nationally. Market integration can be described in terms of connection to the mainstream economy at regional and national levels, the operation of commodity value chains, the presence and operation of entrepreneurs access to finance, etc.

Development: in many countries, and particularly at the extremity of the centre–periphery continuum, rural environments can be characterised by (long-term) political, physical and socio-economic marginalisation and, thus, relative under-development. Under-development may be expressed in terms of limited accessibility and the established road network; limited infrastructure; limited accessibility, availability and quality of services (education, health) and utilities (power, water); and poor access to markets. Relatedly the limited presence of industry limits local experience of participation in industrial activity, a regulated work environment, etc. Largely as a consequence of the preceding, under-development can also be observed in key human development indicators of the population in rural areas (i.e., education, literacy and numeracy, health, life span, poverty).

Infrastructure and Services and Utilities: the state of infrastructure development and the availability, access to, level and quality of services (health, education, water and sanitation) and utilities (power, water) is often poorer in rural environments. Therefore, most rural communities and rural households do not have ready access to the full complement of basic services and utilities. As such, the basic needs of rural communities are often not met.

Population: a rural population and the individuals, households and communities that comprise the population can be described in terms of their primary natural resource-dependent livelihood activity (i.e., hunter-gatherers, shifting cultivators, sedentary agriculturalists, pastoralists, fishers). Depending on the livelihood system and the status of the attributes listed above, rural populations invariably have less access to education (through secondary school, vocational and higher education) and health services and practice subsistence (and to a lesser extent commercial) production systems earning poverty-line incomes. As noted above, as a consequence rural populations generally score lower on human development indicators.

Land and Resource Tenure, Governance and Use: household and community access and use of natural resources may be governed by a combination of traditional and formal institutions and resource access regulations that have seasonal, social and cultural dimensions. Assumptions regarding resource availability, especially for common property and open access resources, require validation.

Natural Resource-Based Production Systems: most of the population inhabiting rural environments operate natural resource-dependent livelihoods. As described above, primary livelihood systems may be used to characterise the population. However, in practice almost all rural households operate diversified livelihood systems. Refer to Section 'Diversified Livelihood Systems' for a description of diversified livelihood systems.

Vulnerability: by virtue of location and state of development, rural households and rural communities have greater interaction with the environment and greater exposure to environmental shock and stresses, while market and state (emergency) response and support mechanisms may be limited if not non-existent. Therefore, their livelihood objectives and systems are likely to place more emphasis on mitigating risk, reducing vulnerability and ensuring resilience (e.g., cultivation of fallback staple crops such as cassava, the existence of social networks that provide safety nets) than the less vulnerable and more individualised livelihoods of urban populations.

Diversified Livelihood Systems

Most rural households operate diversified livelihood systems including natural resource-dependent activities, enterprise, employment and remittances (Figure 5.1).

Typically, rural households and communities are described by their natural resource-based activities. These may include:

- agriculture – both subsistence and commercial production systems including shifting cultivation/short- or long-fallow rotational production systems; annual cropping; house gardens; perennial cash crop production (cashew, cocoa, coconut, coffee, cloves, fruit tree orchards, nutmeg, pepper, rubber, etc.)
- livestock – intensive and extensive livestock production systems that may involve rearing of poultry, goats, sheep, cattle and camels, etc.
- collection of aquatic produce and fishing involving access to common property aquatic resources (i.e., lacustrine, riverine or marine)
- harvesting and/or processing of timber and non-timber products from other common property or open access terrestrial resources including firewood, charcoal production, construction timber, thatch, medicinal plants, wild foods (wild vegetables, honey, insects, wild animals), etc.

Household members may participate in other activities including enterprise and the supply of goods and services (e.g., grocery stores and kiosks; local artisans such as house-building, baking, tailoring, solar energy kiosks, repair of punctures, repair of engines; local transportation). Local

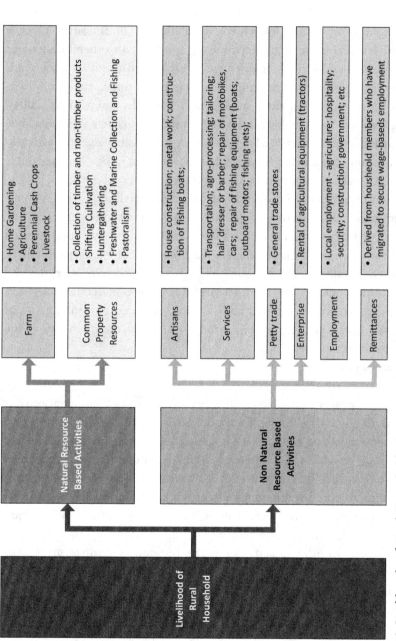

Figure 5.1 Livelihoods of Rural Households Comprising Natural Resource-Dependent Activities, Provision of Goods and Services, Trade, Employment and Remittances

employment opportunities may exist with government and enterprise and may be formal or informal and on-going or seasonal in nature. Finally household members may leave their household and community to practice natural resource-dependent activities (e.g., fishing) in other locations or seek informal and formal employment in urban environments often sending remittances home. Such migration may be seasonal, circular or represent more permanent rural–urban migration (Ellis and Allision, 2004). Taken together, households can be understood to operate a livelihood system that allocates household resources across possible sectoral activities with the aim of achieving household objectives. Taken together the household's sectoral activities may be described as a livelihood portfolio.

Notwithstanding the operation of diversified livelihoods, households, communities and indeed the population as a whole are often characterised by their primary natural resource-based livelihood activity, being referred to as, for example, hunter-gatherers, shifting cultivators, agriculturalists, fishers, pastoralists or other terms which describe their primary natural resource-dependent livelihood activity. Key aspects of community and household settlement patterns and housing, resource governance, social relations, assets, etc., are usually strongly linked to the operation of the primary livelihood system(s).

Based on the above:

- typically, it is possible to identify primary and secondary natural resource-dependent livelihood activities reflecting the resource endowment and allocation of household resources (primarily land and labour) towards various activities. Primary natural resource-dependent livelihood activities can be expected to make a more significant contribution to core livelihood subsistence or income needs. However, this observation does not diminish the importance of secondary activities, nor mandates a focus on primary livelihood activities only.
- different livelihood activities make different contributions to the household livelihood potentially addressing different objectives, e.g., subsistence, income, risk management, increased resilience, reduced vulnerability and social obligations. In this sense ensuring an ability to maintain diverse livelihoods and further enabling diversification are critical to sustainable household livelihood re-establishment and development and poverty reduction. Means to encourage household

diversification should consider the institutional context, household vulnerability (and reduction thereof) and social attributes of affected households and communities.

- household-level diversification of livelihood activities may serve different objectives for different households. For the majority of rural households, diversification is a risk mitigation strategy. For more well-to-do households, diversification may be a means for asset accumulation. In general, diversification is recognised to widen people's options, reduce reliance on specific natural resources, encourage spatially diverse transactions, increase cash in circulation in rural areas and enhance human capital through the acquisition of new skills and experiences (Ellis and Allison, 2004). Social attributes including migration, mobility, flexibility and adaptability as well as ease of engaging in spatially diverse transactions are identified as critical enablers for household diversification (Ellis and Allison, 2004).

- households with diversified livelihood activity portfolios and income sources may change the relative balance of the portfolio based on context, opportunities and challenges or change the means through which diversification is maintained (e.g., the substitution of own labour by using increased disposable income earned from employment to support contract farming). Livelihood assessment should assess the dynamic nature of livelihoods, describing the breadth of portfolios and the rationale for changes over time.

Understanding the basis for the households' diversified livelihood systems is critical to support:

- understanding of household objectives, priorities and resource allocation between activities.
- categorisation of households, allowing the grouping of households operating a similar diversified livelihood system.
- the identification, assessment and evaluation of impacts associated with disruption of household and community lives and livelihoods.
- the identification, assessment and evaluation of options to support the re-establishment and development of sectoral livelihood activities and effective targeting, design, planning and execution of selected livelihood re-establishment and development interventions. Such interventions may address the conventional focus on improving the

productivity of specific livelihood activities (returns relative to land or labour) or consider related issues including institutional challenges to diversification (e.g., fees, licences, permits, fines, bribes) (Ellis and Allison, 2004); changes in the enabling environment to support diversification (e.g., addressing reduced access/increased cost of access to selected resources); inter-dependency of activities (e.g., cost of labour migrating to project workforce); addressing relative resource demand/requirement for activities; and/or scheduling/phasing of interventions to match household resource availability.

Natural Resource-Based Livelihood Activities

Figure 5.2 illustrates the relationship between the rural population and natural resources in defining primary natural resource-based livelihood systems. Specifically, the figure seeks to classify and characterise primary livelihood systems based on the mobility of either the population or the natural resource that forms the basis of the primary livelihood activity.

The assessment of livelihood activities and elucidation of key land access, involuntary displacement and resettlement issues[2] in relation to these (primary) livelihood activities can be complex and often require specific expertise and experience of the livelihood systems and activities under consideration. Appendix 4 sets out a summary of considerations for assessing the impacts of land access, involuntary displacement and resettlement impacts on primary natural resource-based livelihood systems.

Experience demonstrates that the re-establishment and development of natural resource-based livelihood activities is most straightforward in contexts where: (i) livelihoods involve households having formal (or otherwise

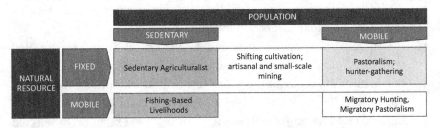

Figure 5.2 Categorisation of Primary Natural Resource-Based Livelihood Systems and Activities

recognised) land tenure and that are implementing sedentary agricultural systems and (11) resettlement involves land-for-land compensation involving land with similar productive characteristics. As noted in Chapter 3, land access and involuntary displacement policies, standards and guidance have generally been informed by experience gained in such contexts.

The assessment and re-establishment and development of livelihoods and livelihood activities become increasingly complex in other resource-dependent livelihood contexts including natural-based livelihoods reliant on open access/common property natural resources (e.g., fishing-based livelihoods, pastoralism and hunter–gathering). IFC (2013) addresses project impacts on fishing-based livelihoods. Limited guidance for other natural resource-based livelihood systems (e.g., pastoralism; forest-based livelihoods) is available.

While approaches to livelihood assessment are described in Chapter 6, it should be noted that there are multiple international research and development institutions focussed on various livelihood systems that may provide useful guidance and support. Examples include (i) the United Nations Food and Agriculture Organisation (FAO); (ii) the network of Centres

Table 5.1 Centre of International Agricultural Research (CIAR)

Acronym	Name	Location
Africa Rice	Africa Rice Centre	Cote D'Ivoire
Biodiversity International and CIAT	The Alliance of Biodiversity International and the International Centre for Tropical Agriculture	Italy/Columbia
CIFOR	Centre for International Forestry Research	Indonesia
CIP	International Potato Centre	Peru
CIMMYT	International Maize and Wheat Improvement Centre	Mexico
ICARDA	International Centre for Agricultural Research in the Dry Areas	Lebanon
ICRISAT	International Crops Research Institute for the Semi-Arid Tropics	India
IFPRI	International Food Policy Research Institute	Washington DC/USA
IITA	International Institute of Tropical Agriculture	Nigeria
ILRI	International Livestock Research Centre	Ethiopia
IRRI	International Rice Research Institute	Philippines
IWMI	International Water Management Institute	India
World Agroforestry ICRAF	World Agroforestry/International Centre for Research in Agroforestry	Kenya
WorldFish	WorldFish Centre	Malaysia

for International Agricultural Research (Table 5.1); (iii) the International Institute for Environment and Development; and (iv) the Institute of Development Studies. Similar institutions may be found at the national level, while the experience of donor assistance programmes and NGOs in promoting livelihood development in the area of interest should also be assessed.

Conclusion

Whether in the context of emergency response, development assistance or resettlement programming, livelihood development is based on an understanding of the rural environment and rural livelihoods. This chapter has set the basis for the more detailed approach to describing and assessing the rural environment and rural livelihoods presented in Chapter 6. Both Chapters 5 and 6 point to the need to:

- place the affected population in the context of the broader environment in which they live and secure their livelihoods.
- recognise that households have livelihood strategies involving the allocation of their resources across diverse sectoral activities. Existing household livelihood strategies are defined by the broader political–economic–social environment in which households operate, household objectives and the specific resources available to the household. Typically, livelihood strategies include primary and secondary activities (reflecting prevalent resource governance systems and the allocation of household resources).
- go beyond the description of the rural environment and household livelihoods to achieve a better understanding of the rationale, construction and operation of household livelihood strategies and component activities. Too often assessment is little more than description – the challenge is to move from the descriptive 'what it is' to the 'why it is' and 'what it means' (from the perspective of the household and communities). Further the truism that a generic description begets a generic programme with less confidence in outcomes needs to be recognised and addressed.
- opportunities for livelihood re-establishment and development should consider the external environment that helps define livelihood options,

the household livelihood strategy and the activity portfolio including primary and secondary activities. Accordingly, livelihood development requires a multi-disciplinary team capable of: (i) assessing local and regional development opportunities and challenges; (ii) understanding household livelihood strategies; and (iii) providing technical expertise for specific sectoral livelihood activities. The multi-disciplinary team should comprise expertise to consider the institutional, economic, social, cultural and gender dimensions of livelihoods.

Notes

1 Merriam-Webster defines rural as "of or relating to the country, country people or life, or agriculture."
2 Including nature of impact (scale, intensity, duration, significance); identification of affected households and communities; the valuation of losses, entitlement and compensation; and re-establishment and development of livelihoods.

Bibliography

Ahearn, A., and Namsrai, B. (2022). Filling a Hole? Compensation for Mining-Induced Losses in the South Gobi. In Sternberg, T., Toktomushev, K., and Ichinkhorloo, B. (Eds.), *The Impact of Mining Lifecycles in Mongolia and Kyrgyzstan, Political, Social, Environmental and Cultural Contexts*. Routledge, London and New York, 76–89.

Catley, A., Lind, J., and Scoones, I. (Eds.). (2013) *Pastoralism and Development in Africa, Dynamic Change at the Margins*. Routledge, London and New York.

Chambers, R. (1983). *Rural; Development, Putting the Last First*. Longman, London.

Chambers, R. (1999). *Whose Reality Counts? Putting the First Last*, 2nd edition. Intermediate Technology Publications.

De Haan, L. J. (2017). *Livelihoods and Development, New Perspectives, Koninkjlijke*. Brill, Leiden, The Netherlands.

Ellis, F., and Allison, E. (2004). *Livelihood Diversification and Natural Resource Access*. Livelihood Support Programme, FAO, Rome.

IFC (2013). *Addressing Project Impacts on Fishing-Based Livelihoods, A Good Practice Handbook: Baseline Assessment and Development of a Fisheries*

Livelihood Restoration Plan. International Finance Corporation, Washington, DC.

Loison, S. A. (2015). Rural Livelihood Diversification in Sub-Saharan Africa: A Literature Review. *The Journal of Development Studies,* 51(9), 1125–1138. https://doi.org/10.1080/00220388.2015.1046445.

McCabe, J. T. (2004). *Cattle Bring Us to Our Enemies: Turkana Ecology, Politics and Raiding in a Disequilibrium Environment.* University of Michigan Press, Ann Arbor, MI.

Mphande, F. A. (2016). Rural Livelihood. In *Infectious Diseases and Rural Livelihood in Developing Countries,* 17–39. Springer Science+Business Media, Singapore.

Scoones, I. (2015). *Sustainable Livelihoods and Rural Development.* Practical Action Publishing.

6

ASSESSMENT OF THE RURAL ENVIRONMENT AND RURAL LIVELIHOODS

DOI: 10.4324/9781003358725-8

For some the assessment of the rural environment and rural livelihoods serves to describe the pre-project context and establish the baseline which will serve as the nominal minimum objective for 'livelihood restoration.' This chapter argues that the pre-project baseline should serve to inform resettlement design and planning about the resettlement-affected population's point of departure rather than their point of return. Assessment and analysis of household livelihood strategies and particularly the categorisation of households based on their livelihood strategies should serve to inform resettlement design and planning about the point of departure – their objectives, the current capabilities, assets and activities and the broader environment – and how to optimise the design of livelihood re-establishment and development in light of the changes wrought by resettlement, project development and the broader-based area development that may occur. As such the challenge is to move from the descriptive 'what it is' to the 'why it is' and 'what it means' from the perspectives of affected households and communities, resettlement and livelihood re-establishment and development.

An Overview of the Approach

This chapter elucidates the recommended approach for the assessment of the rural environment and rural livelihoods and its relationship to the development of a (Land Access and) Resettlement Action Plan or a Livelihood Restoration Plan (Figure 6.1).

At the outset, it is recognised that the resettlement-affected population is a subset of the local population. The resettlement-affected population is defined by the project's need for land; impacts on the area, access to and/or use of land and natural resources; or need to mitigate health and safety impacts that make continued in situ residence and use of land and resources impossible. For most projects, the broader population located in the immediate vicinity of the project is likely to face a similar context and operate livelihoods that are similar to the resettlement-affected population. As such, resettlement may require, and also provide the opportunity for, broader-based livelihood re-establishment and development initiatives that benefit both the resettlement-affected population and the general population.

Based on the above, the first step in the assessment process involves the *assessment of the broader rural environment* (Section 'The Rural Environment'). The purpose of such an assessment is to develop a profile of the broader context

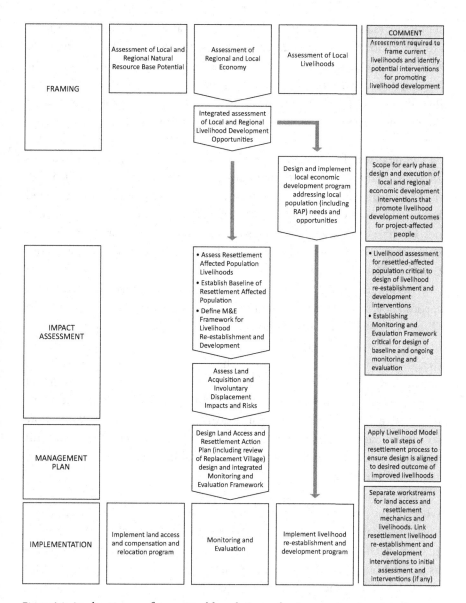

Figure 6.1 Application of a Livelihood-Centred Approach in Involuntary Displacement and Resettlement Design, Planning and Execution

in which the resettlement-affected population exists, facilitate the identification of local and regional economic development opportunities and challenges and determine what is required to enable development. Thus, in addition to a general profile of the rural environment, the assessment should include (i) an assessment of the natural resource potential of the area (both local and regional); (ii) an assessment of the local and regional economy; and (iii) an assessment and description of the prevalent livelihood systems. By looking at these different aspects, the assessment informs the potential opportunities and the pathways for development, including the potential for the development of natural resource-dependent production systems.

The next step focuses on the resettlement-affected population, with (i) an assessment of the resettlement-affected population's livelihood objectives, strategies, activities and outcomes; (ii) a categorisation of affected households by livelihood strategy; and, (iii) an evaluation of opportunities for (targeted) livelihood re-establishment and development (Section 'Assessing the Livelihoods of Resettlement-Affected Households and Communities').

Together these steps help inform an *assessment of land access, involuntary displacement and resettlement impacts and risks*, leading to the development of a (Land Access and) Resettlement Action Plan (LA)RAP. To help ensure that livelihood considerations are identified, assessed and integrated into every step of the resettlement process in the (LA)RAP, Chapter 7 provides an example of the application of a livelihood model to the entire resettlement process. Early definition of the livelihood re-establishment and development M&E framework during the (LA)RAP design phase will promote consistent data collection throughout the project life cycle, and a continuous focus on the intended livelihood re-establishment and development outcomes (Chapter 9).

The ensuing (LA)RAP implementation phase should comprise two main workstreams, firstly, land access, compensation and relocation and, secondly, re-establishment and development of livelihood activities. As argued in more detail in Chapter 10, these should be implemented simultaneously as parallel but related workstreams. Chapter 8 focuses on the re-establishment and development of livelihood activities.

The Rural Environment

As noted, resettlement-affected communities are a subset of the local population impacted by project development, identified by the project's need for land; restriction of area, access to and/or use of land and natural resources; and project health and safety impacts.

To properly understand the lives and livelihoods of the resettlement-affected population requires that we consider the affected population within the broader environment. Such an analysis will demonstrate how the resettlement-affected population (and the general population inhabiting the same area) live. Such a contextual assessment may be needed for both the resettlement-affected population's pre- and post-displacement location, particularly if the latter involves a distant resettlement site or otherwise significantly different context (for example, differences in ethnicity, culture, faith, natural resource base, ownership and/or access resources). In this way, the livelihood assessment places the resettlement-affected population in the political–economic–social–cultural context in which they secure their livelihoods.

Beyond understanding the current context of the resettlement-affected population, an assessment of the rural environment is also required to understand the opportunities and challenges for market-driven development. This includes the identification of interventions that may help unlock entry, development or expansion of economic activities and markets that have the potential to promote livelihood development opportunities for the resettlement-affected population and the broader population.

Implicit in the above is the recognition that resettlement design, planning and execution should consider resettlement-driven investment in activities beyond the 'resettlement footprint,' thereby simultaneously benefitting the general population. Put differently, to be successful, resettlement-sponsored interventions promoting re-establishment and development of livelihood activities should not be viewed as being tied to the location of households to be displaced or to the proposed resettlement site and not necessarily providing exclusive benefit to the resettlement-affected population. For example, activities to enable or facilitate local economic development (e.g., unlocking commodity value chains and markets) that create opportunities for livelihood development for the resettlement-affected and general population are potentially a powerful contribution to the success of resettlement, the socio-economic development of proximate populations, the creation of an enabling environment and ultimately the project social licence. Based on the preceding, one can understand that interventions to promote livelihood re-establishment and development may (need to) be implemented well beyond the resettlement-affected communities themselves.

Assessment of the Rural Environment

The general description and assessment of the rural environment should include:

- **Regional and local government administration**: the structure of regional and local government administration (including decision-making powers, authority and budget), the human resources (number, capability) and the services (presence, accessibility, level, quality) provided by the government to the population (e.g., education, health, agricultural extension, business development) are important aspects of the context. The profile of government will identify both government leaders and departments relevant to resettlement design, planning and execution, the handover of resettlement infrastructure services and utilities, the re-establishment and development of livelihood activities and the key stakeholders within the identified departments.

- **Capacity and Resources of Regional and Local Government**: beyond the structure of the administration and identification of key stakeholders, an assessment of the capacity and resources of regional and local government in terms of their ability to provide support to the local population (including resettlement-affected communities) and as a potential partner with the project is needed. It is important to recognise that given the range of social issues associated with resettlement, identification and engagement of diverse government stakeholders may well be necessary. While engagement with the government should be considered a given, understanding to what extent the project can rely on an interface with the government is critical in design and planning, this being especially the case with regard to the administration of the replacement village and operation, maintenance and repair of infrastructure services and utilities. Early interventions in assessing and building requisite capacity may be critical to ensuring longer-term sustainability and independence.

- **Regional and Local Economic Opportunity**: mapping of the natural resource potential, assessment of the business environment and activity, and economic analyses identifying sectors with growth potential help identify and assess potential livelihood (activity) re-establishment and development (refer Section 'Assessing the Local and Regional Economy').

- **Accessibility (roads) and transportation**: the road network comprising primary, secondary and tertiary roads determines access to natural resources, commercial centres, markets and government services. Beyond the road network, the availability and cost of transportation to facilitate exchange is an important aspect of linking people to resources and markets.
- **Provision of services (education, health, social security, financial services, extension services for sectoral livelihood activities)**: access to services – including education, health, financial services and extension services for sectoral livelihood activities – is an important indicator of the ease with which the local population can address basic needs and the readiness of a population to participate in project construction and operations and the area development that project development may catalyse.
- **Access to utilities (e.g., power, water, telecommunications)**: access to utilities – primarily power, water and telecommunications – is an important indicator of development, helping to increase labour availability and providing inputs for economic activity.
- **Population**: description of key information of the area population including the history of settlement, ethnic groups/tribes, language, faith, settlement, housing, household composition, age, education, employment, etc.

Assessing the Potential of the Natural Resource Base

Assessment of the potential of the natural resource base to support various livelihood sectors/activities (often characterised as *land use suitability*) provides the basis for the identification of existing and potential land uses and their scale and extent. Such an assessment may demonstrate current and potential land use and identify the potential of the natural resource base to support expansion and/or intensification of existing activities or the introduction of new activities at scale. In addition to biophysical characteristics, one should also assess the socio-cultural aspects of land and natural resource ownership, access and use. In this way the assessment will also help inform the potential for market-driven development of sectoral activities.

Assessing the Local and Regional Economy

Assessment of the local and regional economy aims to build awareness and understanding of (i) local and regional economic activity; (ii) how current livelihood systems interact with markets; and (iii) the potential to attract existing market actors and build commodity value chains in the project area of influence. The assessment of local and regional economic opportunity is based on the integration of component studies as discussed below:

- **Local and Regional Markets**: a profile of local and regional markets in proximate commercial centres can reveal the sectors, types and scale of economic activity and help identify the main entrepreneurs active in various sectors. It is worth noting that larger – and perhaps more distant commercial centres – often defined by better access (road, sea), infrastructure, services and utilities and serving as a regional economic hub/node may demonstrate activity and potential that are not evident at the local level.
- **Profile of Informal and Formal Activity of Micro-, Small and Medium Enterprises**: a business assessment focusing on micro-, small and medium enterprises in regional and local commercial centres can demonstrate sectors, types and scale of economic activity that exist today and – through the engagement of entrepreneurs – help identify potential sectoral opportunities and challenges for entry, development and growth of a business.

Box 8.1 describes the process through which the market-driven development of natural resource-dependent production systems is assessed and supported.

Assessing the Local and Regional Prevalence of Livelihood Systems

Area-wide mapping of livelihood systems aims to place the livelihoods of the resettlement-affected population in the context of the local and regional population and seeks to assess if there is a critical mass of primary producers who might be targeted for development interventions and market development.

There are various approaches to defining and mapping household farm typologies (Cramb and Newby, 2015) including:

(i)   farming systems research and recommendation domains
(ii) agro-ecosystems analysis and agro-ecological zoning
(iii) agrarian systems analysis and multi-level typologies
(iv) rural livelihoods analysis and diverse livelihood strategies
(v)   household types in policy analysis

The Save the Children Household Economy Approach (HEA)[1] focused on assessing household food security and vulnerability sets out one approach to the description and characterisation of area livelihood systems.

Assessing the Livelihoods of Resettlement-Affected Households and Communities

A comprehensive livelihood assessment together with the implementation of a socio-economic baseline and census of the resettlement-affected households are the building blocks for informed resettlement design, planning and execution, including interventions supporting the re-establishment and development of livelihood activities. This section uses the livelihood concepts and models presented in Chapter 4 to inform approaches to the assessment of rural household and community livelihoods and the design and implementation of the socio-economic baseline and census. Additional dimensions (e.g., demographic analysis, vulnerability and development trajectories) that may contribute to a more dynamic and meaningful analysis of household livelihoods, livelihood development and livelihood trajectories are addressed in Section 'Additional Considerations.'

Description of Household and Community Rural Livelihoods

A comprehensive description of rural livelihoods should include:

• a description of the village(s), settlement(s) and household biophysical resource base (e.g., village territory, land uses including residential, agricultural land, pastoral land, forest resources, aquatic and marine resources).

- description and analysis of traditional and existing land tenure and ownership and governance systems including individual and household land ownership and access to and use of common property resources (land, pasture, forest, aquatic resources). In addition, the assessment of land and housing markets may be relevant in certain circumstances.
- description of existing (village) infrastructure (administration, meeting halls, markets, places of worship, recreational facilities, housing) and services (health, education, waste management) and utilities (electricity, water and sanitation). For household infrastructure and utilities, it is important to understand differences in both provision and use between households.
- the socio-economic profile of affected households and communities including:
  (i)   description of the recent history of settlement reflecting an understanding of reasons that people choose to settle in a given location. In principle it might be assumed that, for historical or current reasons, the existing settlement(s) convey some comparative advantage for the resident population, e.g., relative autonomy, territorial, security, accessibility, seasonal access to resources (e.g., water, pasture), trade routes. In addition, consideration should be given to the possibility of seasonal occupation, e.g., proximity to fishing grounds, or seasonal migration, e.g., urban employment.
  (ii) description of the ethnic and socio-cultural characteristics of the resettlement-affected people including tribe-ethnic groups; village leadership and administration; village community–social organisation and networks; family and household structures; gender relations, roles and responsibilities; vulnerable groups including tenants, squatters, female- or child-headed households, elderly, infirm; etc.
- demographic profile of the resettlement-affected population including age, gender, education, health, faith and capabilities. Beyond a static point-in-time profile, the assessment should also describe trends in household and settlement growth, the extent of local and non-local migration and settlement, etc. This information is useful for the following reasons: (i) to understand pre-project population dynamics

including natural household growth and extended family groupings; (ii) to predict the impact of the construction of replacement housing and the resettlement village which, due to improved housing standards and access to services and utilities, may encourage stabilisation of the relocated population and influx of population; (iii) to predict the impact of project development on in-migration (of extended families); and (iv) to predict the impacts of increased disposable income (from wage employment) on housing and settlement behaviour.

• assessment of stock of household assets/capitals – human, social, natural, physical and financial. It is important to assess the total stock of household assets irrespective of location. In this sense assets located within the project-affected area and beyond it are necessary to understand livelihoods.

• description of household and community livelihood strategies and existing capabilities, assets and livelihood activities (not limited to considering economically productive activities) including primary production (agriculture, timber and non-timber forest products, pasture, aquatic resources), commercial activities (enterprises providing goods and services) and wage employment (including remittances). The description should include:

  ○ individual, household, group (e.g., fishing, hunting) and community activities practiced.

  ○ the resource requirements (natural and physical capital) and resource use (primarily labour) for identified activities. Natural capital may include land (with a recognised need to identify all household landholdings including those outside the land being acquired by the project) and common property resources. Physical capital may include agricultural implements, fishing boats and equipment, etc.

  ○ distribution of activities (including key component activities) through each season of the calendar year.

  ○ the allocation and use of labour between productive, domestic and leisure activities; map labour requirements for each activity and the distribution of labour across activities developing a labour allocation and use graph for all economically active household members; ensure due consideration of gender- and age-related roles and responsibilities.

o   production and productivity (returns to land and labour) of activities (both in-kind and cash income).

It is important to characterise the land, labour use and capital intensity of the existing livelihood strategy. Livelihood re-establishment and development interventions may require significant increases in land, labour use and/or capital intensity compared with traditional systems and many therefore face significant challenges in household uptake. In more built-up areas where informal and formal commerce occurs, component studies of markets, etc. may be appropriate.

o   analysis of political, economic, social and cultural determinants of livelihood strategies and livelihood activities including the relationship between the individual/household/community and the broader market.

o   assessment of household income and expenditure – estimates of in-kind and cash income and/or expenditure and standards of living.

BOX 6.1 ASSESSING ACCESS, UTILISATION AND PRODUCTIVITY OF COMMON PROPERTY RESOURCES

Common property resources include terrestrial and aquatic systems including agricultural lands, pasture, forests and freshwater and marine fisheries. Common property resources may be characterised in terms of their communal ownership and (to a greater or lesser extent) communal management although national administrative systems often characterise these resources as belonging to the state and coming under the jurisdiction of a government ministry or department.

Typically, the contribution of common property resources to livelihoods is difficult to quantify. Often the resource encompasses multiple niche ecosystems in which specific products grow and may be harvested (opportunistically) by different household members at different times/seasons. Consequently, the impacts stemming from the loss of common property resources, whether through reductions in the resource base (e.g., through conversion/transformation) or through loss of access, are difficult to quantify and are often under-estimated. Such under-estimation leads to a failure to adequately address resource access in resettlement design and planning and inadequate replacement and/or compensation (i.e., a form of impoverishment).

Typically, for terrestrial systems, extensive forest fallow-based agricultural systems that also permit the collection of timber and non-timber forest products are replaced with smaller areas. Similarly extensive grazing lands may be replaced with smaller areas. Reductions in the area may be associated with increased vulnerability and with increased intensity of usage, reduced resilience and medium-to-long-term degradation of the resources.

For artisanal fisheries, projects may have a wide range of impacts including reductions in the size of fishing grounds (e.g., through the establishment of marine exclusion zones), reduced access to fishing grounds (e.g., increased distance to fishing grounds, increased risks in accessing fishing grounds), increased risks regarding safety and security, potential damage for equipment, declining productivity (e.g., through acoustic disturbance, increased turbidity, pollution events), all of which lead to reduced livelihoods. These impacts affect the operational cost of the activity, the returns of the activity (i.e., harvest/unit effort) as well as the economics of the livelihood activity.

Further it is important to note that communities with a long history of accessing common property resources have well-established and intimate knowledge of these resources. Relocation to alternative resources is associated with transition costs for communities to locate and become familiar with replacement resources. Any intensification of resource use may require new management systems.

Considering the above, both expert and thorough assessment of pre-resettlement household and community access to and use of common property resources is needed. Baseline information can then inform impacts associated with loss of or changing access to and use of common property resources. For example, if a small community has access to 1,000 ha of forest in which they practice long-fallow shifting cultivation and collect specific forest products to meet household food needs (including the hunting of wildlife), to manufacture household items (mats, baskets, etc.), for medicinal purposes, house construction (thatch, wood), as well as for sale (e.g., jungle vegetables and fruit), how large a replacement area is required? Should one verify the existence of key species used by the community; the area required for wildlife; and demonstrate that pre-relocation management regimes can continue and will not adversely affect the resource?

BOX 6.2 DETERMINING FISHING PARTICIPATION RATES AT THE TANGGUH LNG PROJECT (IFC 2015). PERMISSION: IFC

At the Tangguh LNG project site in West Papua, Indonesia, the Tanah Merah community members practised diversified livelihoods comprising fishing, agriculture, hunting and gathering, and employment. Key informants described the evolution of livelihood activities and participation rates in terms of economic opportunity – whereas fishing has always been part of their livelihood strategy, participation rates have varied in accordance with the availability of alternative economic opportunities

In the early 1990s, participation rates in fishing increased with the establishment of a local prawn processing facility and increased demand for prawns from Sorong-based traders. However, participation rates declined gradually from 2004 as project-related wage labour opportunities became available.

As such, depending on when an assessment is conducted, assessment of household fishing activities through surveys of household participation rates and resource use intensity could yield markedly different results from household surveys documenting ownership of assets and equipment for fishing. Nonetheless, most households would have identified themselves as fishermen, irrespective of their day-to-day participation in fishing or other activities such as construction.

BOX 6.3 INTEGRATING GENDER CONSIDERATIONS INTO FISHERIES ASSESSMENT (IFC 2015). PERMISSION: IFC

At the Tangguh LNG project in West Papua, Indonesia, the key fishing activities of residents of Tanah Merah village comprised drift net fishing for prawns and fish, line fishing and collecting shellfish on the tidal mudflats. Drift net fishing involves the use of small canoes (powered by paddles and sails or outboard motors to reach the fishing grounds) that drift along the shoreline on the incoming/outgoing tides. Harvested prawns were sold to traders in the village. This activity was male-dominated (until project employment removed men from village-level economic activities). However, the collection of shellfish on mudflats near the village, which was carried out by small groups of women and children, involved little more than a digging stick and bucket. However, the assessment of fishing activities only identified the driftnet fishing activities of the affected households, despite the completion of a baseline household survey.

While efforts to address the combined impacts of the project exclusion zone and greater resource utilisation stemming from the combination of the host village and resettlement village population were finally addressed by the project through the provision of outboard motors to households, there was no assessment of the importance of shellfish harvesting, the capacity of the resettlement site to support the activity or, ultimately, the impact of resettlement on the activity.

BOX 6.4 THE IMPACTS OF SEASONALITY
(IFC 2015). PERMISSION: IFC

The initial scoping and preliminary environmental and social impact assessment of the Sadiola Gold Mine, which is in the Sahel region of landlocked Mali, approximately 150 to 200 km south of the Sahara Desert, was undertaken in the middle of the dry season. There was no surface water in the area at the time, and the nearest perennial river (the Senegal River) was 70 km from the project. Comprehensive stakeholder focus groups and household livelihood and food security questionnaires failed to elicit any mention of fish consumption in the area.

The researchers subsequently returned to the project site in the middle of the wet season to find that the previously dry tributaries of the Senegal River at the project site were flowing intermittently and contained significant fish populations (which had migrated upstream from the Senegal River) that were being harvested by local Bambara households and migrant Bozo fishermen. The fishing season was short but provided important supplemental food supplies for local households. Thus, it was recognised that it was important to assess the impacts of the mine on local seasonal stream catchments.

Photo 6.1 Tributary of the Senegal River in the wet season Credit: Arjun Bhalla

BOX 6.5 ASSESSING THE (SOCIAL) BOUNDARIES OF PROJECT FISHING IMPACTS (IFC 2015). PERMISSION: IFC

Initial assessment of project's impacts on fishing activities in the vicinity of the Tangguh LNG Project in West Papua, Indonesia, derived from work being conducted to assess the impacts of involuntary displacement and resettlement on the Tanah Merah community. Consequently, the assessment focused on the villagers' prawn-harvesting activities that occurred offshore and notionally in front of the village. The activities relied on the use of small canoes, which were paddled, sailed or motored up to 1 km from the shore, where driftnets were cast, and the canoe and net allowed to drift with the incoming/outgoing tides. The fishermen would then return later in the day with the aid of the reverse tide. (Various other fishing activities were not assessed, including the value chain for prawns and women's activities involving the harvesting of bivalves from the muddy intertidal shoreline.)

After relocation, when the Tanah Merah community settled into their new village located opposite the host village Saengga and the project commenced nearshore and onshore construction activities requiring establishment and enforcement of an exclusion zone, the

Saengga community protested that they too were entitled to compensation regarding fishing impacts, claiming that they had used the
same fishing grounds and were thus also impacted by the imposition of the exclusion zone. Consequently, Saengga households also
received compensation in the form of outboard motors that allowed
them to access alternative fishing grounds more readily. This issue
would have been identified earlier if the environmental and social
impact assessment had conducted a more thorough assessment of
fisheries activities proximate to the proposed LNG site and recognised that households from neighbouring villages made use of the
same fishing grounds.

Analysis of Household and Community Livelihoods

As noted in Chapter 1, the assessment of household and community livelihoods is often limited to a generic description of the affected population
and their livelihood activities, failing to work through the livelihood hier-
archy (objectives, strategy, activities, outcomes) and differentiate between
households in the affected communities.

At the outset, one must recognise that households do not share one
household livelihood strategy nor is an individual household strategy necessarily fixed in time. In any one community, one might expect that:

- household livelihood strategies exist to achieve multiple goals
  simultaneously.
- households have different capabilities, and this may affect their current
  and potential range of livelihood activities.
- households are at different stages of their life cycle affecting labour
  availability and the mix and relative importance of their livelihood
  activities.
- households have differential access to livelihood assets, and this differential access determines the mix and relative importance of their
  livelihood activities.
- households combine different activities to meet the objectives of their
  livelihood strategies in different ways.

- changing circumstances (including unanticipated events) may cause a relative change in emphasis between goals (with survival being deemed to be the primary goal) and activities.

Based on the above, livelihood assessment and analysis needs to move beyond a generic description of household livelihoods and component activities with the aim of understanding:

- the influence of the external environment on household livelihood strategies.
- the rationale for individual household livelihood strategies.
- the relationships between capabilities, assets and activities for different households and how they help define household livelihood strategies.
- the basis for categorisation of a resettlement-affected population into livelihood groups that may be usefully targeted with specific livelihood re-establishment and development interventions. This process will also help improve the assessment of resettlement impacts on livelihoods and lead to the identification of groups that may be more vulnerable to livelihood impacts and other changes introduced by resettlement.

While there is no set way for conducting a livelihoods analysis, it is important to gain an understanding of key themes (Ashley and Hussein, 2000). The key themes and derivative questions are presented below. Multiple approaches, methods and tools may be used to investigate these themes (Section 'Methods for Description and Analysis of Livelihoods'). Generally, the investigation does not involve asking households the identified questions directly, especially given that the questions may be abstract in nature and interest lies in specific examples and detailed accounts. In this way much can be deduced from focused discussion with household members of affected households. Once complete, conducting validation exercises with the households and communities is important to confirm that the derived understanding is both valid and comprehensive.

Theme No. 1: Current Livelihood Strategies, Achievements and Priorities

The analysis should identify livelihood strategies and their component activities and attempt to define the rationale (i.e., goals) for household selection of these livelihood strategies and activities, whether this is defined at the individual, household and/or community level. These goals might include income; risk mitigation; food security; labour allocation between productive, domestic, social and leisure activities; livelihood stability and/ or resilience; social status; etc. Key questions include:

- what are individual, household and community livelihood objectives and priorities?
- what livelihood strategies and activities do households pursue? What are the underlying priorities and preferences that influence household livelihood strategies?
- how do households allocate their (limited) resources across competing activities?
- are these activities competitive or complementary with regard to household resources (labour; capital, etc.)?
- what livelihood outcomes do people achieve?

Theme No. 2: Factors That Influence Livelihood Strategies and the Combination and Scale of Livelihood Activities

Determinants of household livelihood strategies and activities may be identified while describing current livelihood systems. These may include the following:

(i)   the households' circumstances (stage of family life cycle, labour availability, health, capacity, assets)
(ii) group- or community-level determinants (e.g., structures, governance regulating access and use of resources, and empowerment)
(iii) the natural conditions (e.g., climate and seasonality)
(iv) institutional issues (e.g., the power balance between local institutions)
(v)   the broader political–economic–social–cultural environment including security, accessibility and transportation, markets, etc.
(vi) the policy environment (e.g., tenure or credit policies)

It is useful to distinguish between determinants that cannot readily be changed (e.g., women's lack of time to participate) and those that are more amenable to change.

Theme No. 3: How and Why Are Livelihoods Changing?

Analysis should investigate both how and why household and community livelihoods' have changed over time, including drivers/causes of change, household and community coping and adaptive mechanisms, etc. A timeline of the dynamics of livelihood activities (including land use change, annual and perennial cash crops, fishing, etc.) over the last 5–10 years including household adoption, participation, employment and income should be developed and interrogated. Through this process, one may come to understand the entry, expansion and/or decline of key activities and land uses, especially those which are dependent on external markets. For example: (i) land use managed by pre-independence colonial actors; (ii) land use change associated with entry of perennial cash crops (e.g., pepper, cloves, nutmeg, cocoa, coffee, coconut, cashew, palm oil) including government incentives and availability of private sector markets; (iii) activities associated with specific local or regional market demand, e.g., charcoal, dried fish, or entry of middlemen in commodity value chains; (iv) land use changes as opportunity for and participation in wage based employment increases, etc.
      Key topics to consider include:

(i)   assess the stability of key livelihood activities in terms of participation, scale and production and identify key determinants of stability/instability.
(ii)   how are livelihoods evolving?
(iii)   how have households adapted to changing circumstances?
(iv)   identify events (internal and external) that led to changes in livelihoods and/or relative importance of livelihood activities. Changes may include natural disasters, man-made disruptions (e.g., conflict), improved access (e.g., roads), improved access and participation in education leading to outmigration in search of employment, the entry/exit of commodity-specific markets, the entry of large-scale projects, development-assistance projects, etc.
(v)   explore how affected households and communities cope with shocks including natural disasters (e.g., extreme weather events) or man-made disruptions?
(vi)   explore how and why change has affected households differently. How did different households respond to change? What were the

outcomes achieved? Are there examples of success or failure? Which household characteristics were associated with successful coping or adaptation strategies and which were associated with failure to cope or adapt?

(vii)   identify if and when new livelihood activities were introduced. For example, in terms of agriculture, significant changes in livelihood activities may be correlated to improved access, the introduction and adoption of improved crop varieties or new crops, perennial cash crops or market demand for specific products, government incentive schemes, etc.

(viii) identify which changes are long-term 'adaptive' strategies (adapting to either new opportunities or constraints) and which are short-term 'coping' strategies (Scoones, 1998).

(ix)   assess the current livelihood trajectory of different household categories? Which households are most/least successful? Why?

Theme No. 4: Livelihood Analysis – Categorisation/ Grouping of Households

As noted in Chapter 4, livelihood concepts are usually applied at a household level. In practice, interventions promoting livelihood re-establishment and development generally target the resettlement-affected population (whether comprising a group, a single community or multiple villages) and to a greater or lesser extent, treating them as a homogenous population. However, a more granular approach is needed if appropriate interventions are to be identified and be successful.

Livelihood analysis requires exploration of the existence and nature of the different livelihood strategies used by the individual households that together comprise the target population. The process of household categorisation based on livelihood strategy aims to address the challenge of delivering relevant livelihood development interventions, moving from considering that the population is (relatively) homogenous towards developing tailored interventions for individual households.

Categorisation and grouping require an analysis of household livelihood strategies including capacity, assets and activities to explore if there is any basis for differentiation between the households who comprise the resettlement-affected population. The categorisation and grouping of the displaced households provide the basis for the selection and design of tailored (either in target, content and/or scheduling) livelihood re-establishment and development programs targeting identified groups within the resettlement-affected population. The attributes of the identified groups (e.g., size, composition) then provide the basis for defining target participation and success rates. Through this approach, it is possible to provide more relevant interventions based on inputs from the identified category group, ensure the appropriate baseline to evaluate the success/failure of a livelihood intervention and increase household ownership and participation. Taken together such an approach will help save project resources.

Generally, a useful approach to identifying different household livelihood strategies includes:

(i)   use of Participatory Rural Appraisal (PRA) and Focus Group Discussions to understand different stakeholders' perspectives (including elders, men, women, youth, community) on the identification and categorisation of groups.[2] In so doing it is critical that assessment provides the opportunity for separate exercises for men and women, recognising that household roles and responsibilities differ by gender and that often women's roles and responsibilities and thus labour allocation are insufficiently recognised and often under-valued

(ii)   a limited number of in-depth household case studies (preferably identified through PRA exercises) mapping change in their livelihood strategy; capabilities; assets and activities; and trajectory, over the last 5–10 years.

BOX 6.6 UNDERSTANDING COMPLEX SOCIAL AND LIVELIHOOD ACTIVITIES AMONGST THE PASTORALIST TURKANA, KENYA

Tullow Oil implemented exploration activities involving seismic campaigns and well drilling in Turkana, NW Kenya, from 2014 to 2018. Traditional Turkana (*Ng'iTurkana*) are pastoralists seasonally migrating with their goats, sheep, donkeys and camels (and to a lesser extent cattle) over 300 km to ensure livestock access to pasture and water resources. In this sense, to understand the Turkana is to understand the relationship between people, land (environment), livelihoods (livestock) and external pressures such as drought, disease and raiding. Within this context, understanding traditional social structures, leadership, governance and decision-making and the inter-relationships between genealogy (clans), territorial geographical affiliation and settlement and migration patterns are fundamental to understanding how the Turkana survive in a challenging semi-arid and arid environment and how project activities may impact them. Beyond pastoralism, in recent decades (i.e., post-1980) 'traditional' Turkana have been changed by various factors including emergency relief, settlement in rural areas, increased urbanisation, higher levels of participation in higher education (generally outside Turkana) and, most recently, devolution following the adoption of a new Constitution in 2010.

Tullow Oil ESIA supporting seismic and exploration drilling failed to adequately describe (i) the Turkana traditional social structures, leadership, governance and decision-making and the inter-relationships between genealogy (clans), territorial geographical affiliation and settlement and migration patterns; (ii) pastoralism; and (iii) their management of resources within the arid landscape, thus limiting their ability to assess the occurrence and nature of potential economic displacement impacts associated with their activities.

Development of the Project Stakeholder Engagement Plan sought to partially address this gap, starting first with Project Community Liaison Officers (CLOs). While useful, the CLOs represented a class of educated Turkana, who received such education by virtue of their pastoralist leaders' recognition and commitment to improve livelihoods. Given the limited availability of educational services locally, access to secondary and higher education required Turkana to leave the county and board at regional schools. Consequently, the CLOs lost some of their connection to traditional Turkana society and pastoralism and could only partially describe the attributes of their system, also struggling to identify English-language equivalents to describe the Turkana system.

The final summary description of the Turkana (Ng'iTurkana) was derived from multiple sources including literature, Tullow Oil Kenya Turkana staff, key informants and communities within the area influenced by Tullow Oil Kenya's activities. The information was subject to validation sessions with representatives from communities as well as civil society and County Government.

BOX 6.7 AGRICULTURALISTS AND FISHER-FOLK OF TANAH MERAH VILLAGE, BINTUNI BAY, WEST PAPUA, INDONESIA

The BP Tangguh Liquefied Natural Gas (LNG) Project is in the Bintuni Bay on the Bird's Head Peninsula of West Papua, Indonesia. Construction of the project started in 2001 and was completed in 2006; operations commenced in 2007. The Tangguh LARAP provides an overview of household livelihood activities including agriculture and forest resource use; intertidal and fishing activities; trade; and employment – in summary, households operated a diversified livelihood system. The description of natural resource-based livelihood activities is general in nature with limited detail of activities, participation rates, labour allocation, productivity and contribution to the household. While it is recognised that the assessment of livelihood activities has shortcomings, an interesting detail not captured in the description is that of the largest clans occupying Tanah Merah (i.e., Wayuri, Agofa, Kamisopa, Masipa), the Wayuri and Agofa could be described as agriculturalists and fishers while the Kamisopa and Masipa were essentially seafarers focusing on fishing-based livelihoods and trade. (Other differences between clans were also identified including origin, faith, residential location within the village, etc.) The orientation to agriculture is, in some ways, a first-level stratification of the population in relation to agricultural livelihood re-establishment and development.

The bases for categorisation and grouping of the affected households according to livelihood strategy may vary and may involve multiple variables depending on context. Possible bases for categorisation of the affected/target population into different groups include:

- livelihood objectives and strategies
- household activities
- household asset base (land, labour, etc.)
- capacity of household head and household working age population
- profession – different households may vary by the degree of specialisation/dependence – primary and secondary livelihood activities
- household mobility and availability of remittances

- household labour resource
- household labour allocation by activity
- household income by activity
- household wealth
- vulnerability – poverty; health; marital-family status; age
- number and diversity of household livelihood activities

Figures 6.2–6.4 provide conceptual illustrations of possible categorisation and grouping of a population by labour, productive assets (land) and wealth. Each figure highlights how stratification of the population can help identification and targeting of groups, including more vulnerable groups. Note however that stratification and categorisation may be based on a combination of the factors identified above.

Figure 6.2 illustrates stratification by household labour availability during the family life cycle. The figure illustrates specific challenges for nuclear families with young children and for the elderly. Similar patterns are observed for vulnerable families although many of these families are already characterised by lower family labour availability. For these households, the provision of resettlement- and/or project-related employment will compete directly with livelihood re-establishment and development activities.

Figure 6.3 illustrates stratification by productive assets. Households with marginal or no productive assets may be identified as more vulnerable.

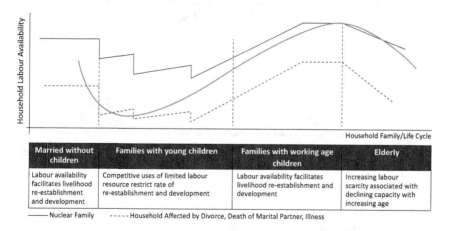

Married without children	Families with young children	Families with working age children	Elderly
Labour availability facilitates livelihood re-establishment and development	Competitive uses of limited labour resource restrict rate of re-establishment and development	Labour availability facilitates livelihood re-establishment and development	Increasing labour scarcity associated with declining capacity with increasing age

——— Nuclear Family   - - - - - Household Affected by Divorce, Death of Marital Partner, Illness

Figure 6.2 Stratification of Households by Household Labour Availability

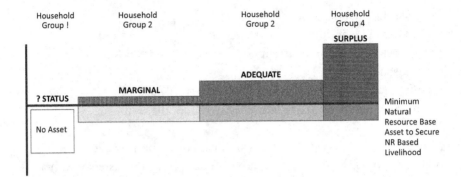

Figure 6.3 Stratification of Households by Household Productive Assets

Measures to address these households, e.g., tenant farmers and sharecroppers, need careful consideration as the continuation of their livelihoods – and hence prevention of impoverishment – relies on securing access to assets or a continuation of the prevailing livelihood system. Note that in situations where households are heavily reliant on common property resources, this analysis is considerably more complex (i.e., issues with access, area or uniformity in distribution of resources).

Figure 6.4 illustrates the stratification of household livelihood strategies by wealth/poverty. Like the previous figure regarding assets, this figure highlights the vulnerability of poor households. Poverty affects household decision-making regarding diversification and the management of risk, vulnerability and resilience. Understanding the underlying causes of poverty, e.g., poor asset base and limited labour due to the stage of the family life cycle, allows for targeted assistance in livelihood re-establishment.

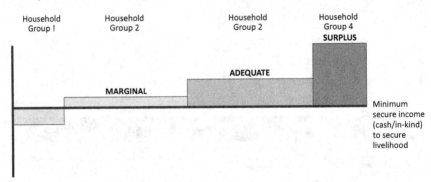

Figure 6.4 Stratification of Households by Household Livelihood Strategy and Household Poverty–Wealth

Ultimately what should be understood is that households may have different livelihood strategies based on their livelihood objectives and current capabilities, assets and activities and the livelihood outcomes achieved through the use of these factors.

Methods for Description and Analysis of Livelihoods

Livelihood re-establishment and development can only be successful if the target households assume ownership and participate in the assessment, design, planning and implementation of livelihood development interventions. Accordingly, it is critical to establish an approach that ensures community, group and household ownership and participation throughout the project cycle from initial assessment to design, implementation and evaluation. The recommended approach would combine the methods and tools of assessment with the community development processes, promoting awareness, understanding, participation and ownership. For example, the process for the assessment should serve to establish the building blocks to enable the establishment of livelihood development groups (at the group or community level as appropriate) with whom the project and specific livelihood development programs can work on an on-going basis.

Without such a deliberate, participatory, trust-building and development-oriented approach, many project-sponsored livelihood interventions will be seen as 'what the project is doing' (a position exacerbated by experiences with aid or government development-assistance programming) and opportunities for controlling benefit distribution and/or capture (e.g., inputs). Further, poorly designed livelihood interventions will be associated with limited participation and uptake rates, wasted resettlement (project) resources and, ultimately, failure to contribute to livelihood re-establishment and development.

The Rapid Rural Appraisal (RRA) and Participatory Rural Appraisal (PRA) approaches have generated many relevant methods and tools through which to build an understanding of household and community livelihoods. Table 6.1 presents some of these methods and tools. Nonetheless it must be recognised that even the most comprehensive efforts to describe and analyse livelihoods will miss aspects of livelihoods by virtue of seasonality, respondents' perceptions of what is important (e.g., prioritisation of income generating, male domain activities) and the relative value placed

Table 6.1 Activities to Support Participatory Livelihood Assessment (Adapted from Ashley and Hussein [2000])

No.	Topics	Activities	What Can Be Learned
1	Categorisation of households by livelihood strategy	Categorise households and seek an explanation of the basis for such categorisation	• Identify household livelihood strategies • Distribution of households between livelihood strategies • Identify key determinants of livelihood strategies • Provide a basis for interrogating household survey data
2	Welfare/wealth ranking	• Carry out welfare/wealth ranking of participants and explanation of criteria • Explore occurrence of changes in welfare/wealth ranking and causes thereof	• Identify local criteria for welfare/wealth • Categorise households based on welfare/wealth ranking • Correlate welfare/wealth and livelihood security
3	Current assets and resources	Identify and discuss household assets and resources currently used to support the family (building blocks). How?	Identify livelihood assets and relative importance
4	Current livelihood activities	List pros and cons Rank according to: • Preference • Contribution to household objectives • Labour requirements • Contribution to income • Importance to household (HH). Discuss. Generate criteria for scoring activities and construct a matrix	• Identify livelihood activities and household objectives • Assess the relative contribution of livelihood activities to household objectives • Use pros and cons to identify challenges, constraints, etc. • Identify livelihood activities and assets • Derive ballpark figures for income from different activities • Establish values other than cash income • Criteria can then be discussed/expanded/ranked As above but more complex. Focuses on locally generated criteria (which can then be ranked). Scoring against criteria is easier to visualise for consensus-building and comparing across stakeholder groups

(Continued)

Table 6.1 (Continued)

No.	Topics	Activities	What Can Be Learned
5	Seasonality	Construct a matrix of activities and needs Construct a matrix or discuss the seasonality of natural resource-based activities, work, food availability, income, etc.	• What needs are, which activities are pursued and why. • Which activities have multiple functions? • Livelihood strategies • Main needs • Availability of human capital
6	Expenditure	• Rank/matrix of items of expenditure • Who decides?	• Impact of earnings (e.g., on needs, HH assets) • Who benefits
7	Scenario building (what if)	Paint a picture (verbally or literally) of a positive and negative future – in general or resulting from resettlement	• Long-term trends without project • Long-term impacts of resettlement and project • Identification of key community issues (both current and future)
8	Constraints	Discuss what are the constraints that prevent livelihood improvement	Encourages focus on household, community and external influences
9	Changes and causes	Construct a matrix of recent major changes and their causes; rank the most influential causes of each change; and discuss how changes impacted households and their activities	• Map changes in livelihoods (capabilities, assets, activities) over time • Identify drivers of change, e.g., the role of external influences • Map individual, household and community responses to change
10	Timeline and trends	Construct timeline. Discuss key events and gradual trends. How people coped or adapted? How are they preparing for the next change? Household action, and community action	• Understand household adaptive and/or coping strategies and mechanisms • Understand relation between intervention and response including (i) potential influence of external policies and organisations and (ii) role of community and household organisation

on different activities (e.g., men and women's activities), etc. Accordingly, it can be reasonably anticipated that the stakeholder engagement and resettlement livelihood teams will need to continue to build on awareness, knowledge and understanding throughout the resettlement program and adapt livelihood programs as necessary. As such, it is important that key staff are familiar with both the livelihood assessment and available methodologies and tools and can assess if and when further assessment and validation are required.

Key approaches, methodologies and tools to describe and analyse livelihoods include:

- *Existing literature and records*: available literature should be collected and reviewed. Potential sources include government, sectoral development plans, other private sector actors within the project-affected area, etc.
- *Observation and Participation*: albeit relatively time-consuming direct observation of people going about their daily activities and participation in selected activities can be the best way to make sense of oral and written information on livelihoods and can provide much that words do not describe. (Ashley and Hussein, 2000).
- *Interviews with Key Informants*: semi-structured interviews with individuals can provide (i) a rapid overview of livelihoods; (ii) specific and detailed information that may not be elucidated through group meetings (for example, who does what in the household, time input to activities, income/expenditure items); and (iii) the basis for triangulation to verify observations, etc.
- *Participatory Assessment of Livelihoods*: RRA and PRA define a broad range of participatory approaches, methods and tools through which to develop an understanding of livelihoods. While these have largely been applied towards the description of livelihoods and livelihood activities, these approaches can also be utilised to facilitate livelihood analysis. Table 6.1 presents some of these methods and tools. Table 6.2 applies the Sustainable Livelihoods Framework to the participatory analysis of household and community livelihoods.
- *Household Surveys*: the establishment of a household socio-economic baseline is an accepted practice for the management of resettlement, and this is generally achieved through the implementation of household surveys. Such surveys provide the means through which substantial

Table 6.2 Group Assessment of Livelihoods (Adapted from Ashley and Hussein [2000])

	Activity I	Activity II	Activity III	Issues to Explore
Assets/Capital				**Dependence and Impact on Assets:**
Human				• Describe activity dependence/use of assets
Physical				• Does the activity affect access to assets, or change their quality or productivity?
Financial				• If natural resources are used, are they used sustainably?
Natural				• Does the activity rely on community co-operation and institutions, particularly institutions for common property resource management?
Social				• Does the activity rely on access to social networks of households or the broader community?
				• Does the activity change the community's relations with the outside world, in terms of influence, co-operation or conflict?
				• Are cash earnings invested in human capital (education, health) or other reserves (financial, physical assets)? Are skills acquired that enhance human capital?
				• Are assets used up in the activity?
Capacity				• Identify and describe the capacity required for each activity
Activity I				• Describe gender roles and responsibilities for activities/component activities
Activity II				
Activity III				
Activity IV				
Activity V				
Activities				**Conflicts and Complementarities with Other Activities:**
Activity I				• Does time spent on this activity compete with other activities?
Activity II				• Does the activity conflict with or complement the seasonal timetable of other existing activities?
Activity III				• Is there competition for inputs (e.g., land, resources) between activities (i.e., what is the opportunity cost)?
Activity IV				
Activity V				

	Activity I	Activity II	Activity III	Issues to Explore
Livelihood Outcomes Increased income Food security Improved well-being (health, education) Sustainability of resource use Empowerment				**Direct Contribution to Outcomes:** • How does the activity contribute directly to improved livelihood outcomes, e.g., cash, food, physical security, empowerment, sustainability? • How significant is the contribution compared to other sources, e.g., how do cash earnings compare with other sources of cash? What is the value in terms of what can be bought? Is the timing of earnings of any significance?
Strategy Diversify Minimise risk Maintain liquidity				• Ascertain the relative contribution/importance of strategic objectives in defining livelihood activities and determine why any one objective takes primacy in defining livelihood strategy
External Policies and Institutions Market Access Attitude Access to decision makers				**Impacts on and of External Influences:** • Does the activity enterprise involve any external forces – organisations, institutions, policies markets and social norms – that influence local livelihoods?
Sustainability, Stability and Resilience Sustainability Stability				• Does the activity affect the sustainability of the natural resource base? • Does the activity play a role in the stability of livelihoods? • Does it help people 'cope' with temporary change, or 'adapt' to a permanent change?
Reduce vulnerability/increase resilience				• How does it relate to long-term trends – does it counter or amplify them? • Does the activity help people cope with shocks or capitalise on positive trends? • Does the activity play a role in reducing the vulnerability of livelihoods?

amounts of information can be collected to inform the description and analysis of livelihoods including household demography and education; household assets; household activities (including participation, labour and other input requirements, productivity, returns); and household income/expenditure. Survey design is important to (i) avoid the often time demanding collection of information more efficiently collected through other means (RRA, PRA, FGD) and (ii) ensure that adequate quantitative and qualitative data is collected to facilitate the description and analysis of livelihoods and subsequent monitoring and evaluation.

• *Financial Data*: beyond an analysis of household income/expenditure patterns that may be secured through focus group discussions or household surveys, other financial data may also be useful. Exploration of markets provides insight into what is sold/purchased, when and for how much. Surveys of markets and shops allow the collection of local price information (e.g., the price of staple foods). Understanding the provision, use and cost of credit as a component of livelihoods can be achieved by visiting creditors (often traders involved in the collection and sale of primary products, provision of key inputs and/or general shop-keepers).

Additional Considerations

This section provides additional considerations necessary to move beyond the static 'point-in-time' assessment set out in the preceding sections. The need to move beyond static assessment – articulated as the need to identify, assess and plan for predictable change associated with the population or stemming from resettlement, project construction and operations and induced area development – has been articulated in preceding chapters. Three key areas have been identified for consideration, namely demographic change, vulnerability and livelihood development trajectories.

Demographic Change: the social baseline and census include the collection of point-in-time demographic data that allows the description of the resettlement-affected households and community; helps identify impacts and defines eligibility, etc.; and informs resettlement design (e.g., household size, gender issues). The demographic data can and should be further analysed to predict how the resettlement-affected population will evolve over time and the implications thereof for the planning and design of the replacement village and housing, adequacy of services and utilities, adequacy of replacement land and evolving livelihood strategies. The most obvious example relates to a rural population where the proportional representation of youth is high and their access to education and opportunities that derive therefrom is low. In such contexts one can anticipate near- and medium-term demand for housing as youth mature and establish their own families and consider the implications thereof (e.g., the requirement for empty house plots to reflect anticipated growth, availability of modular low-cost housing, ease of connection to utilities). Similarly, with regard to livelihoods, if the youth have no option but to continue natural resource-based livelihoods, they will need access to land and resources. Further if they perceive that they have missed out on construction-phase opportunities and are unable to access land and resources and/or diversify and improve their livelihoods, frustration may be directed towards the project.

Vulnerability: the need to account for individual and household vulnerability in resettlement – for example, for the poor, single-female and child-headed households, the physically challenged, and the elderly – has been recognised. In addition there is a need to consider the overall evolving contextual vulnerability and how resettlement, the project and induced area development may impact the vulnerability of the resettlement-affected population. Generally large projects in an underdeveloped environment are associated with an increase in the level of general contextual vulnerability (e.g., through reduced access to land and natural resources, decreases in the diversity of livelihood activities, increasing dependency on selected activities, entry of more capable and better resourced external parties, etc).

For a project involving physical displacement, the implementation of the Resettlement Action Plan may be associated with high levels of cash compensation; ownership titles for land and house; a high-value replacement house; improved infrastructure; and access to services and utilities. These benefits may have adverse impacts on household and community vulnerability – high levels of cash compensation may lead to rent extraction by extended family, neighbouring communities and corrupt officials; ownership titles combined with a high-value asset may promote more permanent settlement and a loss of spatial flexibility to respond to shocks and stresses; opportunists may pressure or otherwise incentivise relocated households to sell replacement houses at discounted prices; access to utilities involves cash income for operation, while maintenance and repair may be hampered by the lack of supplies in the local market; project impact management and social investment programs may encourage enclave development and adversely impact social relations and networks across the area of influence as well as divert government investment away from project-affected areas. In this way, without careful design, planning and implementation, the safeguards defined in the land access, involuntary displacement and resettlement standards and guidelines may well increase the overall vulnerability of the resettlement-affected households.

Finally, and as described in the next section, project construction and operation catalyse change. Without understanding the near- and medium-term nature of such change, it is not possible to increase the resilience and adaptability of the affected population to secure their livelihoods in the face of such change.

Livelihood Development Trajectories: the concept of livelihood development trajectories describes the evolution of household livelihood development strategies over time. Household livelihood strategies may evolve in response to the changing socio-economic environment, changing household objectives and changing household capabilities, assets and activities.

Does project development in undeveloped rural contexts lead to a predictable evolution of livelihood strategies? While context- and country-specific research is limited, evidence from a case study of mining in a South American context[3] indicates that traditional poverty-line subsistence livelihoods may evolve towards:

- commercialisation of agriculture and employment
- diversification to higher value products often with contract labour
- greater production of products relevant to peri-urban and urban markets
- establishment of rural industry and employment
- formal employment and greater investment in selected resource-dependent activities

- perpetuation of rural communities through family remittance payments from elsewhere in the country
- migration/departure – investment outside of an environment

Considering the above, the project should inform the affected population of the likely livelihood development trajectories and encourage strengthening their capabilities to adapt and manage in a changing environment. Although investment in subsistence agriculture is often thought to be an essential first step in promoting improved household welfare (by improving food security and enabling the sale of surplus produce) and enabling investment in other activities, experience in livelihood development suggests this is not necessarily the case. As further described in Chapter 8, deliberate on-going investment in the education of resettlement-affected households (and more generally the project-affected population in the project area of influence) beyond the construction of primary and secondary schools has merit.

Conclusion

Assessment of the rural environment and rural livelihoods allows for the integration of three related streams:

- the area-wide assessment that provides an overview of the environment in which households secure their livelihoods and situates the resettlement-affected population in the broader population
- the description and analysis of the resettlement-affected households' and communities' livelihoods
- an understanding of project construction and operation and anticipated induced socio-economic change

Together such assessment and analysis should inform impact and risk assessment and guide all aspects of resettlement design, planning and execution. Chapter 7 illustrates this concept through the application of the SLF to the component steps of resettlement.

Notes

1 Seaman, J., Boudreau, T., Clarke, P., and Holt, J. (2000) The Household Economy Approach: A resource manual for Practitioners, Save the Children;

Boudrea, T., (2002) Practitioners' Guide to Household Economy Approach. Save the Children.

2 Cramb et al. (2004) provide an example of the use of participatory assessment of rural livelihoods in Vietnam.

3 Refer Bury (2004), Bury (2007) and Castillo and Brereton (2018).

Bibliography

Ashley, C., and Hussein, K. (2000). Developing Methodologies for Livelihood Impact Assessment: Experience of the African Wildlife Foundation in East Africa. Working Paper 129. ODI.

Bainton, N. A., Owen, J. R., and Kemp, D. (2018, September 5). Mining, Mobility and Sustainable Development: An Introduction. *Special Edition Sustainable Development*, 26, 437–440.

Boudreau, T. (2002). *Practitioners' Guide to Household Economy Approach.* Regional Hunger and Vulnerability Program, Food Economy Group and Save the Children.

Bury, J. (2004). Livelihoods in Transition: Transnational Gold Mining Operations and Local Change in Cajamarca, Peru. *The Geographical Journal*, 170(1), 78–91. https://doi.org/10.1111/j.0016-7398.2004.05042.x.

Bury, J. (2007). Mining Migrants: Transnational Mining and Migration Patterns in the Peruvian Andes. *The Professional Geographer*, 59(3), 378–389. https://doi.org/10.1111/j.1467-9272.2007.00620.x.

Castillo, G., and Brereton, D. (2018). Large-Scale Mining, Spatial Mobility, Place-Making and Development in the Peruvian Andes. *Sustainable Development*, 26(5), 461–470.

Catley, A., Lind, J., and Scoones, I. (Eds.). (2013) *Pastoralism and Development in Africa, Dynamic Change at the Margins.* Routledge, London and New York.

Cramb, R. A., Gray, G. D., Gummert, M., Haefele, S. M., Lefroy, R. D. B., Newby, J. C., Stür, W., and Warr, P. (2015). Trajectories of Rice-Based Farming Systems in Mainland Southeast Asia. Australian Centre for International Agricultural Research (ACIAR) Monograph No. 177.

Cramb, R. A., Purcell, T., and Ho, T. C. S. (2004). Participatory Assessment of Rural Livelihoods in the Central Highlands of Vietnam. *Agricultural Systems*, 81(3), 255–272.

De Haan, L. J. (2012). The Livelihood Approach: A Critical Exploration. *Erdkunde*, 66(4), 345–357.

De Haan, L. J. (2017). *Livelihoods and Development, New Perspectives, Koninkjlijke*. Brill, Leiden, The Netherlands.

Department for International Development (1999). Sustainable Livelihoods Guidance Sheets. https://www.livelihoodscentre.org/documents /114097690/114438878/Sustainable+livelihoods+guidance+sheets.pdf /594e5ea6-99a9-2a4e-f288-cbb4ae4bea8b?t=1569512091877.

Emery, M., Gutierrez-Montes, I., and Fernandez-Baca, E. (2013). *Sustainable Rural Development, Sustainable Livelihoods, and the Community Capitals Framework*. Routledge, New York.

FAO & ILO (2009). *The Livelihood Assessment Tool-Kit, Analysing and Responding to the Impact of Disasters on the Livelihoods of People*. FAO, Rome and ILO, Geneva.

Holzmann, P., Boudreau, T., Holt, J., Lawrence, M., and O'Donnell, M. (2008). *The Household Economy Approach, A Guide for Programme Planners and Policy-Makers*. Save the Children.

https://www.livelihoodscentre.org.

IFC (2009). *Projects and People, A Handbook for Addressing Project-Induced in-Migration*. International Finance Corporation, Washington, DC.

IFC (2013). *Addressing Project Impacts on Fishing-Based Livelihoods, A Good Practice Handbook: Baseline Assessment and Development of a Fisheries Livelihood Restoration Plan*. International Finance Corporation, Washington, DC.

IFRC (2010). *IFRC Guidelines for Livelihoods Programming*. International Federation of Red Cross and Red Crescent Societies, Geneva.

Levine, S. (2014). How to Study Livelihoods: Bringing a Sustainable Livelihoods Framework to Life. Working Paper No 22 Secure Livelihoods Research Consortium Overseas Development Institute, London.

Price, S. (2017). Chapter 17, Livelihoods in Development Displacement – A Reality Check from the Evaluation Record in Asia. In van den Berg, R., Naidoo, I., and Tamondong, S. D. (Eds.), *Evaluation for Agenda 2030, Providing Evidence on Progress and Sustainability*. International Development Evaluation Association (IDEAS), Exeter/UK, 273–289.

Scoones, I. (2015). *Sustainable Livelihoods and Rural Development*. Practical Action Publishing.

Seaman, J., Boudreau, T., Clarke, P., and Holt, J. (2000). *The Household Economy Approach: A Resource Manual for Practitioners*. Regional Hunger and Vulnerability Group, Food Economy Group and Save the Children.

Tabares, A., Londoño-Pineda, A., Cano, J. A., and Gómez-Montoya, R. (2022). Rural Entrepreneurship: An Analysis of Current and Emerging Issues from the Sustainable Livelihood Framework. *Economies*, 10(6), 142. https://doi.org/10.3390/ economies10060142.

Tefera, T. L., Perret, S., and Kirsten, J. F. (2004). Diversity in Livelihoods and Farmers' Strategies in the Hararghe Highlands, Eastern Ethiopia. *International Journal of Agricultural Sustainability*, 2(2), 133–146. https:// doi.org/10.1080/14735903.2004.9684573.

UNDP (2013). *Promoting Sustainable Livelihoods, Reducing Vulnerability and Building Resilience in the Drylands, Lessons from the UNDP Integrated Drylands Development Programme.* United Nations, United Nations Development Program, New York.

Yumiko, K., Joffre, O., Laplante, B., and Sengvilaykham, B. (2017). Coping with Resettlement: A Livelihood Adaptation Analysis in the Mekong River Basin. *Land Use Policy*, 60, 139–149.

Part III

APPLICATION OF A LIVELIHOOD MODEL TO THE RESETTLEMENT PROCESS

7

APPLYING THE SUSTAINABLE
LIVELIHOOD FRAMEWORK TO
THE ASSESSMENT, DIAGNOSIS
AND DESIGN OF LAND ACCESS
AND RESETTLEMENT

DOI: 10.4324/9781003358725-10

Introduction

The introduction of this book proposes that the term 'restoration of liveli-hoods' be replaced with 're-establishment and development of livelihoods,' the latter better reflecting the reality of the changing circumstances asso-ciated with resettlement, project development and the broader regional development that project development may catalyse. With regard to reset-tlement, while the focus is on addressing the impacts of physical and eco-nomic displacement and resettlement, it should be recognised that the project itself may drive changes in the resettlement- and project-affected peoples' aspirations and expectations including their livelihood objectives and strategy.

Livelihood assessment and re-establishment and development needs are determined by the context and the type and nature of project-induced involuntary displacement associated with securing project land access. Where the context and nature and scale of project-induced involuntary displacement necessitate substantial resettlement, it is recommended that the livelihood re-establishment and development criterion be applied as a guiding principle for the entire resettlement process.

This chapter presents an approach to ensuring the consistent and sys-tematic application of a livelihood lens to the entire resettlement process: from the initial livelihood assessment, socio-economic baseline and census through diagnosis, design and planning of resettlement to implementation and ultimately monitoring and evaluation.

This approach is demonstrated in this chapter through the application of the Sustainable Livelihoods Framework (SLF). In applying the SLF to the resettlement process, the household assets are used to frame key livelihood re-establishment and development considerations and questions for each step of the resettlement process.[1] Answers to these questions – drawn from the project's livelihood assessment, socio-economic baseline and census and guided by recognised good practice and resettlement experience – should be used as input into the design and planning of each step.

Where issues remain, the questions facilitate the identification of gaps and thereby point to priorities for additional interventions to support livelihood re-establishment and development. Together, the questions guide implementation and monitoring and evaluation.

Resettlement Process

Table 7.1 provides a description of the key steps of a resettlement plan addressing both physical and economic displacement. Steps 6–14 may not all be relevant in specific contexts or where only economic displacement occurs. Stakeholder engagement (including a community grievance

Table 7.1 Key Steps for a Land Access and Resettlement Action Plan (LARAP)

	Step	Description
1	Scoping physical and economic involuntary displacement and resettlement	Following identification of the need for involuntary displacement, scoping to assess the nature and magnitude of displacement impacts and resettlement and livelihood requirements
2	Livelihood assessment, socio-economic baseline (including identification of vulnerable groups) and census	Design and implementation of a livelihood assessment, socio-economic baseline and census to inform the development and implementation of the Resettlement Action Plan
3	Impact analysis – resettlement, project and induced development	Assessment of the impacts associated with physical and economic displacement
4	Entitlement Matrix, Compensation Framework, Vulnerability Prevention Plan	Development of a Resettlement Action Plan/Livelihood Re-Establishment and Development Plan
5	Compensation	Provision of compensation for lost assets (e.g., crops, perennial crops, structures – often mandated by government regulation), reduced and/or loss of access to common property resources and temporary economic displacement, impacts on business activity, etc.

(Continued)

Table 7.1 (Continued)

	Step	Description
6	Site selection	Consultative process culminating in the selection of site for construction of replacement village and/or replacement housing for households affected by physical displacement. Note the importance of replacement land (Step 14) for agricultural and other land-based production including grazing, timber and non-timber products, etc.
7	Design of replacement village and replacement housing	The design of the replacement village and replacement housing involves consideration of (i) design and layout of the replacement village and replacement housing (Step 8); (ii) replacement housing (Step 9); (iii) public infrastructure, services and utilities (Step 10); and, (iv) handover of and on-going management of replacement village and replacement housing (Step 11)
8	Site preparation	Preparation of site for the construction of replacement village including public infrastructure, services and utilities and replacement housing
9	Construction of replacement village and replacement housing	Construction of replacement village and replacement housing including design and layout; selection of technologies for incremental improvement of housing and access to services and utilities including access to solar power, rainwater collection, appropriate water and sanitation systems
10	Replacement housing	Construction of replacement housing for households affected by physical displacement. Generally involves compliance with relevant legislation and regulations, government support and consultation of the resettlement-affected population with regard to design and construction. Such engagement includes both design and evaluation of a demonstration model house
11	Public infrastructure, services and utilities	Construction of: • Public infrastructure (i.e., village administration, community hall, recreational areas [parks, playgrounds], health, education, places of worship, cemeteries, green spaces) • Services (i.e., health, education) • Utilities (power, water, sanitation)

Table 7.1 (Continued)

	Step	Description
12	Handover of replacement village and replacement housing	The process includes (i) processes to ensure formal administrative recognition of new settlements which are relevant to registration, budget allocation, etc.; (ii) readiness of local administration to assume responsibility for the operation, care and maintenance and replacement of village. This includes issues of capacity, human resources (including for services and utilities) and budget; (iii) handover and operation of the replacement village, services and utilities to government and utility providers; (iv) handover of replacement houses to physically displaced households including the title. In addition management of vacant plots, capacity to connect to services and utilities; availability of modular expansion capacity, etc. should be considered
13	Physical relocation	Physical relocation of physically displaced households generally comprising pre-move orientation to new house and settlement; health checks; packing and move of personal effects; relocation of family members
14	Replacement land and on-going access to and use of common property resources	Identification and preparation of replacement land; re-start cultivation of crops as per traditional agricultural systems with progressive improvement through programs initiated as part of Step 15. Ensure appropriate consultation and governance, accessibility, use and sustainability of residual or alternate common property resources
15	Re-establishment and development of livelihood activities	Design, contracting and execution of programs to promote the re-establishment and development of livelihood activities of resettlement-affected communities
16	Monitoring and evaluation and corrective actions	On-going monitoring and evaluation of execution and outcomes of the Resettlement Action Plan
17	Close-out	Formal external evaluation allowing closure of Resettlement Action Plan and constituent programs

mechanism) is not listed as a step as it is deemed to be a continuous activity throughout the resettlement process.

When presented as a linear process, it is clear why the re-establishment and development of livelihood activities is often seen as an activity that occurs after relocation to a new site, and therefore, relatively late in the resettlement process. The flowchart of the resettlement process may itself suggest that the re-establishment and development of livelihood activities should occur relatively late in the process itself because of the need to establish enabling conditions. However, if we consider the activities that are part of efforts to promote the re-establishment and development of livelihoods,[2] there is no reason why many cannot start at the time, or even before, the steps associated with physical displacement and relocation commence.

Figure 7.1 illustrates the application of the SLF model to the resettlement process.[3] The figure applies the SLF asset categories to the assessment, diagnosis and design of the resettlement plan and thereby informs implementation and monitoring and evaluation.

While Figure 7.1 assumes that the SLF is applied pro-actively to every step of the resettlement process, it can also be used as a gap analysis at any stage of the design, planning and execution process. For example, such an application may demonstrate shortcomings in livelihood assessment; site selection; design of the replacement village and replacement houses; handover of infrastructure, services and utilities; and availability, quality of replacement land; and livelihood re-establishment and development. When used to facilitate gap analysis, the process allows for early identification of shortcomings, thereby providing opportunities for early course-correction during the resettlement process.

Assessment

Scope of Resettlement

The project ESIA will evaluate the project, its footprint and activities and identify the type, nature and scale of involuntary displacement, the impacts of involuntary displacement and the need for, type, nature and scale of resettlement. When impacts are deemed to be sufficiently significant, this will lead to the development and implementation of a Land Acquisition and Resettlement Action Plan (LARAP)[4] or Livelihood Restoration Plan (LRP) in cases of projects involving economic displacement only) by the project or government. In certain cases a Resettlement Framework may be developed.

A statement defining the type, nature and scale of involuntary displacement and the impacts of involuntary displacement is essential to understanding the need for resettlement and the type, nature and scale of

DEFINE SCOPE OF RESETTLEMENT	

ASSESSMENT Human Social Natural Physical Financial Political	Conduct livelihood assessment, socio-economic baseline and census commensurate with type and nature of resettlement impacts	
	Analyse project-level potential threats and opportunities for resettlement-affected communities and process	Will the pre-project context continue to exist? What will change?
	Analyse potential induced local and regional development threats and opportunities for resettlement-affected communities and process	

DESIGN Human Social Natural Physical Financial Political	Apply livelihood lens to design of key steps of resettlement process	Most component design activities require consultation with the resettlement-affected communities and key stakeholders. A livelihood lens driving design and evaluation is needed for all steps.
	Compensation	
	Site Selection	
	Replacement Settlement and Housing	
	Infrastructure, Services and Utilities (Site and Local/Regional Context)	
	Replacement & Access and Use of Common Property Resources	
	Re-establishment and Development of Livelihoods	

IMPLEMENT	• Implement to design • Ensure timely start of administrative processes required to recognise new settlement and assume administrative responsibilities • Build requisite capacity of physically displaced households and government prior to relocation • Engage local providers (electricity, water, sanitation, waste management) prior to relocation • Ensure early start of livelihood re-establishment and development

M&E	• Plan M&E to be commensurate with nature and scale of resettlement impacts • Where appropriate ensure that M&E and close-out are scheduled to occur after conclusion of project construction/start of project operations and situation has stabilized • Monitor outputs and outcomes • Use monitoring as a tool for improving livelihood re-establishment and development

Figure 7.1 Application of Sustainable Livelihoods Framework to Component Resettlement Activities

resettlement required. In turn, this will help define the scope of the LARAP or Livelihood Restoration Plan.

The livelihoods assessment, socio-economic baseline and census together inform the assessment of resettlement impacts. The key questions to be considered are:

(i) how do project development, land access and involuntary displacement differentially impact the households comprising the identified

Table 7.2 Potential Livelihood Impacts of Physical and/or Economic Displacement by Household Livelihood Category

Impact On	Impacts of Physical and/or Economic Displacement					
	All Households		Livelihood Category #1 of Displaced Households		Livelihood Category #2 of Displaced Households	
	Positive	Negative	Positive	Negative	Positive	Negative
Context						
Natural, economic and demographic context						
Household assets/capital [explain how involuntary displacement will impact household assets]						
Human						
Social						
Natural						
Physical						
Financial						
Household livelihood activities (add more rows as required) [explain how impacts on households assets will impact activities]						
Activity I (specify)						
Activity II (specify)						
Activity III (specify)						
Household livelihood outcomes [explain how impacts on specified activities will impact livelihood outcomes]						
Adequate shelter						
Food security						
Income/Wealth						
Well-being (health, education)						
Social status/Networks						
Empowerment						
Sustainability of resource use						
Household livelihood strategy and objectives [explain how impacts may impact household livelihood strategy and objectives]						
Diversity of activities/income sources						
Risk management						
Maintain liquidity						
Sustainability/resilience/vulnerability [consider how impacts may affect household sustainability/resilience/vulnerability]						
Stability						
Increase resilience/reduce vulnerability						

household livelihood categories/groups within the resettlement-affected population?

(ii) what are the diverse, positive and negative, short-term and long-term ways in which displacement and resettlement will affect the livelihoods of identified household livelihood groups within the resettlement-affected population?

Table 7.2 provides a tool to help assess the potential livelihood impacts of physical and/or economic displacement. The tool can be used prior to any decisions regarding resettlement being made, thereby making it an integral part of the overall assessment of the potential impacts.

BOX 7.1 ASSESSMENT OF ECONOMIC DISPLACEMENT

Economic displacement involves the loss of assets or access to and use of assets or other means of livelihood. Economic displacement may stem from land acquisition or the nature of development, e.g., the establishment of rights of way or environmental impacts such as dust, noise and vibration. For example:

* where project land take involves only a fraction of a household's landholdings, the household may experience a loss of production and associated income without experiencing a loss of viability.
* projects involving altered water management regimes (e.g., irrigation, dams, seasonal access to water sources) may reduce household's access to water and thereby reduce agricultural productivity.
* projects affecting household and community access to natural resources – often common property resources including grazing lands, forests and fisheries – may cause economic displacement in different ways, reflecting the users, patterns of resource use and multiplicity of products.

While the assessment of the nature, magnitude and significance of such losses at both the activity and household level is the basis for mitigation and compensation, there is limited guidance for such assessment. In principle such assessment involves the determination of the: (i) actual change in household assets and activities; (ii) potential household economic (and other) losses; and (iii) determination of the relative significance of these losses in relation to the viability of the activity (and where relevant household) and overall household welfare. To achieve the latter determination requires consideration of the relationship between the losses and:

- household Viability/Needs – how does the economic displacement affect the viability of the activity and ability of the household to meet its needs (both current and future)?
- household Vulnerability – how does the economic displacement impact household vulnerability (i.e., the household may remain viable but be more vulnerable/less resilient)?

The loss of a fraction of a household's landholdings presents the most straightforward example of economic displacement. The loss of the land and production therefrom is readily calculated and the significance of such losses vis-à-vis the household's ability to achieve subsistence and/or overall income can be determined. The vulnerability of the household can be integrated by considering basic/surplus production and the overall level of poverty. However the assessment of economic displacement is considerably more difficult in contexts involving access to and use of common property resources. This is because of challenges in: (i) identifying discrete, directly impacted, user groups; (ii) assessing impacts on specific resource uses; and (iii) designing and implementing suitably detailed socio-economic surveys assessing individual and household activities, the activity's contribution to the household and project impacts.

Assessment of Land Access and Resettlement

Livelihood Assessment

Conduct Livelihood Assessment commensurate with the context of resettlement-affected households and communities, type of involuntary displacement and nature and magnitude of displacement impacts

The design, delivery, monitoring and, ultimately, the success of efforts to re-establish and develop livelihoods should be informed by a comprehensive pre-project livelihood assessment that provides sufficient information for the entire resettlement process. As described in Chapters 4–6, livelihood models can be used to define the information to be collected by the livelihood assessment and increase understanding of the livelihood system. In addition, consideration of how livelihood re-establishment and development will be monitored and evaluated throughout the resettlement process may also inform key data to be collected consistently throughout the resettlement process (refer to Chapter 9).

The livelihoods assessment,[5] specifically the type of information and the level of detail required, is determined by the livelihood context of the resettlement-affected households and communities, the type of displacement and the nature and magnitude of displacement impacts. Where land acquisition entails: (i) physical displacement of only a small number of households on the same resource base and/or (ii) economic displacement with limited impact on household activities and overall viability, the livelihood assessment and programming requirements may be relatively straightforward. In all other cases, a more thorough and rigorous process is required.

Figure 7.2 identifies key factors and a continuum for each factor that is typically associated with increased information requirements and as such, a more complex and comprehensive livelihood assessment. Hence livelihood assessment is more complex when there is physical displacement, when entire communities are affected, when the resettlement-affected households are dependent on common property/natural resources for their livelihoods and when resettlement-affected people are indigenous.

Potential Project-Related Resettlement Threats and Opportunities

Analyse potential project-related threats and opportunities for resettlement-affected households and communities and resettlement process

Baseline Socio-Economic Assessment		
Insitu and/or limited impacts	**Nature of Displacement**	• Significant Physical and/or Economic Displacement impact
Limited number of Households	**Scale of Displacement**	• Entire settlements and communities
Wage-based formal employment	**Primary Source of Livelihood**	• Natural Resource Dependent • Reliance on Common Property Resources
Mainstream	**Characteristics of Affected Population**	• Indigenous or Vulnerable

Figure 7.2 Factors Affecting Requirements of Livelihood Assessment

The construction and operation of the project may be associated with direct project-related opportunities and threats for resettlement and the re-establishment and development of the livelihoods of the resettlement-affected population. Project factors that change the household assets – human, social, natural, physical or financial – should be identified, the potential impacts identified and their potential effect on resettlement-affected households and communities assessed.

It is recognised that in many instances key resettlement decisions (e.g., decisions whether resettlement will occur within the project area of influence or outside of it, choice of potential alternative resettlement sites and replacement land), number of resettlement-relocation sites that will be considered are limited by project requirements and the state (refer Chapter 2 concerning area development planning and the political economy). Where such limitations are evident prior to engaging the resettlement-affected communities, they should be explicitly identified at the outset of the resettlement process.

Early project proponent's or government decisions regarding assets (i.e., land and natural resources) may limit or otherwise define opportunities for livelihood re-establishment and development and have implications for the need for improved or different capabilities and activities. In cases where resettlement involves substantial intensification of the use of land, labour and/or capital or where people are moved from a rural to an urban setting (or vice versa), the livelihood objective of resettlement is better defined as establishing new livelihoods. In cases where resettlement occurs within the project area of influence, it should be recognised that the resettlement-affected population is likely to adopt a new goal, specifically on-going participation in the project.

Project-Induced Development Impacts and Resettlement

Analyse potential project-induced local and regional development threats and opportunities for resettlement-affected households and communities and process

Livelihood restoration has typically been seen to mean the restoration of pre-resettlement (and, to a greater or lesser extent, pre-project) traditional livelihoods. However, depending on the context, the construction and operation of a project will disrupt a reasonably stable, predictable environment and catalyse potentially significant induced local and regional development.

The impacts associated with such development may include increasing accessibility (roads); greater availability of transport; improved market linkages; higher levels of secondary investment with higher visibility; creation of new markets for land, housing, goods and services; project-induced in-migration including replacement village hotspots; increased opportunities for wage employment, etc. As a consequence, during the project construction phase, project development is often associated with accelerated rates of landscape-level change. Resettlement and livelihood re-establishment and development must consider these impacts with a view to taking advantage of opportunities and mitigating threats. Put differently, resettlement must take into account the affected population's on-going and changing relationship with the evolving local and regional economy.

The type, magnitude and significance of project-induced development impacts will vary according to context and project. Figure 7.3 identifies several factors and continuums for each factor that reflect a higher likelihood of induced impacts. Hence projects developed in remote locations, insulated from the mainstream economy, with populations that are rural and primarily dependent on natural resources and primary production are likely to be associated with higher levels of induced impacts and/or creation of bubble economies. As noted, higher levels of project-induced development impacts may create both opportunities for and, threats to, resettlement and household livelihood re-establishment and development. Key issues for resettlement include high levels of uncertainty, accelerated rates of change over and above that caused by resettlement (and how such change impacts aspects of pre-project livelihoods) and building the capacity to benefit from the opportunity and manage threats.

Project development and resettlement in rural, undeveloped areas with insulated economies are generally adversely impacted by the pre-existing

Lesser Impact	Project Setting/Context	Greater Impact
Integrated	Accessibility	Insulated
Accessible	Economy	Remote
Urban	Primary Livelihood Source	Rural
Wage based formal	Impact of Project Induced Development	• Informal urban and rural market • Natural resource dependent activities

Figure 7.3 Assessing the Impacts of Project-Induced Development on Livelihood Re-establishment and Development

lack of development in the area as seen in limited accessibility; limited availability of transportation; poor infrastructure, services and utilities; a rural population scoring low on human development indicators; and limited economic opportunities. In such situations, the project and project-related employment offer the potential to secure significant increases in real income and household welfare and expenditure, and as a consequence, there is little incentive to return to the pre-project way of life after resettlement has taken place. Sustainable livelihood re-establishment and development is especially challenging in circumstances where the project is transformational in nature and becomes the driving force for the economy (i.e., a project-generated bubble economy).

Examples of projects that are transformational at a landscape-level demonstrate the meaning of real and/or induced changes in livelihood strategies where the new goal of on-going project participation (primarily through employment) and/or sustaining higher income levels are associated with increased expectations, increased levels of dependency and the loss of the skill base needed to operate traditional livelihoods. This is often seen with Oil, Gas and Mining (OGM) development in relatively remote, under-developed areas. In these circumstances, the arrival of the project may lead to fundamental changes in livelihood strategies for the affected population, thereby ensuring that a return to the pre-project situation is not preferred, probable or perhaps even possible.

Application of the SLF to Land Access and Resettlement Diagnosis and Design

This section applies the Sustainable Livelihoods Framework (SLF) to the key steps of a resettlement program involving physical and economic displacement as the basis to inform and improve resettlement design. For each step, considerations and questions pertaining to the livelihood assets (human, social, natural, physical, financial and political and institutional[6]) and, in this way, to livelihood re-establishment and development are identified.[7] During diagnosis and design, the practitioner should answer these questions using the results of the livelihoods assessment, socio-economic baseline and census and thereby help ensure appropriate design for each step of a resettlement program. Following design, the gaps that were not satisfactorily answered during the design process would be identified for corrective actions and integrated into targets for further livelihood re-establishment and development programming.

Some overarching considerations include:

- **need to adopt a landscape view to the improvement of access and transportation, basic infrastructure, access to services and utilities and commodity value chains (including input and output markets):** the identification of potential landscape-level interventions that simultaneously help the re-establishment and development of the livelihoods of the resettlement-affected population and broader livelihood development for the general population needs to be considered. Such development interventions do not need be restricted to the resettlement-affected population and resettlement footprint.

- **need to approach physical displacement and the construction of new settlements and replacement housing with a greater emphasis on the area-wide human and social dimensions of resettlement:** the development of new settlements, public infrastructure, services and utilities and replacement housing of a disproportionately high standard relative to surrounding (host) communities may result in a deterioration in relations within and between communities and run counter to the aspiration of building communities. The landscape approaches detailed in the preceding paragraph as well as design considerations (e.g., promotion of sustainable rural housing) that may be extended to neighbouring communities have the potential to address this issue. Put differently the challenge is to identify and design a housing model that caters to the resettlement-affected households and their evolving requirements (i.e., plot size, modularity and potential for expansion), the next generation (i.e., replicability) and proximate communities (i.e., self-driven progressive improvements in housing).

- **need to assess and address intra- and inter-generational requirements:** design, planning and execution of resettlement programs tend to be based on the enumeration of the affected population, definition of entitlement and establishment of cut-off dates. While resettlement projects do consider population growth, there is often insufficient consideration of its implications, including (i) design of replacement housing and allowances for modular expansion and/or replication; (ii) capacity of services (health, education, sanitation) and utilities (power, water); and (iii) availability of empty house plots and assessment of the adequacy of available replacement land and residual natural resources. Where population growth is considered, insufficient attention may be given to changing social practices and norms that may be associated with resettlement. This could include the (opportunistic) establishment of child-headed households, early marriage leading to the establishment of independent housing, entry of extended family to benefit from improved infrastructure, services and utilities and economic opportunities or higher rates of divorce and/or polygamy.

• **need to integrate key issues of cost, care and maintenance and repair into the design of replacement housing and access to services and utilities:** experience demonstrates a consistent failure to adequately consider issues of cost, care and maintenance, repair and ultimately replicability of housing and services and utilities into the design. If materials are not available locally; if households are unfamiliar with key technologies (windows, locks); if the cost of use, repair or replacement is disproportionately high compared with monthly incomes; or if the technologies are over-designed for the context, design should be re-visited or efforts to develop local supply chains for these inputs need to added to the resettlement scope of work. With regard to replicability, if house plots are not available, the house design is too expensive to construct, materials are not available locally, or if services and utilities are difficult to connect, how are subsequent generations to live independently?

Compensation

The ease and utility of providing cash compensation (for land preparation, crops, structures) is dependent on the availability and accessibility of banking services and the affected households' possession of relevant documentation for opening and operation of bank accounts. The level of compensation – based on government rates – can be substantial and may be associated with a range of adverse impacts. Specifically cash compensation for resettlement-affected people has the potential to negatively affect livelihoods by affecting:

(i) beneficiaries' investment behaviour, encouraging dependency and further extraction of additional compensation

(ii)   inter-family relations as members of extended family seek to extract benefits from the compensated household

(iii)   inter- and intra-community relations between individuals, households and communities receiving different types and levels of compensation

(iv)   social relations between resettlement-affected communities and other proximate communities and administrative officials (i.e., jealousy, rent extraction, theft)

(v)   the on-going political and administrative position of households and communities in receipt of resettlement benefits (especially land and housing) who experience the likelihood of being characterised as 'project villages' and may be excluded from on-going government planning or budget allocations

For these reasons, ensuring early awareness, understanding and support of the resettlement project and how it fits into the overall project development cycle the compensation framework and the proposed compensation for resettlement-affected people among the broader population of project-affected people and in government are critical. Further implementing resettlement with development will mitigate the early concentration of benefits on the resettlement-affected households and communities.

Typically individuals and households are the identified beneficiaries of in-kind and cash compensation. Good practice guidance identifies (i) the need to address gender issues in developing the compensation framework and (ii) that in-kind compensation is generally preferable to cash compensation.

Community-level compensation for reduced access to and/or loss of common property resources may be channelled to affected communities in various ways. A common approach has been the establishment of community foundations. While the utility of this approach from the project perspective is clear, the use of a foundation generally proves difficult to operationalise for the following reasons:

•   often the basis for the calculation of compensation is unclear and projects may contribute more to such funds over an extended period of time.

- the time required for and cost of establishment and operation of foundations is under-estimated and often disproportionately high relative to compensation provided. Significant effort is required in developing intra- and inter-community governance frameworks and building individuals' capacity. As a consequence, timeframes imposed on resettlement programming when it is identified as a CAPEX expense are too short.
- the broader population in the project area of influence and the resettlement-affected population cannot usefully distinguish between the different benefits (i.e., household and community resettlement as well as socio-economic development). Further, in the medium to long term, the development of a foundation for resettlement-affected households may be difficult to integrate with broader area-wide efforts to establish development foundations (Table 7.3) and, in this sense, runs counter to the idea that resettlement-affected population re-integrating with the general population.

Site Selection

Project land access requirements and the circumstances of displaced households and communities requiring resettlement are unique. In general terms, in rural areas it is fair to assume that the existing site confers a degree of (comparative) advantage to the inhabitants. Put differently, there are reasons for the development of settlements or habitation in any one location, with these reasons giving the site a comparative advantage for its inhabitants. Reasons may be either historical or current and may include autonomy/independence from central administrative systems; existence of individual, household and community rights of residence, access and resource use; ease of access to natural resources including water, pastures, forest, riverine or marine systems and fisheries; proximity and access to trade routes, transport, services, employment, business; natural protection, human safety and security, etc. Local and regional development and the evolving relationship with the mainstream economy often affect the relative importance of these advantages. Unless these aspects of (comparative) advantage are identified, recognised and where relevant addressed in site selection, resettlement may be associated with a degree of marginalization/ compromise on the one hand or with missed opportunities to take advantage of new scenarios on the other.

Table 7.3 SLF Criteria for Compensation

Compensation	
Human	• Are resettlement-affected individuals, households and communities able to understand the basis of compensation? • Have resettlement-affected individuals, households and communities been effectively engaged regarding the approach to compensation and has their input been sought on the optimal approach to the provision of compensation? • Do resettlement-affected individuals, households and communities have the relevant capacity to manage cash compensation (including investment)?
Social	• Does the proposed compensation meet the requirements of relevant national, regional and local legislation, regulations and other requirements? • Has the compensation framework, processes for the determination of eligibility and anticipated levels of compensation been shared with the resettlement-affected population and have they confirmed the acceptability thereof? • Has the potential for the compensation approach to adversely impact resettled and host community relations and with other communities in the project area of influence been considered? For example, will compensation lead to competition, jealousy, loss of trust and social harmony among the resettlement-affected population and with other project-affected people, not in receipt of resettlement benefits? • Is there an increased risk of extortion, theft and other means of benefit extraction from compensated individuals and households? • Has the potential for compensation to lead to an increase in anti-social behaviour (e.g., alcoholism, gambling, drug taking, prostitution, divorce) been considered?
Natural	• Does the proposed compensation adequately reflect the true value of assets, especially with regard to perennial crops and fruit trees which may take years to reach maturity and peak production?
Physical	• Does the compensation approach adequately take account of the preference for land-for-land compensation? • Has an assessment of potential replacement land demonstrated the adequacy of quantity and quality of land to re-establish and sustain existing land use systems without substantial changes in practices (e.g., intensification of land and/or labour use)? • If cash compensation will be provided, is suitable land available in the market and are appropriate procedures in place to ensure the intended use of funds for land acquisition?

(Continued)

Table 7.3 (Continued)

Compensation	
Financial	• Have appropriate investment options been provided to households receiving relatively high levels of cash compensation? • Has the process and requisite supporting documentation required to open bank accounts been investigated and where necessary factored into the approach to delivering compensation? For example, in rural areas generally not serviced by financial institutions nor necessarily all dimensions of government administration, there may be a need to secure birth certificates, IDs, proof of residency, proof of tax payment, etc.
Political and institutional	• What is the local government's perception of and attitude to the compensation package? • What is the likelihood that receipt of resettlement benefits may lead to loss of administrative and political recognition of the resettlement-affected population, with the government deeming the resettlement-affected population to be the project's responsibility and no longer allocating resources to them?

Typically the choice of alternative sites is limited by political, biophysical, economic, social and cultural considerations. In addition project considerations may also influence the potential resettlement options (e.g., project willingness to support multi-site development, commitment to achieving sustainable livelihoods). Within the limited choices available, identification and selection of the (optimal) site is probably the decision which has the most impact on in situ livelihood re-establishment and development (or the progressive abandonment of the site).

Where possible, the resettlement-affected communities' (including potential host communities') local government and the project should participate in identifying, assessing and making informed decisions about potential sites, their characteristics and their potential impacts on livelihood re-establishment and development. Community decision-making processes may be affected by their leadership and representation and local perceptions of what is best. Hence "communities" may opt for: (i) proximity to the project with the expectation of on-going participation and benefit; or (ii) proximity to roads with the expectation of benefitting from improved access. Yet the anticipation of an on-going direct relationship with the project is often not reflected in project construction and operational planning, where resettlement is seen as a step towards project execution. Needless to say, other strategies to mitigate the effect of distance from the project, i.e., transportation services, exist.

In summary it is critical to have a broad-based awareness and understanding of:

- the innate qualities of potential sites
- potential development challenges to address site limitations
- the likely pattern of local and regional development
- the relationship to the political and economic elite
- how communities may evolve over one to two generations (i.e., life-cycle analysis)

Table 7.4 uses the SLF framework to identify key questions to guide the evaluation and comparison of alternative resettlement sites.

Site Preparation

Site preparation includes the design (site layout, settlement patterns) and physical development of the site and the agreed approach to the allocation of land to relocated households. Any tension between the impacted population's preferred settlement pattern and mechanism for plot/land allocation to households and ease (and cost) of construction should be addressed (Table 7.5).

Construction and Handover of Replacement Village

This step refers to the construction and handover of the replacement village. This encompasses various component steps including the design of new settlements (or integration into host communities), public infrastructure, services and utilities and replacement housing. However given their importance these steps are also addressed separately in subsequent sections (Table 7.6).

Table 7.4 SLF Criteria for Site Selection

Site Selection	
Human	• Has the potential existence of site factors affecting the incidence of disease (e.g., malaria) been investigated? • Are proposed sites proximate to existing natural resources and existing and potential employment and commercial opportunities? If not, have accessibility and availability of transport been factored into livelihood re-establishment and development planning? • Is the replacement site located in a similar environment, thereby ensuring on-going relevance and application of existing knowledge, skills, etc.? If not, how will resettlement address the need to develop new knowledge and skills?

Social	• Has the project considered the alternatives and ability to accommodate the development of a single replacement village and thus need to co-locate households from separate hamlets or maintain separate settlement areas by multi-site development?
	• Has due diligence of replacement sites included consideration of social factors including:
	    ◦ Avoidance of areas affected by historical disputes (land, warfare, etc.)
	    ◦ Avoidance of areas that may involve current or future social and ethnic tension and conflict between resettled and host or otherwise proximate populations
	    ◦ Acceptability of alternative sites to traditional leadership, with regard to existing natural resource institutions and governance systems
	• Does the proposed site have sufficient area to accommodate medium-to-long-term growth of relocated households and the broader community?
	• Does the proposed site have sufficient area to facilitate the maintenance and development of established networks between individuals, households and communities?
	• Do the proposed site and its location relative to natural resource-based and other livelihood activities provide the ability for households to maintain their distribution of labour between productive, domestic and leisure goals as well as returns to labour?
	• What are the Implications of the proposed site for existing and potential livelihood strategies, the stability and resilience/vulnerability of households? For example, where the available sites are associated with reduced access or loss of quantity and/or quality of resources, how will the livelihood strategies and activities of resettled households be impacted?
	• What is the risk that the proposed site becomes a locus of project-induced in-migration (i.e., hotspot) during project construction and beyond?

(Continued)

Table 7.4 (Continued)

Site Selection	
Natural	• Is the proposed site large enough to accommodate the preferred settlement layout and land and resource use? • Is the proposed site large enough to accommodate requirements for expansion whether driven by the government (e.g., the establishment of primary and secondary schools and dormitories, increased requirement for government staff housing) and/or the resettled population's inter- and intra-generational requirements for expansion? • Has an assessment of soil fertility demonstrated adequacy and sustainability of productivity? • Has an assessment of water sources to meet domestic needs and agricultural production demonstrated the adequacy and sustainability of intended water sources? • Has the adequacy of the proposed site to maintain natural resource-based activities been demonstrated? For example, the proposed site may facilitate the continuation of natural resource-based livelihood activities by including adequate land areas and/ or providing adequate access to agricultural lands and common property resources.
Physical	• Has the accessibility of the site – to natural resources, to proximate communities and to commercial centres – been assessed? • Is the site located sufficiently far from the project site and associated facilities to avoid the impact of project operations (e.g., noise, dust, vibration) and the risk of repeated resettlement while allowing the population to participate and secure project benefits? • What is the scope and need for physical development to overcome site limitations or maximise opportunities? • What measures may be required to address identified site limitations? For example, levelling; runoff management and erosion control; intensification, use of fertilisers, weedicides and pesticides; need for irrigation?
Financial	• Has the approach to and cost of land development been included in resettlement planning and compensation? • Has the absence of dis-proportionate demands on income (relative to household average monthly income) through increased cost to access the site, for transport to natural resources, markets, communication, water supply, inputs for livelihood activities including fuel and transport costs, fertiliser, weedicide, pesticide, etc. been demonstrated?

(Continued)

Table 7.4 (Continued)

Site Selection	
Political and institutional	• What is the likelihood that new settlements become host to relevant levels of local government administration and what are the implications thereof? • Is there an opportunity to link improved infrastructure and services to a broader area development trajectory (e.g., development of access roads; establishment of secondary school; establishment of agricultural extension facilities; development of input, storage and processing facilities [e.g., ice and cold storage for marine produce; establishment of produce markets])? Do such infrastructure and services need to be co-located with the resettlement location or is there an opportunity to simultaneously service other communities? Put differently does the site for replacement housing have to be the same for administration and services that are of benefit to the broader population? • What is the relationship between the proposed site and the broader local and regional development plans? • What is the relationship between the proposed site and (i) local political and economic elite; (ii) village administrative leaders; and (iii) traditional authorities? • Has the project considered the requirements for administrative recognition of new areas; process of formalisation for new settlements; the government budget and resource allocation process; etc. so as to ensure effective handover and continuity of operations? • What is the prospect of government land zoning and re-allocation to support industrial development?

Table 7.5 SLF Criteria for Site Preparation

Site Preparation	
Human	• What is the scope for the resettlement-affected population to participate in site preparation? Will such participation be through employment by a contractor or own responsibility for development? • Skills development requirements to enable participation of resettlement-affected households?
Social	• Do the proposed layout and settlement patterns take account of ethnic, faith-based or other potential criteria? • Have the resettlement-affected households and communities been consulted on the approach to the allocation of individual replacement houses and plots? Is the proposed approach acceptable to all households?

(Continued)

Table 7.5 (Continued)

Site Preparation	
Social	• Will plot/land allocation for housing and productive activities occur on the basis of single plots or separate plots? • Has retention of green spaces, communal areas and recreational activities (parks, playgrounds, etc.) been included in design considerations? • Is there a need for separate land allocation to accommodate the government footprint to address responsibilities for operation, maintenance and repair as well as potential future development? • Is there a need for separate land allocation to accommodate state-provided services (education, health) and utilities?
Natural	• Do plans allow for the retention of vegetative cover (especially trees), transplanting or early re-planting to create social rest, networking and recreation areas? • Is there a need to incorporate environmental protection into site development plans, e.g., runoff and erosion control, cover of steep slopes, stream buffer zones, coastal buffer zones?
Physical	• What is the extent of site development required, e.g., clearing, levelling, infill? Does such development adequately address site constraints and risks including risks that may derive from climate change?
Financial	• What is the cost of the site development?
Political and institutional	• What is the likelihood that new settlements become host to the relevant level of local government administration and the implications thereof?

Table 7.6 SLF Criteria for Construction and Handover of Replacement Village and Housing

Construction and Handover of Replacement Village and Housing	
Human	• Do the design and layout of the new settlement consider the human dimensions of how the newly relocated community will function – access to markets, places of worship, land and other natural resources including fuelwood? • Do the design and layout adequately address issues of health, safety and security, e.g., sustainability of potable water supplies, management of vector-borne disease, likelihood of flooding, erosion, both within and in areas proximate to settlement? • What is the scope for a resettled-affected household to participate in the construction of a replacement village and replacement housing?

(Continued)

Table 7.6 (Continued)

Construction and Handover of Replacement Village and Housing	
Human	• What investment in skills and capacity development is required to ensure participation in construction? • Does such participation in resettlement-related construction provide the basis for on-going development of skills and capacity and participation in project construction? • Has there been adequate consideration of the need to develop capacity for everyday operation, maintenance and repair, e.g., locks, windows, plastering, painting of housing and village? • Has design included water and sanitation and waste management considerations especially if settlement brings together disparate settlements creating a larger settlement?
Social	• Do the design and layout of the new settlement consider the social fabric of communities. For example, the relations between different clans, the relations between people of a different faith, the existence and adequacy of spaces for social interaction and leisure (for men, women and children), for informal enterprise and markets, especially if disparate communities are being consolidated. Such considerations also extend to proximate (host) communities, especially with regard to potential discrepancies in the standards of housing, the population's access to services (education and health) and utilities, etc. • Has the project considered management of key replacement housing issues including allocation; social preparation; titles and relevant documentation for land and house; household contracts for services (electricity, water, etc.)? • What is the anticipated distribution of employment opportunities associated with a replacement village and house construction, including for physically and economically displaced and the host village?
Natural	• Has the project confirmed the adequacy of key natural resources (e.g., land area for additional house plots, water, fuelwood) to sustain a larger population?
Physical	• Has the project ensured household awareness and understanding of critical design and implementation aspects of construction and utilities? For example, use of above- or below-ground electrical cables; layout of drainage pipes; need for seasonal flushing of gutters and water storage tanks; management of pit latrines?
Financial	• Have resettlement-affected households been made aware of and understood the costs associated with house operation, maintenance and repair and access to utilities?
Political and institutional	• Has the project included local government and service providers in the design, construction, handover and operations of village infrastructure and services? • Has the project defined the required documentation for land, replacement housing, public housing and infrastructure (education, health, water provider)?

BOX 7.2 THE HANDOVER OF RESETTLEMENT PUBLIC INFRASTRUCTURE, SERVICES AND UTILITIES TO GOVERNMENT

The handover of the village to local government including (i) administrative recognition of new settlements (which is often a pre-requisite for national-level resource [i.e., staff and budget] allocation) and (ii) the operation, maintenance and repair of infrastructure, services and utilities (for which a formal government staff and budget allocation is required) deserve standalone treatment, given implications for efficient handover and the sustainability of the village and improvements provided through design.

Administrative Recognition of New Settlements: the relocation of a population from one settlement to another and the subsequent demolition of the original settlement represent part of the resettlement process. However timely assessment of requirements, engagement of government stakeholders and planning of processes to ensure government administrative systems recognise the removal and/or addition of settlements and movement of a population are often an after-thought in resettlement programs. These processes may require specific interventions (e.g., delimitation of new settlements and village boundaries, community consultation, submission of budgets for staffing and budget to manage new settlements) and may take considerable time. Administrative recognition can often be an important pre-condition for state resource allocation including staff and budget for operation, maintenance and repair. Protracted transition periods may result.

Village Handover to Local Government: the handover of the village (including public infrastructure, services and utilities) to local government assumes the availability and capacity of staff and budget to operate the infrastructure, services and utilities. Depending on the context, the government may have to recruit additional staff or re-assign staff from other locations. Further, with enhanced services (e.g., addition of a health facility, provision of a secondary school) there is a need to assess how such services will be operated and delivered, again being reliant on staff, capacity and budget. As with the process of administrative recognition, these issues are often an after-thought in resettlement.

BOX 7.3 GOVERNMENT–PRIVATE SECTOR RESETTLEMENT COOPERATION (CONTRIBUTED BY ROBERT BARCLAY)

For a large private sector petrochemical project in Guangdong/PRC, the host city established a dedicated "Project Headquarters" to oversee resettlement and other infrastructure development associated with the project. About 150 staff were seconded to the headquarters from local and city government specialist bureaux. Staff were drawn from departments of land acquisition, resettlement, land planning, public utilities and power supply, environmental protection, construction management, labor, social welfare, finance, construction management and public security.

A high level 'Resettlement Steering Committee' made up of representatives from both the city government and the project sponsor was established. The project sponsor funded a team of international and PRC resettlement specialists to assist the city government to develop a RAP to assist with securing external financing and to conduct external monitoring. There was an agreement for the project sponsor to work closely with the host city to identify direct and indirect employment opportunities arising from the sponsor's operations.

The project sponsor and local labor department worked closely to provide trade skills training relevant to the demands of the project (construction and operations), downstream industries catalyzed by the project and other local industries. Displaced villages were granted industrial land to enable them to capitalize on commercial opportunities arising from the petrochemicals project.

The formation of the Project Headquarters had many benefits:

- it drew on government officers' cumulative experience from previous large scale resettlement projects undertaken by government.
- it enabled direct integration with government functions to manage registration of replacement housing and people; provision of social assistance for vulnerable households; delivery of transitional support; and, registration of the un-employed, trade skills training and job placement.
- housing and resettlement development plans were integrated with the host city government's plan to use the core petrochemicals project to catalyse an industrial park and new residential neighborhoods.
- it facilitated smooth allocation of replacement housing and agricultural land, efficient provision of servicing.
- it facilitated the establishment of new replacement neighborhood administrative systems and their seamless integration within the host government.

Replacement Housing

Resettlement standards and guidance require improvement in one or more aspects of housing and infrastructure, services and utilities. In some countries, requirements (particularly house and room size and number and, to a lesser extent, building materials) are also defined in housing or resettlement legislation/regulations. Further, often resettlement-affected people seek to have the 'best' option, the perception of what is 'best' being based on what is deemed to be 'modern,' what is seen in urban environments or what is utilised by western societies. Finally, for various reasons both the population and the project default to 'brick and mortar' design and construction.

Irrespective of the driver, 'best or preferred' housing is not always the best option for the specific situation. As a matter of best practice, improvement should be incremental rather than transformational such that the resettlement-affected communities do not face excessive additional demands on knowledge, capacity to adapt, costs of operations, maintenance and repair, etc. Key questions regarding economic, social and cultural suitability; operations, maintenance and repair of replacement housing (availability of inputs, cost, local capacity); and extension and replicability of replacement housing (modular design; local availability of materials, cost, capacity) should guide design. As with site selection, the project has the responsibility to ensure that the affected communities are fully aware of and understand the implications of any one design (Table 7.7).

Table 7.7 SLF Criteria for Replacement Housing

Replacement Housing	
Human	• Does design address environmental, social, cultural and livelihood considerations?
	• Will replacement housing be constructed by the project or by the RAPs or a combination thereof?
	• Are houses readily constructed, maintained and repaired (i.e., match local-level capacity)?
	• Are houses readily extended or replicated (e.g., modular design) so as to allow both natural and in-migration-related expansion and maintain the integrity of community/village and house design? Will the project provide scaled-down design and invest in the capacity to build and connect to utilities?
	• Has consideration of the needs of vulnerable households, including those with physically/mentally challenged individuals, been included?

(Continued)

Table 7.7 (Continued)

Replacement Housing	
Social	• Is house design (including electricity; water delivery, storage and use; sanitation; cooking facilities; and washing) based on the social, cultural and economic characteristics of the resettlement-affected population? • Do improved availability and delivery of utilities imply changes to social networking and relations (e.g., loss of communal washing areas)? Should resettlement site design also include scope for continuity of existing communal activities where they exist? • Are the identified eligibility criteria and proposed land and house ownership mechanisms understood and accepted by resettlement-affected households? • Do the proposed land and house ownership and allocation mechanisms adequately address risks for all members of the affected population including women and vulnerable groups such as female-headed households, the elderly, the infirm? • Does the proposed house allocation process reflect existing social, cultural and economic attributes and is it understood and agreed with the resettlement-affected households?
Natural	• Does the design of housing take account of weather extremes (rainfall, temperatures [heat/cold], storms/cyclones/typhoons) and natural disasters (e.g., earthquakes, flooding)? • Does the house design integrate appropriate technology including use of solar panels, rainwater collection, use of grey water, etc.?
Physical	• What is the anticipated durability of the construction material? • Are designs for scaled-down versions or options for modular expansion that can be built by relocated households to accommodate growth in family size and eventually household numbers available? • Are building materials for the construction of houses and relevant supplies for operation, maintenance and repair available locally or regionally (i.e., nearest commercial centre)?
Financial	• Are houses cost-effective (and reflect local financial capacity)? • Are materials for the construction, operations, maintenance and repair affordable? • What is the availability of designs for scaled-down versions or options for modular expansion that can be built by relocated houses to accommodate growth in household numbers?

(Continued)

Table 7.7 (Continued)

Replacement Housing	
Political and institutional	• Is the design of the replacement house based on local standards for housing, services and utilities (allowing for improvements in electricity, water and sanitation) including tendency (if any) for modification? • Does the project address minimum requirements stipulated in resettlement policy, legislation and regulation? • Is the project aware of the expectations of (i) local, regional and national political elites and (ii) local leaders and how these considerations may influence design? • Has the project ensured local-level recognition of land and house ownership documents (as documents generally derive from regional or national institutions)? • How will the project ensure continued government administrative recognition and responsibility for resettlement- (and to a large extent project-) affected communities in the project area of influence? For example, receipt of resettlement benefits may lead to loss of administrative and political recognition of the resettlement-affected population, with the government deeming the resettlement-affected population to be the project's responsibility and no longer allocating resources to them. Similarly higher level of social investment for villages in the project area of influence may lead to similar outcomes. • What protection from extortion – undue pressure to sell at discounted prices – by state or private actors is included?

BOX 7.4 DESIGN OF REPLACEMENT HOUSING

It is hard to be excited about well-executed but over-designed replacement housing when one is well aware of the challenges that displaced communities will face with their new replacement houses and settlements. The enthusiastic imperative to 'do good' can often have quite the opposite outcome. The failure to address sustainability issues guarantees that relocated households and communities will face increasing challenges in cost; operation, maintenance and repair of their housing; and, with expansion and/or addition of housing, with implications for their families and for the village. The promise of improved conditions can be lost for the next generation if not within years of relocation.

One of the objectives of IFC PS5 Land Access and Involuntary Resettlement addresses living conditions – specifically, the objective is 'To improve living conditions among physically displaced persons through the provision of adequate housing with security of tenure at resettlement sites.' This is further elaborated in the Guidance Note for PS5 as follows:

> GN13. Performance Standard 5 requires provision of adequate housing and a degree of security of tenure to displaced persons at resettlement sites. Adequate housing or shelter can be measured by quality, safety, size, number of rooms, affordability, habitability, cultural appropriateness, accessibility, security of tenure and locational characteristics. Adequate housing should allow access to employment options, markets, and other means of livelihood such as agricultural fields or forests, and also basic infrastructure and services, such as water, electricity, sanitation, health-care, and education depending on the local context and whether these services can be supported and sustained. Adequate sites should not be subject to flooding or other hazards. Whenever possible, clients should endeavour to improve aspects of adequate housing mentioned in this paragraph, including security of tenure, in order to offer better living conditions at the resettlement site, particularly to those without recognizable legal rights or claim to the land they occupy, such as informal settlers (Performance Standard 5, paragraph 17 (iii)) and/or those who are vulnerable as described in Performance Standard 1. Creation of improvement options and setting priorities for such improvements at resettlement sites should be done with the participation of those being displaced as well as host communities as appropriate.

Despite the guidance provided, resettlement plans often involve the construction of replacement housing that may be characterised as follows:

- house design that may not be adequately informed by the livelihood assessment. The design of a replacement house may follow externally defined specifications regarding house size, the number and size of rooms and improvement in access to water, sanitation, electricity, etc. These specifications and approval often derive from government urban architects and town planners who may not have awareness, understanding and experience of rural livelihoods.

- Insufficient exploration of alternative approaches to the development of sustainable rural housing. Alternative approaches should consider both the technical aspects of design and construction and the social dimensions of housing (i.e., social acceptability, affordability, durability, modularity, replicability, supply chain issues for construction and care and maintenance).
- an approach to replacement village and replacement housing that is driven by civil engineering and construction criteria. This approach may drive preferences for a single site, specific site characteristics, project design to maximise efficiencies in schedule and cost and over-design of housing relative to context. By considering alternative design, alternative construction methodologies may be associated with reduced cost, reduced time, increased flexibility and ultimately generate more suitable housing tailored to household needs and capabilities. Where appropriate technologies are included in house design, it is likely that houses will be more sustainable and more replicable.
- many projects do engage physically displaced households to review the proposed design and allow for adaptation of the design based on feedback. However consultations generally do not involve a detailed review of all aspects of housing and especially consideration of critical sustainability issues. The validity of engaging household members to evaluate modern, relatively large, permanent housing when their dwelling may only be a wattle and daub structure may be questioned. In any event, at the very minimum, the project proponent should discuss sustainability issues with those households that will be physically displaced and receiving a new house. Subsequent to this it may be useful to design and build various designs with sustainability criteria incorporated in the design for evaluation.
- failure to adequately consider and address sustainability issues including the operation, maintenance and repair of housing and the ability and cost of independently replicating houses. Specifically these issues include:
  - integrated design to minimise cost and/or improve the use of renewable resources – solar energy, rainwater collection and harvesting.
  - cost of housing and scope for replication.

- capacity for physically displaced households to construct, expand and maintain and repair their replacement house (e.g., through modular design).
- ease of expansion and/or replication to accommodate growth in the household family size and evolving requirements as children marry and need their own rooms and/or houses. This includes ease of connection to utilities.
- local or regional availability of construction materials and hardware for maintenance and repair.

The failure to interrogate sustainability issues and ensure these considerations are integrated into design has significant consequences for the household, future generations and the evolution of new settlements, risking dilapidation, squatter-like settlement expansion and inter- and intra-generational conflict regarding access to existing replacement housing. Put differently, what appears to be a contribution to *improved living conditions* for the displaced and relocated households may result in a return to pre-resettlement living conditions (and possibly worse conditions) within years of relocation.

There are substantial benefits for all stakeholders in pursuing sustainable rural housing models. Advantages include:

- improved schedule and cost base for delivery of replacement housing.
- reduced demand on poorly resourced local government.
- increased ability of resettled households to maintain and repair replacement houses throughout the life of the project.
- modular design empowers households to expand housing as needs arise.
- appropriate low cost, modular housing models (taking account of materials, supply chain, ease of construction and cost) enables the adoption of improved housing and thus delivery of improved living conditions within the replacement village, host communities and population in the project area of influence.

BOX 7.5 THE MOLADI CONSTRUCTION SYSTEM: AN ALTERNATIVE APPROACH TO CONSTRUCTION OF REPLACEMENT HOUSING

Rural housing is at the centre of household livelihoods insofar that housing provides shelter and the basis for food storage and food preparation and meals, family health and sanitation, education, enterprise and community engagement (i.e., situated within a community). Given the significance of houses, the limited focus on sustainable rural housing is surprising although there are many inter-related challenges including legal requirements, land tenure, availability of finance, appropriate design, existence of material supply chains, construction skills and cost. Notwithstanding the above, the default to 'block and mortar' construction as the only model for modern durable housing seems unnecessarily limiting.

Alternative approaches to design, materials and construction are available although perhaps not part of a broader discourse. Approaches vary, reflecting various determinants including the need, urgency, cost, etc. For example, natural or man-made causes of displacement may require different solutions as part of the recovery–development continuum, while the importance of rural housing in development may suggest other approaches. What is clear is the need for sustainable rural housing that is driven from the bottom up – i.e., what a household *can* rather than *could* build – hence the importance given to cost, modularity and replicability.

The *moladi* construction system (https://www.moladi.co.za/) is one example of an alternative approach. As described:

- the *moladi* system comprises a reusable, recyclable lightweight plastic injection moulded formwork system with a lightweight aerated mortar mix that produces a cast in situ, steel-reinforced monolithic structure.
- Moladi formwork components are fully interlocking and are assembled into easy-to-handle panels configured into a full-scale mould of the desired structure.
- formwork panels are joined to form the external and internal wall cavities and all the steel reinforcing; window and door block-outs, conduits, pipes and other fittings are positioned within the wall cavity to be cast in place when filled with the mortar mix.

- wall cavities are filled with a mortar mix producing a fast-curing aerated mortar which flows easily and results in a wall that is waterproof and possesses good thermal and sound insulating properties.
- formwork panels are removed after one night set, leaving walls with a smooth flat finish not requiring plastering, beam filling or chasing.

Advantages of the *moladi* construction system include:

- raft foundation that may reduce site preparation
- high-standard permanent structure – permanent, durable, waterproof, thermal and sound insulation
- earthquake, cyclone and tsunami resistant
- simplicity, adaptability
- speed of construction
- limited requirement for skilled labour
- no need for beam filling, chasing, plastering
- low cost
- scope for modular construction

Photo 7.1 Assembly of Wall Panels using Re-useable Plastic Formwork Source: Moladi

Photo 7.2 Formwork Panels Are Erected and Joined to Form the External and Internal Walls Source: Moladi

Photo 7.3 Completed Formwork Panelling Forming Interior and Exterior Walls of the House with Steel Reinforcing, Window and Door Block-Outs, Conduits, Pipes and Other Fittings Are Positioned within the Wall Cavity Source: Moladi

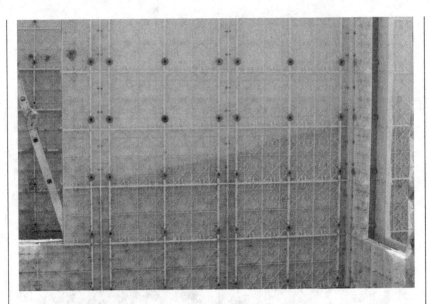

Photo 7.4 Following the Erection of Formwork a Mortar Mix Is Poured into the Wall Cavities Source: Moladi

Photo 7.5 Removal of Re-useable Formwork Panels Following Overnight Setting Source: Moladi

Photo 7.6 Residential House Constructed Using Moladi Construction System
Source: Moladi

Public Infrastructure, Services and Utilities

Resettlement standards require improvement in one or more aspects of housing and infrastructure, services and utilities. Numerous options for the improvement of public infrastructure; services (health, education, waste management); and utilities (electricity, water, sanitation) exist. As a matter of best practice, improvement should be incremental rather than trans-formational such that the resettlement-affected communities do not face excessive additional demands on knowledge, capacity to adapt, costs of operations, maintenance and repair, etc. Key considerations include:

- maximising the use of natural resources (e.g., solar energy, rainwater and rainwater harvesting and storage)
- minimising reliance on external management, externally sourced inputs, etc.
- minimising reliance on single-source high technology options for crit-ical livelihood inputs (i.e., water) thereby also minimising potentially increased vulnerability

- use of systems and technologies that are readily replicated and/or expanded so as to accommodate population growth
- the compatibility with local economic, social and cultural norms and standards for housing, services and utilities
- systems and technologies that reflect local capacity (government, community, household, technicians) for operation, maintenance and repair
- ensuring early integration with and assumption of ownership and management responsibility by relevant local providers
- ensuring local availability of inputs for operations, maintenance and repair
- considering the cost of operations, maintenance and repair, the financial capacity of current livelihood systems to meet these costs and mechanisms to meet costs (including user pay systems [household vs community systems], government, etc.)

Where resettlement involves in-fill relocation or settlement proximate to host communities, the host community requirements for services and utilities (and other improvements) must be integrated into the project design.

Beyond the provision of public infrastructure, services and utilities, their handover to, and assumption of management by, government (or a third party), projects should look beyond access to the infrastructure including promotion of community and household utilisation of improved infrastructure and ultimately improved health, education, etc outcomes. For example, the construction of primary and secondary schools is an important aspect of education but in and of itself provides no guarantee of attendance, improved standards of education and educational outcomes. These attributes may be affected by a wide range of factors including the perceived utility of education; competing demands for labour for household livelihood activities; gender considerations; and availability of teachers (and teacher accommodation) among others. One might argue that 'resettlement with development' requires that the project look beyond the provision of infrastructure to the promotion of improved educational outcomes. This argument – that is based on considerations of the importance of the evolving economy, predicted livelihood trajectories, diversified livelihoods and household capacity to participate in semi-skilled and skilled employment, the relevance and transferability of wage-based occupation and income, etc. – might lead resettlement programs to sponsor interventions that ensure improved participation, standards of education and education outcomes for all school-age youth including the 10–20-year-old age category that was unable to access education prior to resettlement (and thus are now lagging) as well as the current pool of primary school children in all resettlement-affected communities. Such interventions would be part of a broader mandate to ensure individual and household capacity to include livelihood activities involving enterprise and wage employment in their livelihood strategies (Table 7.8).

Table 7.8 SLF Criteria for Public Infrastructure, Services and Utilities

Public Infrastructure, Services and Utilities	
Human	• Are the public infrastructure, services and utilities readily operated, maintained and repaired (i.e., match local-level capacity)? • Does the local administration have the resources and capacity to operate, maintain and repair infrastructure, services and utilities? • Are the public infrastructure, services and utilities readily replicable so as to allow both natural and in-migration-related expansion?
Social	• Has the project adequately accounted for all public infrastructure including local administration; health; education; markets; bus stops; community centres; places of worship and associated facilities (cemeteries); etc.? • Is the design of public infrastructure, services and utilities based on local standards for housing, services and utilities? • Is the design of public infrastructure, services and utilities (including electricity; sources of water, delivery, storage and use; sanitation) based on social, cultural and economic characteristics of the resettlement-affected population including tendency (if any) for modification? • Do management requirements characteristic of the design of public infrastructure, services and utilities reflect social norms (e.g., individual vs collective)? • Are the proposed tenure and ownership systems for public lands, public infrastructure, services and utilities understood by the resettlement-affected group and will these systems be sustained in the face of existing practices? • Has the ownership and responsibility for operations, maintenance and repair whether involving local providers or to be managed by RAPs been established and where necessary, relevant stakeholders engaged prior to relocation?
Natural	• Does the design of public infrastructure, services and utilities take maximum advantage of naturally available sustainable resources, e.g., solar energy (or other renewable energy sources – wind, hydroelectricity, tidal energy), rainwater collection?

(Continued)

Table 7.8 (Continued)

Public Infrastructure, Services and Utilities	
Physical	• Does the design of public infrastructure, services and utilities match the local-level (i.e., nearest commercial centre) availability of materials for construction, maintenance and repair?
Financial	• What are the operational, maintenance and repair costs associated with the public infrastructure, services and utilities?
	• What assumptions are made regarding the requirement for inputs (e.g., energy/fuel to operate water pumps and water treatment plant, chemicals for water treatment) and associated costs (i.e., household usage, cost of fuel)?
	• Does the local administration have the financial resources to meet the predicted costs of operation, maintenance and repair associated with the public infrastructure, services and utilities on a sustainable basis without project support?
	• Receipt of resettlement benefits may lead to loss of administrative and political recognition of the resettlement-affected population, with the government deeming the resettlement-affected population to be the project's responsibility and no longer allocating resources to them.
Political and institutional	• Have the project and government assessed local area development trajectories and needs and optimised siting of infrastructure, services and facilities in relation to the proximate communities?
	• Does the project address minimum requirements stipulated in resettlement policy, legislation and regulation?
	• Have local providers been integrated into the design, construction and management of public infrastructure and utilities?
	• Have the local government and local providers confirmed their willingness to assume ownership and management responsibilities for the operation, maintenance and repair of public infrastructure and utilities?
	• Have the local government and local providers agreed to provide resources (staff, supplies) for the operation of infrastructure, services and utilities?

BOX 7.6 PROVISION OF PUBLIC INFRASTRUCTURE, SERVICES AND UTILITIES

The critique of the design of replacement housing also applies to the design of public infrastructure, services and utilities for which the local government and service providers will assume on-going responsibility.

While the critique of design will not be repeated here, attention needs to be drawn to:

- design and retention and/or early revegetation of green spaces – in many rural contexts central market areas and large shade trees serve as social gathering points. Often the construction of replacement villages and housing is associated with site clearing and levelling, leaving a desolate, exposed site for occupation by relocated households. Subsequent re-greening may take 5–10 years. Assessment of vegetative cover, integration into design and deliberate protection prior to the start of construction would ensure maintenance of vegetation and facilitate rapid re-establishment of social networking.
- assessment, planning and design of public services (i.e., health, education) should consider the scope to serve a broader population, in addition to the resettlement-affected population. For example, opportunities to strengthen the area hospital in addition to providing a village-level clinic could be considered. Similarly, the construction of a secondary school should consider area requirements.
- over-designed utilities beyond the capacity of local services providers to operate, maintain and repair and for which inputs are not available locally, e.g., water treatment plants and associated inputs.
- failure to integrate waste management facilities into resettlement village design. Rural households and communities tend to dispose of their limited waste through burning, burial or dumping, these practices being enabled by the distribution of houses in villages. New settlements are often provided with more defined, structured living spaces where traditional practices are less feasible and acceptable. With further changes in the style of living, increased disposable incomes, etc., the quantity and type of waste are likely to change. Finally in-migration may lead to changes in population and volume of waste. The project should integrate waste management facilities into the site design.
- cost of utilities (electricity water, waste) to be borne by households – the problem of over-design and failure to include local utility providers in design and discussions regarding handover and operations often leads to unwelcome surprises when the village is constructed and ready for handover. Issues include high costs of monthly utility bills (as a percentage of household monthly cash income); limited availability of technology for payment/recharge; on-going dependency on the project for operation, maintenance and repair of utilities and payment for household utilisation of utilities.

Physical Relocation (Including Transition Costs)

The transitional and re-establishment costs associated with physical and economic displacement are varied, diverse and real. Examples of these costs include:

(i)   compensation is usually provided for the loss of annual and perennial crops. However beyond the loss of the standing annual crop or perennial crop, resettled people also face a transition period associated with land clearing and cultivation, planting and growth before harvest. The provision of food baskets until such time that the first crop is harvested mitigates this gap in subsistence production.

(ii) where businesses are displaced and need to be relocated, they are typically compensated for the relocation of the business infrastructure as well as the temporary loss of income associated with the relocation of the business (Table 7.9).

Replacement Land and On-Going Access and Use of Common Property Resources

Replacement land is generally recognised as the key determinant for the success of re-establishment and development of the livelihood activities of physically displaced communities practising sedentary forms of agriculture.

For other primary livelihood activities – pastoralism, fishing – a suite of other concerns including adequacy of residual and additional common property resources; existence of governance, resource access and use issues; relations with other users (hosts) need to be addressed. Put differently, one should not assume the direct transferability and continuity of resettlement-affected populations' use of common property resources nor that such transfer will not cause adverse impacts on existing (host) users. For example, one cannot transfer inter-tidal collectors of molluscs and shellfish into proximate areas without impacting existing users. Further such transfer may have significant impacts on harvests and the sustainability of resource use (Table 7.10).

Table 7.9 SLF Criteria for Physical Relocation (Including Transition Costs and Village Handover)

Physical Relocation (Including Transition Costs and Village Handover)	
• Human	• Has the project addressed the loss of generational knowledge base regarding the pre-resettlement environment including land, common property resources, vulnerability, resilience, etc.?
	• Has adequate allowance been made for transitional costs?
Social	• Has the physical relocation process factored in approaches to minimise loss of social networks and relations (see settlement design and house and land allocation)?
	• Has the project engaged the community to assess what, if any, events need to be implemented to facilitate the relocation of places of worship, departure from cemeteries and sacred/spiritual sites; departure from the village/ arrival in the new village?
	• Has the project adequately prepared for the loss of access to established places of worship, cemeteries and other cultural heritage and arranged for an access agreement or for their relocation or replacement?
Natural	• Is the loss of access to common property resources and their replacement based on adequate analysis regarding products, productivity, resource resilience and household vulnerability?
Physical	
Financial	• Are relocation, re-establishment and transitional costs associated with involuntary resettlement recognised, assessed and compensated or otherwise mitigated?
Political and institutional	• Has the process for administrative recognition of new settlement and allocation of resources (budget, staff) been defined and started at the appropriate time?
	• Is there alignment with government administration and resources (staff, budget) for the operation of the village, infrastructure, services and utilities?

Re-establishment and Development of Livelihood Activities

This section presents SLF criteria for the re-establishment and development of livelihood activities. Chapter 8 provides a comprehensive description of the re-establishment and development of livelihood activities (Table 7.11).

Table 7.10 SLF Criteria for Replacement Land and On-Going Access and Use of Common Property Resources

Replacement Land and On-Going Access and Use of Common Property Resources	
Human	• To what extent do required land use management approaches differ from existing practices, e.g., intensification, fertility management, labour use? • To what extent do new management approaches require the adoption of new practices, adoption of new technologies, etc.? • To what extent do new management approaches increase labour demand (i.e., intensification) or operational costs (inputs such as fertiliser, weedicide; pesticides; irrigation)?

Social	• Has project due diligence on potential sites ensured:
	  ○ Avoidance of areas affected by historical disputes (land, warfare, etc.)?
	  ○ Avoidance of areas that may involve current or future social and ethnic tension and conflict between resettled and host or otherwise proximate populations?
	  ○ Acceptability of site to traditional leadership, with regard to existing land tenure systems, etc.?
	  ○ Adequacy of land area – scope to accommodate medium-to-long-term development of households and the broader community? In the absence of such an intra- and inter-generational change in the livelihood system will be required.
	  ○ Accessibility of replacement land (on foot, by vehicle) and costs associated therewith?
	• What is the proposed land ownership system? What security of tenure – both legal and social – does this provide? How will the proposed land tenure system evolve over time?
	• How does the project propose to allocate land?
	• Are house plots and garden plots allocated as single units or separately?
	• How does the proposed allocation and ownership system interface with social and cultural norms regarding control and access to land, i.e., the existing land tenure system?
	• How will the proposed allocation and ownership system meet challenges introduced by the project including project-induced in-migration, induced development, etc.?
	• Is there a need to develop safeguards to protect household land and community land allocation and management from exploitation?
	• What is the extent to which common property resources are replaced or alternatives are provided and adequate consultation with other users (hosts) been conducted? What are the implications for resource governance and resource sustainability?
	• Have resettlement-impacted households and communities been consulted regarding the need for ceremonies ahead of ground-breaking?

(Continued)

Table 7.10 (Continued)

Replacement Land and On-Going Access and Use of Common Property Resources	
Natural	• Has the adequacy of the area of replacement land been confirmed? • To what extent do the natural characteristics of replacement land reflect land lost – area, fertility, water availability, etc.? • What measures are required to address these different characteristics – intensification, fertiliser, weedicide or pesticide use, need for irrigation? • Adequacy of common property resources (new or residual) to meet requirements? Is there a need for targeted interventions to address specific uses, e.g., fuelwood, medicinal plants, or are alternatives provided?
Physical	• What measures may enhance productivity and or returns from natural resources, e.g., development of road networks, access to markets? • Who will assume responsibility for the demarcation and physical development of the land?
Financial	• Does access to replacement land involve costs, e.g., transportation? • What one-off land improvement costs are associated with ensuring replacement land has requisite productivity? • What on-going costs are associated with ensuring replacement land has requisite productivity? • How do these costs compare with current and anticipated average monthly household income? How will these costs be met? • Can operational costs associated with new land and land use management systems be met by resettlement-affected households on a sustainable basis without project support?
Political and institutional	• Does the project address minimum requirements stipulated in resettlement policy, legislation and regulation? • What are the risks that replacement land will be absorbed by project-induced in-migration, induced economic development, etc.?

Summary Resettlement Livelihood Impact Statement

This chapter has demonstrated the application of a livelihood model to the key steps of the resettlement process with the aim of ensuring that livelihood re-establishment and development issues are integrated into the design. It is intended that initial consideration of these questions occurs during diagnosis (i.e., after the initial livelihoods assessment and baseline socio-economic assessment) and appropriate responses are integrated into the design. Nonetheless it is likely that a number of issues will remain unanswered. Hence following diagnosis and integration into the design, a further review is required to identify the key livelihood impacts that

Table 7.11 SLF Criteria for Re-establishment and Development of Livelihood Activities

Re-establishment and Development of Livelihood Activities	
Human	• Does the range of livelihood activities address the multiple goals characteristic of pre-resettlement households and communities?
	• Will resettlement-affected people want to continue pre-project livelihood activities?
	• What is the anticipated area development trajectory and how does this impact likely livelihood development trajectories?
	• What degree of intensification (land, labour, capital) of land use is required relative to the pre-project situation? If intensification is required, how will the re-allocation of household resources (labour) impact the overall household livelihood system?
	• Can pre-project livelihood activities be re-established on a sustainable basis without the development of new capabilities? If new capabilities are required, what is the anticipated approach to training? What uptake rates over what time period are anticipated?
	• Has the project assessed the capabilities and needs of vulnerable people?
	• Has the project conducted a life-cycle analysis to better understand the relevance and capacity of households to participate in planned livelihood re-establishment and development activities?
	• Will resettlement-affected households be prioritised for project construction and operational employment? Has an assessment of household labour availability for the project employment vs re-establishment of livelihood activities been conducted and how does this inform the livelihood re-establishment and development strategy?
Social	• What impacts will resettlement have on resource base and stability, resilience/vulnerability of households and communities through impacts on natural resources (e.g., water) or common property resources (e.g., fisheries, timber and non-timber forest products)?
	• What percentage/number of affected households can realistically be expected to adopt and integrate new livelihood activities into their livelihood strategies?
	• What is the socio-political dimension of selected new livelihood activities? Are they available to all households?
	• Has the project included social protection measures for the vulnerable and immediate-near-term emergencies?
Natural	• Has the project considered likely increased intensity of use for specific resources – fuelwood, lumber, fishing – during the re-establishment period?
	• Can pre-project natural resource-dependent livelihood activities be re-established on a sustainable basis on replacement land and residual common property resources?
	• Is residual and/or replacement common property sufficient to meet anticipated household needs and uses? Does it have the same product range and productivity?

(Continued)

Table 7.11 (Continued)

Re-establishment and Development of Livelihood Activities	
Physical	• Does the viability of proposed livelihood activities rely on physical infrastructure (market, jetty) and/or the development of natural resources, e.g., irrigation?
Financial	• What are the financial costs associated with the adoption and operation of new livelihood activities?
	• Is there a market for alternative livelihood activities – skills and/or products?
	• Does the economic viability of proposed livelihood activities rely on the project and/or induced development? That is, are they associated with high levels of project dependency or do they rely on entry and operation of market actors to be successful?
	• Can the combination of income-generating livelihood activities meet additional costs associated with resettlement, e.g., transport; inputs; services and utilities; operation, maintenance and repair?
Political and institutional	• Has the project confirmed jurisdiction and governance associated with access to alternative common property resources (potentially used by other households and villages)?

remain and that should become the focus of livelihood re-establishment and development activities. This review may be presented as a summary resettlement livelihood impacts statement (Table 7.12).

Nonetheless the reality is that resettlement is rarely implemented as an optimal process – the political economy may limit options; choices of alternative sites may be limited; replacement land may be limited in area or quality; key decisions may have already been taken (e.g., site selection,

Table 7.12 Residual Livelihood Re-establishment and Development (RE&D) Issues

	Resettlement Step	Residual Livelihood RE&D Issue	Proposed Livelihood RE&D Action
1	Site selection		
2	Site preparation		
3	Village construction and handover		
4	Replacement housing		
6	Infrastructure, services and utilities		
7	Relocation		
8	Compensation		
9	Replacement land		
10	Re-establishment and development of livelihood activities		

compensation framework, design of houses and new settlements) or indeed much of the resettlement may have been completed. In these circumstances, the framework may be used as a gap analysis leading to the identification of key issues to be addressed in the livelihood re-establishment and development plan.

Conclusion

This chapter has applied the Sustainable Livelihoods Framework to the key component steps of resettlement. In this way the chapter has elucidated the livelihood dimensions of each component step, and in the process demonstrated that:

(i)   interpreting the livelihood restoration and/or improvement objective of the current standards and guidance as only applying to livelihood activities is inadequate

(ii)   the deliberate use of a livelihood framework facilitates the identification of livelihood re-establishment and development challenges and facilitates their resolution through design, allocation of resources and development of targeted interventions

(iii)   livelihood and resettlement project challenges frequently occur in relation to specific component steps, including site selection; design of replacement settlements; replacement housing and public infrastructure, services and utilities; the handover of the settlement and public infrastructure, services and utilities to government; and re-establishment and development of livelihood activities

To complement this chapter, Chapter 8 focuses on the re-establishment and development of livelihood activities.

Notes

1 The SLF approach to assessing project induced involuntary displacement impacts provides benefits in (i) providing a more comprehensive and people-centred picture of a project's impacts on the livelihoods of project affected people; (ii) improved insight into people's potential participation

in project activities; and (iii) improved opportunities to re-shape projects to improve success and reduce negative impacts.

2 For example, in relation to agriculture, commodity value chain development, construction and operation of enabling infrastructure and services (e.g., agricultural training and extension, nursery, input markets), introduction of new agricultural practices including conservation farming, new varieties, soil fertility management, house gardening, small-scale livestock).

3 While Figure 7.1 is largely self-explanatory, it should be noted that the local and regional natural resource base, market and livelihoods assessment described in Figure 6.1 precede the start of the resettlement process and are key inputs into resettlement design, planning, execution, monitoring and evaluation. These activities could be deemed to be part of the resettlement process; however, they serve a broader purpose (i.e., assessment of path-ways to promote positive socio-economic development trajectories) and may be implemented as discrete activities.

4 Appropriate mitigation plans will be determined by the nature, scale and impacts of involuntary displacement. These might include land acquisition and resettlement action plans; land acquisition and compensation plans; fishermen compensation plans; etc.

5 The Livelihoods Assessment is distinct from the socio-economic baseline and census of impacted households and an eligibility survey conducted at the time at which eligibility cut-off dates are established.

6 The author has included a political and institutional dimension in the SLF analysis used in this chapter.

7 The list of questions is not necessarily exhaustive and best practice, on-going experience and lessons learned can be used to further develop relevant questions for this SLF-based analysis.

Bibliography

ADB (1998). *A Handbook on Resettlement, A Guide to Good Practice*. Asian Development Bank, Manila, Philippines.

ADB (2003). *Gender Checklist Resettlement*. Asian Development Bank, Manila, Philippines.

Doloi, H., and Donovan, S. (2020). *Affordable Housing for Smart Villages*. Routledge, New York.

Doloi, H., Green, R., and Donovan, S. (2019). *Housing, Planning and Infrastructure for Smart Villages*. Routledge, New York.

IFC (2002). *Handbook for Preparing a Resettlement Action Plan*. International
    Finance Corporation, Washington, DC.
McDowell, C. (2002). Involuntary Resettlement, Impoverishment Risks and
    Sustainable Livelihoods. *Australian Journal of Disaster and Trauma
    Studies*, 6(2).

Part IV

RE-ESTABLISHMENT AND DEVELOPMENT OF LIVELIHOOD ACTIVITIES

8

RE-ESTABLISHMENT AND DEVELOPMENT OF LIVELIHOOD ACTIVITIES

DOI: 10.4324/9781003358725-12

In many resettlement projects, it seems as if the proponents are going through the motions of livelihood re-establishment and development. First the resettlement project defines potential sectoral (economic) livelihood programs based on a high-level description of the resettlement-affected population's existing livelihood activities (including agriculture, livestock, fisheries, business development and/or employment). Without adequate assessment of livelihoods, categorisation of households and targeted design, the project defines Scopes of Work and contracts implementation partners – serving the project as client – to deliver generic sectoral livelihood development programs to all the resettlement-affected households, hoping that some elements thereof will be successful for some households. Put differently, there is a sense that making generic livelihood programs available to all resettlement-impacted households is sufficient and (hopefully) the rest will follow. In this way the resettlement project spends significant resources on selected programs without really connecting with the resettlement-affected households. At the same time, the resettled-affected households go about re-establishing their livelihoods and livelihood activities in the changing context in which they find themselves.

Introduction

This chapter outlines an approach for the re-establishment and development of sectoral (economic) livelihood activities (i.e., the means of earning a living). This approach takes account of the context and the changing circumstances brought about by land access, involuntary displacement and resettlement, project development and the broader area development that project development often catalyses. Together these frame the potential medium-to-long-term livelihood trajectories within the project area of influence and, in this way, should inform the strategy for the re-establishment and development of livelihood activities.

The chapter starts with a typology of possible interventions aimed at promoting re-establishment and development of livelihood activities. It subsequently describes elements of good practice before addressing the development and evaluation of a strategy for the re-establishment and development of livelihood activities. The next section addresses scoping, contracting and execution of the strategy and component programs. The final section addresses remediation and legacy resettlement.

The chapter does not address the assessment of involuntary displacement impacts upon and, the technical aspects of the re-establishment and development of specific natural resource-based livelihood systems (e.g., hunter-gathering, shifting cultivation, sedentary agriculture, pastoralism, fishing-based livelihoods) that often form the primary basis of livelihoods. As described in Section 'Rural Environment' of Chapter 5, specialist expertise is often required to understand current activities; assess project impacts; assess needs and identify opportunities; and design and plan interventions.

Rural Livelihoods and Development

As described in Chapter 4, livelihoods may be described as comprising the capabilities, assets and activities required by an individual or household (or community) to provide for a means of living (Chambers and Conway, 1992). The chapter demonstrated that analysis of household livelihood strategies is generally informed by a livelihood model – for example, the application of the SLF requires assessment of the broader environment and household and community human, social, natural, physical and financial capital. Most resettlement-related livelihood restoration focuses only on sectoral economic livelihood activities and their productivity.

If our aim is to promote rural livelihood development, the first step should be the assessment and analysis of the rural environment and rural household and community livelihoods (as set out in Chapters 5 and 6), the results of which should provide information on livelihood opportunities and challenges. Such assessment and analysis may demonstrate that interventions that serve to create an enabling environment for the development of household livelihood activities – for example, enabling infrastructure, access to resources, security of tenure, improved health, access to potable water or access to finance, risk management – may be more important than interventions focused on economic activities and may ultimately contribute more to the attainment of a positive livelihood trajectory. In addition, proponents should engage with existing bilateral donors and development assistance projects who often have conducted an assessment and analysis of the causes of poverty and identified opportunities and priorities to support rural (livelihood) development.

While this chapter is concerned with the re-establishment and development of livelihood activities, this focus should be preceded by a holistic assessment and analysis of livelihoods and identification of priority areas for intervention. Put differently, how are we to support improvement in the livelihoods of displaced communities if we do not consider both the limitations of the broader environment in which they secure their livelihoods and the opportunities and challenges to developing specific livelihood activities? Where interventions in promoting an enabling environment are warranted, many aspects of this chapter – including good practice guidance, strategy, program design contracting and execution – are relevant.

Typology of Potential Livelihood Re-establishment and Development Activities

The re-establishment and development of livelihood activities may involve the delivery of sectoral programs reflecting: (i) the resettlement-affected households' existing livelihood systems; (ii) the mitigation of project impacts, land access, involuntary displacement and resettlement; and (iii) project and area-wide development, the opportunities such development brings and impacts of development on livelihood trajectories. As such, these programs may target:

(i)   re-establishment and improvement of existing (pre-project) livelihood activities
(ii)   introduction of new livelihood activities
(iii)   participation in project-related opportunities
(iv)   participation in opportunities associated with local and regional area development

In addition to the four themes above, consideration of longer-term benefit-sharing opportunities with resettlement-affected people and means to address vulnerability are available.[1] These approaches serve to:

(v)   support on-going area development through the deliberate allocation of financial resources (e.g., the establishment of foundations through which development funds and compensation can be managed; allocation of funds through local government to support on-going development)

(vi)   provide on-going compensation for reduced access and/or loss of communal resources

(vii) ensure that community, household and/or individuals receive direct on-going benefits from project operations

(viii) provide medium-to-long-term safety nets for the most vulnerable individuals and households

The following sections discuss each of the types of livelihood interventions in more detail.

Re-establishment and Improvement of Existing Livelihood Activities

The re-establishment and improvement of existing (pre-project) livelihood activities (including use of household assets [land]; use of common property resources [pastures, forests, fisheries]; medium and small enterprises) may involve sectoral programs comprising a wide range of initiatives. Generally, the purpose of these component programs is to improve productivity. Possible interventions include:

- improvement in the resettlement-affected households' access to land and natural resources
- the improvement and development of household land resources
- provision of inputs (e.g., physical inputs, access to finance, savings groups)
- capacity building[2] of household members to develop their ability (knowledge, skills) to improve or adapt (i.e., integrate new practices into) existing activities
- the development of commodity value chains to support market-driven development

Physical displacement to a new geographical location and site may be associated with reduced access to, reduced resource quantity and quality and reduced readiness of the site to start agricultural activities. As such some of the interventions described above may be 'enabling' rather than developmental insofar as they may be required to address the constraints introduced by the resettlement process (e.g., site preparation, intensification to account for reduced land areas, dryland agriculture to account for reduced access to irrigation water).

Beyond addressing the shortcomings of resettlement sites and replacement agricultural land, the improvement of existing livelihood activities must be based on an assessment of current practices, challenges and opportunities. Put differently, interventions are not needed to help resettlement-affected people do what they already know how to do. Rather interventions should be designed to address identified problems and challenges and/or introduce proven improvements to current practice. Given that adoption of new agricultural practices generally only occurs over extended time periods (i.e., multiple cropping seasons), it is better to promote re-establishment based on current practices and identified problems and challenges (i.e., start where the farmers are) and use farmer-driven approaches to introduce improvements and build requisite capacity.

A similar approach is recommended for inter-tidal collection and fisheries where the first step is to ensure that resettlement-affected households can continue their pre-project activities. This may involve addressing issues of access (to address distance from the coast, bypassing marine exclusion zones or accessing more distant fishing grounds), establishing appropriate shelter and processing facilities at new locations, facilitating more rapid access to fishing grounds). With long-lead times, addressing key inputs (fishing equipment, ice, cool boxes), facilitating storage (cold storage) and processing may be addressed before the start of resettlement. New products (e.g., seaweed, sea cucumber) and practices that involve high risk and uncertainty and have external dependencies (i.e., middlemen and markets) should be introduced as development programs (refer to next section).

Introduction of New Livelihood Activities

New opportunities typically involve the introduction of new activities aimed at supporting households to meet their subsistence and income needs (although in principle new activities could be aimed at meeting other identified household objectives) (e.g., vulnerability, stability, savings). New opportunities may be created by project development (including resettlement), improved access, improved connectivity to markets and, more generally, induced area development and the generally increased wealth and higher standards of living that such development brings. For example, this can include the supply of goods and services to either the project (and contractors) or the population in the project area of influence and may include small-scale trading, transport, local construction, communication, catering and accommodation among others. Adoption of new activities may require households to re-allocate resources (land, labour, capital), returns may only be evident in the medium-to-long term and consequently are often associated with higher levels of risk and vulnerability for the resettlement-affected households. Furthermore it is recognised that new activities may be associated with higher levels of dependency on the project and the mainstream economy. Finally, new activities are also likely to be of general interest to the broader population.

Irrespective of the source, a thorough analysis of proposed activities (whether involving the development of existing activities or the introduction of new activities) is required. The Sustainable Livelihoods Framework described in Chapter 4 can be used to inform such an analysis. Each proposed activity should be evaluated in terms of its relationship with the broader environment and household and community's human, social, natural, physical and financial capital. At a minimum, the evaluation should investigate:

(i)   the relationship to existing livelihood strategies and activities (i.e., does the proposed activity complement the current livelihood strategy; is it competitive in time in terms of the resources [land, labour, capital] required for it to be implemented; does it maintain or exacerbate risk and vulnerability of resettlement-affected households?).

(ii) the need for additional knowledge, skills and labour to learn about and implement the proposed activity and, thus, the need for capacity building.

(iii) the social feasibility of the proposed activity (including access to resources; land or marine tenure; labour availability; suitability to identified groups within the resettlement-affected population).

(iv) the economic viability of the proposed activity (i.e., input, production, gross margins, scale and period of adoption required for meaningful contribution to the household, operation of the market) for a range of scenarios (i.e., worst-case, best-case). Comparisons with existing pre-displacement activities should be undertaken to verify that proposed activities compare favourably with the resource requirements and returns to existing household activities.

(v)   the sustainability of the proposed activity as well as its contribution to the household livelihood strategy should be considered in terms of productivity, resource requirements, potential contribution to livelihood outcomes, on-going viability and vulnerability/resilience/sensitivity.

(vi)   for market-dependent interventions, the existence or development of commodity value chains including issues such as entry and operation of entrepreneurs (middlemen), availability of inputs, supporting infrastructure, services and utilities requisite scale of production, availability of markets.

Participation in Project-Related Opportunities

Participation in project construction and operations-related opportunities may be achieved through employment and the supply of goods and services.

Project employment (mostly through contractors) can be an important component of livelihood re-establishment and development for displaced people. Where project employment is promoted as a livelihood activity and commitments are made to the employment of the resettlement-affected population, projects need to consider whether the employment opportunities provided are meaningful, ensuring that the duration of employment and the provision of employment contracts with appropriate working terms and conditions (especially if employment occurs through contractors) are defined and monitored. Put differently the 'obligation' is not merely to provide employment but to provide **meaningful** employment. Furthermore, irrespective of whether a project targets resettlement, project construction-phase and project operations-phase employment or employment opportunities associated with the developing economy, a compelling argument for early, pro-active and substantial investment in skills development for employment based on potential livelihood trajectories exists.

Construction-phase employment for the resettlement project and the entire project – which together can have a significant requirement for general (non-skilled) or semi-skilled positions – often provides ample opportunity for employment of resettlement-affected people. However, while the provision of such employment ensures the participation of the resettlement-affected households in the project, it is associated with several issues linked to livelihood re-establishment and development:

- it creates direct competition with their participation and investment in the re-establishment and development of their pre-project livelihood activities following relocation.
- construction-phase employment opportunities for the local population typically involve general and semi-skilled labour and generally do not involve substantial investment in improving the skill base of the employees, leaving them with limited options for continuing employment at the end of the construction period.
- if this benefit stream is not used wisely, the overall impact may be a temporal mitigation (albeit a useful one) of impact. This may involve a temporary increase in disposable cash income which decreases as households adopt an increased standard (and cost) of living; use of windfall incomes and savings to adopt higher cost lifestyles and strive to, meet changing social norms, expectations and opportunities; use income to mitigate against vulnerability; or use of income to expand traditional livelihood activities (e.g., farm or herd size), thereby threatening the ongoing sustainability of resource use. As such formal employment and the derivative wage incomes may ultimately be harmful if they enable changes in household livelihoods and welfare without building the base to sustain it.

In summary while a focus on construction-phase opportunity may confer economic benefit, it is not clear how this focus contributes to a positive sustainable livelihood trajectory. Thus the failure to re-establish and develop livelihoods, a progressive tapering off of employment opportunities for general and semi-skilled labour and a lack of suitable investment opportunities may together lead to an increase in the vulnerability of resettlement-affected households in the medium- to long-term.

These issues should be discussed with resettlement-affected households (refer Section 'The Basis for Re-establishment and Development of Livelihood Activities') to help develop a livelihood strategy that promotes skills development and maximises employment while simultaneously facilitating the re-establishment of pre-project livelihood activities. This may be achieved with more flexible working arrangements (e.g., 4-day working weeks), options for resettlement-affected households to bring in labour (e.g., relatives) for employment or to prioritise re-establishment of traditional livelihood activities with guaranteed project commitments to providing employment opportunities at the appropriate time.

Finally, as noted above, the argument is that construction-phase employment for a limited and defined period may allow for wealth accumulation and transfer from one period (i.e., construction) to the next (i.e., operation), with subsequent investment in productive activities. However, this argument may be invalidated by the households' lack of familiarity with wealth accumulation and the lack of an enabling environment (including the lack of services such as banking) together with the lack of productive activities that might allow such investment and accumulation to occur. The provision of incentives to encourage savings of 'windfall earnings' and to promote investment should be considered.

Operational phase employment may involve direct employment or employment through contractors supplying goods and services to the project. Given its longer-term nature, such employment can provide a more reliable and guaranteed contribution to medium-to-long-term livelihood re-establishment and development, taking advantage of opportunities provided by the operation of the project and broader-based area development. However, as noted above in many contexts, the low levels of education, skills and work experience limit local participation to general labour. Effective investment in household capacity to benefit from such growth requires more pro-active assessment and long-term investment and commitment.

Participation in Economic Opportunities Associated with Local and Regional Development

Resettlement projects often focus solely on the resettlement-affected population as potential targets for livelihood interventions and explore pre-project livelihood activities and project opportunities as the main opportunities for livelihood re-establishment and development.

As described in Chapter 6, projects should also assess market-based area development opportunities (e.g., local and regional commodity value chains) to understand if there are opportunities to develop economic linkages that might drive local economic activities (refer Box 8.1). Where opportunities are identified, the project should consider supporting:

- the development of enabling environments to facilitate the introduction and/or strengthening of commodity value chain linkages including the entry of entrepreneurs and middlemen
- investment in enabling infrastructure (e.g., markets, cold storage, aggregation), logistics (e.g., transport) and services (e.g., extension, input markets, output markets)
- building the capacity and reach of value chain actors
- supporting an outreach and capacity-building campaign to reach primary producers

Such interventions are relevant to the entire population and allow resettlement plans and associated resources to provide the means to promote broader-based development. Further, while such interventions are relevant throughout the project lifecycle, they have the most significant impacts when implemented early in the project implementation phase at which time they help mitigate the impacts of the project's inevitable focus on land access and resettlement, the creation of 'resettlement entitlement' and the sense of exclusion and jealousy that households and communities not affected by displacement and resettlement may develop.

BOX 8.1 SUPPORTING MARKET-DRIVEN DEVELOPMENT OF NATURAL RESOURCE-DEPENDENT PRODUCTION SYSTEMS

In broad terms project-supported local economic development may involve one or more of the following areas: (i) development of commodity value chains and supporting critical infrastructure, input and output markets; (ii) enterprise development; (iii) workforce development; and (iv) supplier development. Often local economic development involves some combination of these workstreams.

This section provides a description of the process undertaken to assess and support (natural resource-based) commodity value chain development. In summary there are four steps, namely research and analysis; defining objectives; building a strategy; and developing a plan.

1. **Research and Analysis**
    - prioritise current and potential natural resource-based commodity value chains in the project area of operations (i.e., local and regional)
    - develop business and impact cases for commodity value chains with identified potential

2. **Establishing Objectives**
    - approach to promoting socio-economic development
    - local environment (market opportunities; employment opportunities; local government; financial sector; partners)
    - community's priorities (challenges and needs; needs of Small and Medium Enterprise (SMEs), farmers, fishers, etc.)

3. **Building a Strategy**
    - **suitability** – filter list of economic sectors and key commodity value chains suitable to the area – suitability reflects both agroclimatic suitability/potential and the existence and willingness of market actors including private sector partners to enter and operate in the area
    - **demand** – identify key sources of demand for the target area – market demand, market stability, private and public partner interest
    - **supply** – define supply to meet identified demand – existing supply, barriers to entry, local interest, potential for increased uptake and/or expansion to increase production
    - **strategy** – build a strategy that tackles constraints to meet demand – impact (area, number of beneficiaries, income); etc.

4. **Developing a Plan**
    - agree on prioritisation of commodity value chain development
    - develop detailed plans for selected commodity value chains including geographical footprint; intervention approach; business case for beneficiaries; quantify expected impact and investment; implementation plan; Gantt chart; partners; risk; financing solution, etc.
    - given the limited operation of commodity markets in many rural areas, it is useful to develop a plan that allows for the progressive development of the commodity value chain including processing and marketing. For example, start with production for the local fresh produce market and project catering; introduce primary processing (drying, milling); and promotion of use as input into other products.

On-Going Livelihood Development Post-Relocation

The requirements to close-out the resettlement program and progressive mainstreaming of the resettlement-affected community with other communities in the project area of influence is an important step in the resettlement process (refer to Chapter 9). Some stakeholders argue that the project should provide for on-going funding of area livelihood development, including the resettlement-affected population. This book (i) argues that proponents should pursue land access and resettlement as 'resettlement and development;' (ii) makes the case that resettlement and livelihood re-establishment and development need to occur over longer time frames not aligned to the CAPEX/OPEX planning of project development and (iii) proposes that resettlement livelihood re-establishment and development are seen as a component program of a broader livelihood development program in the project area of influence (Chapter 10), thereby facilitating the transition from resettlement mandated livelihood re-establishment and development to area livelihood development. Put differently integration into area development should be a consideration from the start of land access and resettlement.

Compensation for Reduced Access and/or Loss of Communal Resources

Compensation for reduced access and/or loss of communal resources is a persistent challenge. Common approaches to community-level mitigation of this challenge include (i) promoting the establishment of local common property governance structures aimed at promoting sustainable use (of a more limited residual resource base); (ii) provision of a locally owned and managed endowment fund aimed at supporting on-going development. Experience demonstrates that both the establishment and operation of a local common property management entity and the establishment and sustainable operation of a local foundation are challenging. For both approaches, the issues of integration with traditional resource governance frameworks regulating access and use, aptitude and capacity of local management, and community awareness and understanding should be understood to be development issues requiring medium- to long-term development commitments.

On-Going Provision of Project Benefits

Various stakeholders continue to question whether resettlement and re-establishment and development of livelihoods adequately address the social, cultural and economic losses of displaced households and communities. These stakeholders suggest that allowance for longer-term project-derived benefits should be included in compensation packages. This may occur through the deliberate assignment of revenue streams; providing opportunities for equity shares in the project enterprise; and deliberate assignment of on-going benefit streams (access to employment, more productive lands, electricity, irrigation, etc.).[3] Where such benefits are provided through the on-going allocation of additional development funds, they have the potential to contribute to on-going development beyond the immediate resettlement program. In turn this may address the need for on-going support as the population adapts to a highly dynamic environment.

Safety Nets

Different approaches to managing the resettlement impacts for specific vulnerable groups exist. These can cover households below the poverty line; female- or child-headed households; landless households or households with insecure land tenure and access rights; households reliant on informal market activities; and the elderly for whom wholesale adaptation cannot be reasonably expected. In addition to direct interventions based on resettlement design and planning, the provision of longer-term safety nets might be considered.

General Good Practice Guidance for Re-establishment and Development of Livelihood Activities

Key elements of good practice for livelihood re-establishment and development include:

(i)   promote ownership and participation
(ii)   include host communities in livelihood re-establishment and development

(iii) prioritise re-establishment and improvement of traditional livelihood activities
(iv) ensure appropriate design and delivery (design, target, screening, timing, sequencing and duration)
(v) define what success looks like
(vi) define the basis and process for the transition of resettlement-driven livelihood development programming to area-wide livelihood development programming

Promote Ownership and Participation

The resettlement project has primary responsibility for most of the component steps that make up the resettlement process, with the resettlement-affected population being involved through consultation and participation and, to a large extent, as beneficiaries. For livelihood re-establishment and development, this dynamic needs to change, with a shift from project-driven activities delivering land access, compensation and relocation to community- and household-driven development including ownership and responsibility for the selection, implementation and success of re-establishment and development of livelihood activities by the resettlement-affected population. This change in approach can be achieved in many ways, all of which involve a central role for the community and households in decision-making and participation. For example:

(i) the project could establish a stand-alone livelihood re-establishment and development function for the resettlement- and more generally project-affected population that uses a community- and household-driven development approach (refer Chapter 10).
(ii) the project could promote the establishment of a consultative resettlement livelihood group with sub-groups of households who share a livelihood strategy or for key resource-dependent activities and/ or target groups. The consultative group could agree to the overall purpose and objective; be engaged in the assessment of the livelihood activities, categorisation of households and targeting; assume a key role in the implementation and assessment of pilot projects; and promote diffusion and adoption of innovations.
(iii) as part of the re-establishment and development of livelihood activities, the resettlement project could facilitate community

representatives and lead practitioners to conduct cross-visits to successful projects or communities where alternative technologies and practices are in use.

Include Host Communities in Livelihood Re-establishment and Development

Livelihood development interventions – whether aimed at improving existing activities or introducing new activities – are likely to have general relevance to the resettlement and host communities and proximate project-affected population. From the outset, livelihood re-establishment and development should include the host communities and other communities proximate to the project. Rather than being characterised as 'non-resettlement investment', such interventions should be viewed as investments in the human, social and financial capital of resettlement and host communities and, as such, aimed at promoting relations and networks and mitigating discrepancies, jealousy and conflict.

Prioritise Re-establishment and Improvement of Pre-Project Livelihood Activities

- where possible start with and build upon pre-project livelihood activities and progressively introduce change in the form of improved and new practices over time. One aspect of re-establishment that is often overlooked is that long project development, land access and resettlement planning cycles, interim restrictions on on-going livelihood activities, delayed relocation and availability of replacement land may have already led to a reduction in pre-project livelihood activities well ahead of relocation. As such re-establishment – including allocation, development and cultivation of replacement land aligned with seasonal agricultural practices – may be a significant activity in its own right that may occur only over multiple cropping seasons of reduced activity.
- an initial focus on re-establishment allows households to establish relations with their (new) natural resource base (e.g., new areas, different access, initial development activities, potential restrictions) – whether terrestrial or aquatic – while simultaneously ensuring that issues such as food security, vulnerability and resilience are addressed.

- the progressive introduction of change based on these livelihood activities should build on the household's existing knowledge and practice; assessment of opportunities, challenges and problems; and relevant external technical expertise.
- Given a long history of livelihood-focused rural development work in many countries, a long list of potential interventions should be readily available – as such, the challenge is not the generation of ideas but screening potential interventions for relevance, identifying and creating the conditions required for an intervention to be successful and the time required to promote adoption and its sustainable application.

Ensure Appropriate Design and Delivery (Design, Target, Screen, Scale, Timing, Sequencing and Duration)

Design: to inform the re-establishment and development of livelihood activities and the design of component interventions, the project proponent should engage with past and current livelihood development programs occurring in the vicinity of the project or in similar agro-ecological/socio-economic contexts. These may be associated with government programs, development assistance (aid) programming, long-term engagement through religious institutions, etc. However, it is noteworthy that the design, duration and performance metrics of such programming (especially in the case of aid-supported projects) may differ substantially from resettlement-driven livelihood development – for example, on aid projects beneficiaries may be selected based on interest and capacity; implementation periods may be relatively short (3–5 years); there may be limited medium-to-long-term M&E; and the criteria for project success may be different compared with for resettlement.

Targeting: comprehensive description and assessment of pre-project livelihood activities together with knowledge of resettlement, the project and more general development of the area should form the basis of categorisation of households for the purpose of livelihood re-establishment and development. Identification of 'livelihood categories/groups' in the resettlement-affected population allows targeting and informs key aspects of potential programs as described above (i.e., sector, design, scale, timing, duration). This approach helps ensure the delivery of relevant, bespoke or tailored livelihood interventions to different groups.

That said, decisions to investigate and develop tailored solutions rely on the existence of a critical mass of people. Within identified groups, further targeting is possible based on predicted adoption behaviour, the aim being to identify innovators or champions who will lead the uptake of ideas and, if successful, their promotion.

Screening: as part of the targeting process, conducting individual/household assessments to screen potential participants and understand their capabilities, aptitude, knowledge and experience may be useful to promote active ownership and participation. For example, on the BP Tangguh Liquefied Natural Gas (LNG) Project in West Papua, the resettlement program assessed household's interest in enterprise development (primarily small-scale traders of consumer goods). Most households expressed interest in business, yet the baseline assessment demonstrated that pre-relocation only 10–20% of households conducted business activities with household members having demonstrable business acumen. Higher participation rates in the same sectoral activity would limit viability of the activity.

Scale: although contracting and procurement rules and guidelines may encourage the engagement of a single contractor to address livelihood re-establishment and development, it is recommended to develop smaller-scale initiatives and engage multiple contractors to ensure flexible, adaptive and appropriate targeted programs. Care is needed to ensure that households are not overloaded with multiple implementors and multiple interventions targeting the same households. Effective categorisation/grouping and targeting would minimise generic overload.

Timing: as discussed, when resettlement is implemented as a linear project, livelihood re-establishment and development occur at the end of the resettlement process. When the different types of livelihood re-establishment and development opportunities are considered – including enabling infrastructure; facilitating introduction and operation of commodity value chains, traditional activities, the improvement of existing practices; the introduction of new practices; enterprise development; resettlement- and project-related employment; and opportunities created by broader economic development – there clearly are opportunities to implement re-establishment and development activities throughout the resettlement process, including both before and at the start of land access and resettlement. Examples include (i) skills development for employment could involve early delivery of vocational training; (ii) in the agriculture sector improvement of existing agricultural practices could start before relocation; and (iii) if there is a need to create enabling conditions, i.e., infrastructure, value chains and services, investment and development could occur well ahead of the start of resettlement.

Sequencing: the concept of sequencing refers to:

    (i)   the timing of livelihood re-establishment and development interventions must be scrutinised with respect to labour availability (specifically competing demands for household labour); household absorptive capacity; and time to apply knowledge and skills, new practices, etc. Where interventions target specific household members (i.e., head of household, males, females) or where they provide competing demand for labour (e.g., project employment vs traditional livelihood activity), the project needs to analyse the timing of interventions and ensure availability over time. It may be that different households – at different periods of their family cycle – are able to participate at different times suggesting the need for smaller-scale programs delivered over a longer period of time.

    (ii)   within sectoral programs, there is a need to consider the possibility of incremental livelihood re-establishment and development approaches that start with the re-establishment of traditional activities and progressively introduce new practices, new technologies, capacity building, etc.

Define What Success Looks Like

- in the design, implementation and monitoring and evaluation of livelihood projects, it is important to start with an understanding of what success looks like. In the development assistance sector, household adoption/uptake rates of between 40 and 60% may be deemed as indicators of success. For private sector projects needing to ensure the success of livelihood re-establishment and development in resettlement, a 60% success rate (i.e., a 40% failure rate) will neither be sufficient nor credible. As such it is important to understand success and design programs that respond to the observed patterns of household uptake/adoption.

- Rogers (2003) suggests that the rate of adoption of an innovation is connected to its relative advantages to previous techniques; its compatibility to the individual and to the social system in which it is introduced; the level of technical and theoretical complexity; the trialability of the innovation; the observability of results; and the innovation itself. A theoretical innovation adoption curve can be presented as a normal distribution curve and divided into five broad categories of adopters, namely *innovators, early adopters, early majority, late majority* and *laggards*. Protracted time lags in adoption between an *innovator* and a *laggard* suggest the need for improved diffusion, improved targeting and extended implementation periods.

- terminology aside, variable rates of adoption are likely to reflect specific individual/household characteristics and circumstances (e.g., risk appetite) and confirm the general position that 'one size does not fit all.' This phenomenon has implications for the re-establishment and development of livelihood activities under resettlement. First, livelihood development programming must be supported for a sufficient length of time for different households to engage with the process on the one hand and for the innovation to be demonstrably successful on the other. Thus for agricultural innovations ensuring adequate time to have demonstrable success over multiple (and differing) cropping cycles is critical. Second, improved categorisation and targeting of households should improve the identification of appropriate innovations and, thus, anticipated adoption rates. Third, even with improved categorisation and targeting, it is strategic to offer a basket of opportunities from which households may select what works best for them. A key consideration is how to de-risk innovation and adoption so as to promote household uptake.

Define the Basis and Process for the Transition of Resettlement-Driven Livelihood Development Programming to Area-Wide Livelihood Development Programming

- finally in recognition that a private sector project will gradually wind down specific resettlement programming, it is recommended that, over time, the resettlement-affected population be integrated into broader strategic socio-economic development programming initiatives that focus on the development of sustainable livelihoods. In principle the objective of livelihood re-establishment and development is to ensure that household livelihood activities have been re-established and that the household has a positive development trajectory and as such is positioned to transition to project supported general area development programming. From the total number of resettlement-affected households, different households will reach the target stage at different times, leaving a smaller number of households at the end of the resettlement project that may require on-going support.

The Basis for Re-establishment and Development of Livelihood Activities

This section presents a series of simplistic and hypothetical equations to illustrate the potential changes in the number and type of livelihood activities associated with the changing environment and the trade-offs that households may have to make to participate in preferred activities.

In this hypothetical context, the pre-project situation, household livelihood strategies involve three sectoral livelihood activities identified as LA1 (agriculture), LA2 (poultry) and LA3 (fishing).

$$\text{Livelihood Strategy} = \text{LA1} + \text{LA2} + \text{LA3}$$

The entry of the project creates opportunities for new livelihood activities – these may be directly related to resettlement, direct and indirect project opportunities as well as opportunities associated with induced local and regional area development that are available to the entire population. Some of these are relatively short-term opportunities (e.g., construction-phase employment), while others are long-term (e.g., supply of goods and services to project operations or more generally to the developing economy).

Existing Activities	Resettlement Opportunities	Direct Project Opportunities	Induced Project Opportunities
(LA1+LA2+LA3)	(LA (R1) + LA (R2))	(LA (DP1) + LA (DP2))	((LA (IP1) + LA (IP2))

Existing Activities	=	LA1	+	LA2	+	LA3
		+		+		
		Agriculture		Poultry		Fishing

Resettlement	=	LA (R1)	+	LA (R2))
	=	+		
		House construction		General labour

Direct Project Opportunities	=	LA (DP1)	+	LA (DP2)
		+		
		Bus driver		General labour

Induced Project Opportunities	=	LA (IP1)	+	LA (IP2))
		+		
		Local transport		Baking

With physical and/or economic displacement, the affected population is unable to continue all its pre-project livelihood activities (because of changes in required capabilities, assets and/or activities), while the feasibility, on-going viability and relative importance (scale, intensity) of those that remain may be altered. Resettlement, direct project and project-induced development may create opportunities for new alternative livelihood activities. Households may have insufficient resources (land, labour, capital) to participate in all the opportunities that may arise forcing them to make choices about resource allocation between sectoral activities.

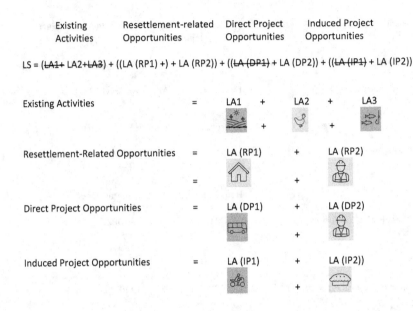

$$LS = (\cancel{LA1} + LA2 + \cancel{LA3}) + ((LA\,(RP1)\,+) + LA\,(RP2)) + ((\cancel{LA\,(DP1)} + LA\,(DP2)) + ((\cancel{LA\,(IP1)} + LA\,(IP2))$$

Finally, following the completion of resettlement and the project construction period, households typically (have to) revert to traditional (pre-project) livelihood activities. Inadequate investment in the development of skills of the current working-age population and limited investment in the education of the next generation may limit opportunities to diversify and participate in the developing economy or through off-farm employment and remittances.

Developing a Strategy for Re-establishment and Development of Livelihood Activities

Section 'The Basis for Re-establishment and Development of Livelihood Activities' describes a situation where a resettlement project commits to interventions to support the re-establishment (and development) of livelihood activities and identifies opportunities associated with resettlement, project construction and/or induced growth and resettled households participate in one or more of these activities opportunistically. The example demonstrates that households have finite resources (labour, land and other assets) to commit to the re-establishment and development of pre-project livelihood activities and participation in resettlement, construction and/ or induced area development opportunities. It should also be noted here that ensuring the availability of options in which households may participate opportunistically should not be equated with a deliberate, strategic approach to the re-establishment and development of livelihood activities (and livelihoods).

Together with the resettlement-affected households (i.e., specifically representatives of identified categories of households with similar livelihood strategies), an overall strategy for re-establishment and development of livelihood activities should be developed. The strategy and design should be informed by:

- comprehensive description and assessment of the context (Section 'The Rural Environment' of Chapter 5) and pre-project livelihood activities (Section 'Assessing the Livelihoods of Resettlement-Affected Households and Communities' of Chapter 6)
- knowledge of resettlement-, project- and more general development-driven change in the area
- consideration of potential household livelihood development trajectories in the medium to long term
- the typology of livelihood re-establishment and development interventions (Section 'Typology of Potential Livelihood Re-establishment and Development Activities')
- good practice guidance for re-establishment and development of livelihood activities (Section 'General Good Practice Guidance for Re-establishment and Development of Livelihood Activities')

Key considerations in defining a strategy include:

- **The Objective of Re-establishment and Development of Livelihood Activities**: while MFI standards default to restoration as a minimum target (and this is often equated with productivity or household income), the objectives of a program addressing the re-establishment and development of livelihood activities should be structured to accommodate short-term re-establishment objectives and medium-to-long-term development objectives (i.e., ensuring positive livelihood development trajectories through development). The strategy should take into account the primacy of re-establishment, the concentration of construction-phase employment and income-earning opportunities and the medium-to-long-term livelihood development trajectories.

- **Re-establishment of Livelihood Activities**: priority must be given to the re-establishment of the traditional (pre-project) primary livelihood activities, i.e., starting with what the affected households know and do and what has been demonstrated to address household resource availability and constraints, needs and vulnerability. Put differently initial activities should not rely on the introduction of new commodities or unproven technical interventions, should not look to produce results over three to four seasons or should not be reliant on non-existent externalities, e.g., inputs, outputs, processing, markets, the establishment of commodity value chains and middlemen.

  Depending on the resettlement project, changes in context and resources (e.g., accessibility and size of landholding, access to marine resources) may reduce either the feasibility or viability of existing activities and the project may need to introduce new infrastructure, services or practices to address these concerns. While the objective of such interventions is to mitigate the impacts of sub-optimal resettlement options, it must be recognised that promoting such interventions and adoption and use thereof takes time, and may be considered to be development interventions. Finally, the urgency of re-establishment must not be compromised by the perceived need for promoting "development goods" (e.g., traditional farming vs conservation agriculture).

- **Participation in Project Construction Opportunities:** project construction-phase employment may compete with livelihood re-establishment and development. Section 'Typology of Potential Livelihood Re-establishment and Development Activities' addresses project construction-phase employment and its relationship to the re-establishment of traditional resource-based livelihood activities.

- **Assessing Area and Sectoral Development Trajectories:** beyond the short-term re-establishment of traditional; (pre-project) resource-dependent activities, understanding current livelihoods, project construction and operations and induced area development allows for consideration of area and sectoral development trajectories. For example, in certain contexts, and for certain types of projects (e.g., linear infrastructure [pipelines, transmission lines], small project foot-print), it might be reasonably anticipated that pre-project, pre-displace-ment livelihoods can continue for most affected households. In other scenarios, for example, mega-projects with large footprints and that catalyse landscape transformation, it is clear that livelihood trajectories will (have to) change in the medium to long term. Typically, such trajectories involve increased infrastructure and services, changing management systems for natural resource-dependent activities, increased interaction with markets, entrepreneurship and employment. In such cases, the resettlement and project interventions should look to facilitate such a transition to ensure continued participation and benefit of local communities. In this way, the project should anticipate livelihood and sectoral development trajectories and build strategies that sequentially address re-establishment, stabilisation and development.

- **Enabling On-Going and Inter-generational Livelihood Development:** beyond the short-term re-establishment of traditional livelihood activities and construction-phase employment targeting the household's adult family members, the project should also consider if and how the affected households – and particularly the next generation – are being enabled to participate in and secure their livelihoods in the context of a changing environment.

For example, where a project delivers improved primary school infrastructure, it improves the basis for participation/attendance. However, education outcomes are dependent on other factors including parent attitude and support, household financial capacity, household family life cycle, staffing, quality of teaching, availability of educational material and scope for progression. Further, in many circumstances where the affected group uses a native language different from that used in formal education, progress in early schooling can be especially challenging. Given the preceding, one must consider how the key human development indicators for the resettlement-affected population are going to be improved sustainably and what role the resettlement project has in supporting such improvement. Pro-active, deliberate investment in enabling continued and increasing participation in a changing economy is necessary. Some examples include:

- the need for broad-based improved literacy at the household level.

- introduction of pre-kindergarten child education and minding to promote education on the one hand and enable child-minders (typically women) to engage in economically productive activities.
- focused investment in primary and secondary education to ensure that subsequent generations are better equipped to deal with induced area development.
- ensuring the development of vocational skills of at least one house-hold member to facilitate employment beyond general or non-skilled labour is critical to ensure continuity of employment and income.
- promoting the entry, development and operation of commodity value chains focusing on annual crops and other resources that are both immediately available and non-seasonal; building the capacity and reach of value chain actors; investment in infrastructure (e.g., markets, cold storage, aggregation), logistics (e.g., transport) and services (extension, input markets, output markets, etc.) at a local/regional level.

BOX 8.2 LIVELIHOOD RE-ESTABLISHMENT AND DEVELOPMENT STRATEGY FOR RESETTLEMENT-AFFECTED HOUSEHOLD, TANGGUH, WEST PAPUA, INDONESIA

The BP Tangguh Liquefied Natural Gas (LNG) project is in the Bintuni Bay on the Bird's Head Peninsula of West Papua, Indonesia. Construction of the project started in 2001 and was completed in 2006; operations commenced in 2007. The project involved the physical and economic displacement of Tanah Merah village to two new settlements, namely Tanah Merah Baru and Onar Baru and the improvement of housing in host villages (Saenga and Onar Lama). Entry to Bintuni Bay usually involves passage through Sorong, a larger town with a port facility that serves as a trading hub for produce.

Pre-displacement livelihoods of the Tanah Merah households involved agriculture (village gardens, shifting cultivation, perennial cash crops), collection of timber and non-timber forest products, fishing (shoreline collection of inter-tidal products and offshore capture of prawns and fish) and petty trade (kiosks). Historically Tanah Merah village was formed by the aggregation of several smaller settlements under the Indonesian government village scheme. Consequently, the population included a diversity of households with different livelihoods and livelihood strate-gies. Two main livelihood strategies could be readily identified, namely fisheries and trade and agriculture, fisheries and trade.

One of the selected resettlement sites, Tanah Merah Baru, was charac-terised by a significant reduction in land area (which impacted land avail-able for agriculture), and reduced access to the sea, due to the extreme tidal flux and presence of extensive mudflats. Further, it was anticipated that the resource use intensity of the marine area in the immediate area of Tanah Merah Baru would increase significantly because of the estab-lishment of a project marine exclusion zone and the increased population density stemming from the proximity of resettlement and host commu-nities. However, Tanah Merah Baru (and the host village of Saengga) was very close to the LNG site, facilitating on-going access for employment.

The strategy for the re-establishment and development of livelihood activities initially focused on re-establishment, supporting the following activities:

- employment (both in the construction of the resettlement village and the LNG facility)
- agriculture – house gardening; intensive fruit tree production (for home consumption and sale)
- increased access to marine resources – boat building; outboard motors
- business development (for existing entrepreneurs)

At the same time, the following opportunities were recognised, and prep-arations were put in place gradually:

- following relocation and re-establishment of livelihoods, it was anticipated that LNG would source vegetables and fruits and marine produce to meet LNG catering requirements for local produce.
- potential for the development of capture and sale of prawns relying on the entry of non-local Sorong-based prawn traders and enabling conditions (village-level processing, water supplies, cold storage) with scope to establish a value chain for many coastal communities in Bintuni Bay.
- the importance of on-going education support – sponsoring opera-tion of primary and secondary schools.
- the importance of on-going vocational training – continued invest-ment in vocational training to promote access to employment.

Challenges

As previously noted, common issues in the development of a strategy for the re-establishment and development of livelihood activities include:

- inadequate livelihood assessment and categorisation/grouping of households by livelihood strategy
- inadequate community engagement, consultation, ownership and support
- relatively late start of re-establishment and development of livelihood activities compared with other land access and resettlement activities
- promotion of unverified approaches (e.g., pilot phase experiments with high uncertainty and risk regarding technology, suitability, product, contribution to subsistence and/or income and markets) and that require households to contribute resources and bear considerable risk associated with large-scale adoption
- conflating re-establishment and development interventions, thereby creating uncertainty regarding intended results, i.e., what will be successful by when while simultaneously introducing new risks to disrupted households
- overloading households regarding expectations to participate, contribute labour and allocate time and labour across opportunities
- compression of all interventions into the project construction phase
- over-optimistic assumptions regarding success

Evaluation of the Strategy and Proposed Sectoral Programs and Interventions

The Strategy

Based on Sections 'Typology of Potential Livelihood Re-establishment and Development Activities,' 'General Good Practice Guidance for Re-establishment and Development of Livelihood Activities,' 'The Basis for Re-establishment and Development of Livelihood Activities' and 'Developing a Strategy for Re-establishment and Development of Livelihood Activities', the resettlement-affected communities, (specifically the identified household livelihood groups) and the project will develop a strategy for the re-establishment and development of livelihood activities. The strategy will include some combination of the following activities:

Area Development

area-wide infrastructure, services and utilities supporting key livelihood
activities

market-driven development – development of commodity value chains in
a specific sector

Community-Driven Development

In areas with low levels of development community-driven multi-sec-
toral development approaches (refer to Section 'Approach to Delivery of
Re-establishment and Development of Livelihood Activities') have merit
as an early entry initiative to drive ownership; facilitate early and responsive delivery of change, thereby building trust-based positive relations; and
improve project understanding of context and livelihoods.

Enabling Environment

interventions to promote an enabling environment for the development
of livelihood activities by addressing recognised challenges and
constraints.

Existing Livelihood Activities

re-establishment of existing livelihood activities
improvement of existing activities

New Livelihood Activities

introduction of new activities

Project Opportunities

project employment (vocational training)
supply of goods and services/entrepreneurship

Inter-Generational Considerations

On-going support to improve human development indicators including:

- ensuring primary and secondary schools are functional
- promoting adult literacy, financial skills
- vocational training
- enterprise development

Further as noted elsewhere, the strategy should consider the importance of:

- community ownership and support
- broader area-wide changes associated with resettlement, project and induced development
- primacy of re-establishment of traditional livelihood activities over development
- categorisation and targeting of households by livelihood strategy
- protracted timelines for development initiatives to deliver results

Assessment of Proposed Strategy and Interventions

In the process of developing and finalising a strategy, it is important to evaluate the strategy – essentially a reality check – by developing an integrated view of the proposed programs and interventions and simultaneously drawing together critical information on all proposed interventions (i.e., type, purpose, target, timing, demand on affected households). Table 8.1 presents a structure, outline and key questions that can be used to assess the proposed livelihood interventions and strategy. Once populated, the table will provide the basis for an overall evaluation of the proposed strategy after which a more detailed integrated plan bringing together the sequence, timing and contracting of interventions for identified household livelihood categories/groups, etc. can be developed. The next section describes the scope for modelling livelihood re-establishment and development.

Table 8.1 Assessment of Proposed Interventions Targeting Re-establishment and Development of Livelihood Activities by Household Livelihood Category/Group [To Be Completed for Each Identified Household Livelihood Category/Group]

| No. | Assessment Criteria | Proposed Intervention – Program/Activities | | | Comment |
| | | Sector 1 | Sector 2 | | |
		Activity 1	Activity 2	Activity 3	
1	**Proposed Intervention/Activity** • Name of intervention/activity • Target group (identified livelihood group) • Estimated no. of households (% of total)				
2	**Type of Livelihood Intervention** • Area development • Enabling environment • Multi-sectoral community-driven development • Re-establish and improve existing activity • Introduction of new activity • Project-related opportunity • Inter-generational development				

3	**Purpose of the Proposed Intervention**
	• Improve enabling environment for the re-establishment and development of livelihood activities
	• Use a multi-sectoral community-driven approach to improve ownership and trust, deliver results and improve understanding of livelihoods
	• Promote re-establishment and improvement of existing activity
	• Intervention aims to address:
	  ○ A recognised resettlement constraint;
	  ○ An identified problem/opportunity; or
	  ○ Generic sectoral improvement program?				

(Continued)

Table 8.1 (Continued)

No.	Assessment Criteria	Proposed Intervention – Program/Activities			Comment
		Sector 1		Sector 2	
		Activity 1	Activity 2	Activity 3	
	• Improve existing activity – aim to improve: participation; productivity (quantity); quality; processing; storage; marketing • Introduction of new activity • Participation in project opportunity				
4	**Assessment of the Proposed Intervention** • Proven potential in the same context or experimental pilot? Y/N • Reliance on external environment – commodity value chain, market actors, key inputs, production levels, etc.? If Y, please explain how identified dependencies are being addressed Y/N • Target of intervention – head of household; male or female household members • Anticipated contribution of household including land, labour and financial resources? • Estimated commitment from household to achieve success? • Requires individual or household capacity development? If Y, explain the relation to current capacity – what additional knowledge, skills, etc. will be required? • Is intervention complementary or competitive to existing household activities and resource/s allocation?Estimated timelines to achieve the expected level of household participation/adoption (between 60 and 80%) • Estimated production/returns (including worst, average and best case) • Estimated timelines to achieve potential returns • Key threats and risks to success				

Table 8.1 (Continued)

No.	Assessment Criteria	Proposed Intervention – Program/Activities				Comment
		Sector 1	Sector 2			
		Activity 1	Activity 2	Activity 3		
5	Relationship to existing and other activities (including resettlement and project employment opportunities)					
6	Contribution to household objectives and risk and vulnerability					

Use of Modelling to Guide Re-establishment and Development of Livelihood Activities

In situations involving medium-to-large-scale resettlement, the development and use of modelling to describe livelihood strategies and the contribution of component livelihood activities may be useful. The development and use of modelling requires the proponent to address many of the general shortcomings that have affected the re-establishment and development of livelihood activities. Specifically, modelling of livelihood strategies and activities:

- requires the collection of adequate baseline information
- requires explicit (and testable) statements of assumptions regarding uptake/adoption and contribution to household income/welfare
- allows separate analysis for identified categories of affected households including vulnerable households (female-headed households, elderly and infirm, disabled, etc.)
- allows for variability analysis for individual activities as well as an overall consolidated livelihood strategy and the assessment of potential impacts on livelihood re-establishment and development with the presentation of worst, intermediate and best-case scenarios
- considers the costs of conducting the livelihood activity as well as increased household expenditure associated with indirect costs such as transport and services and utilities

In addition to the benefits outlined above, modelling can also be used as a design and management tool that clearly demonstrates how changes in the activities, uptake/adoption rates and returns will impact resettled households. The visual application of such analyses demonstrates the importance of assumptions, increases in vulnerability with changing livelihood activities and the combination thereof and ultimately points to the importance of monitoring and evaluation.

Approach to Delivery of Re-establishment and Development of Livelihood Activities

Following the definition of a strategy and component programs, it is also necessary to consider the approach to the delivery of livelihood re-establishment and development programs.

Various approaches exist, ranging from involving community identification of priorities and high levels of community ownership and responsibility to more external, sectoral expert-based needs assessment and program design. Proponents may engage or develop partnerships with a range of partners including government agencies, UN agencies, development NGOs or faith-based organisations, to deliver livelihood re-establishment and development programs. Due consideration of (i) the principles underlying the various approaches; (ii) the requirements, strengths and weaknesses and challenges associated with the various approaches; and (iii) their suitability to the population is required. The two approaches outlined above may be seen as competing models although it may also be the case that they are used sequentially as the awareness and understanding, ownership and capacity of the target population increase.

The most common approach used in the design and delivery of sectoral program interventions is based on a needs analysis and development of a logical framework (also known as logframes) to support the design of the program, contracting of implementation partners, management and monitoring and evaluation of the program. In brief:

- the logical framework helps define the program logic, defining component activities and their respective inputs, outputs and intended outcomes and how, when taken together, these contribute to the intended impact.
- the logframe requires the definition of key risks and assumptions that are beyond the control of the proposed program but potentially have a significant impact on its success.
- while the application of the logical framework could involve community consultation and validation (e.g., problem trees, root cause analyses, needs assessment), typically its use may be characterised as relatively top-down and focused on sectoral interventions.
- program delivery typically involves contracting an external (sectoral) development agency (e.g., NGO) with the expertise and capacity to deliver the required programs to the target population, often requiring the target population to contribute resources (time, labour, land) and participate in initiatives (community group, demonstration plots, etc.) to facilitate delivery of program activities.

In contrast, bottom-up, people-driven, organic, systems approaches are increasingly recognised as a potentially suitable means to promote development among the poor (e.g., the Bangladesh Rural Advancement Committee (BRAC) graduation model). The BRAC graduation approach identifies four key elements to success – namely meeting basic needs, income generation, financial support and savings and social empowerment – and uses a process that first seeks to understand the system by focusing on relationship-building, continuous improvement in understanding the livelihoods and livelihood activities of the target population, and development of locally identified and prioritised results-based interventions. In this way, these systems-approaches offer a broad suite of micro- and small-scale programs to the target population based on the target population's own identification of needs, problems, challenges and opportunities. Through this approach, a process of locally owned growth and development is initiated. Such models have significant advantages in (i) ensuring early engagement and development of trust-based relations; (ii) promoting ownership and self-reliance; (iii) incremental learning regarding livelihoods; and (iv) delivering (quick) results in response to community-identified needs. Such approaches deserve serious consideration during the early stages of project development and resettlement, especially in environments where the general state of development is very low and/or where the population has a very high level of vulnerability.

Scoping, Contracting and Execution of the Strategy and Component Programs for Re-establishment and Development of Livelihood Activities – Requirements and Challenges

Project proponents generally have expertise, experience and aligned to their primary business and often fail to appreciate the scope of work; technical and soft skill requirements; and the relationship and dependency of interventions on the project, the affected population and the broader context associated with livelihood (and more generally social development) programs.

Accordingly, the resettlement team should brief senior project managers, functional leads and the contracting and procurement function regarding resettlement, the strategy and key principles of livelihood re-establishment and development, and key activities and processes. Key considerations include:

(i) Primacy of Livelihood Assessment
(ii) Community-Driven Development as Primary Driver
(iii) Flexibility to Adapt
(iv) Contracting and Procurement (C&P)
(v) Potential Implementation Partners
(vi) Program Management vs Technical Competence

Primacy of Livelihood Assessment

Irrespective of the preferred approach to development, the development of a detailed scope of work (SOW) for livelihood intervention is dependent on a comprehensive livelihood assessment, categorisation of households to determine the relevance of the proposed intervention and an objective/problem statement. In certain contexts, specialist input on the identification and diagnosis of problems and opportunities may be required. While a SOW may aim to promote participation, adoption and productivity, it is important that these objectives and associated targets are specified. Without detail, the risk is that SOW is based on general intentions to 'develop,' 'promote' or 'improve' and in this way become less targeted, more costly and less measurable.

Community-Driven Development as Primary Driver

The primary purpose of re-establishment and development of livelihood activities is to promote the improvement and development of household livelihood activities and practices. In this sense while technical knowledge may well be imparted, the emphasis is on individual and household participation and adoption. Put differently, knowing that an activity, technology or practice is potentially beneficial is essential but confirming its relevance through participation and uptake is the only relevant indicator of success. As such, the SOW needs to confirm the requirement for, and implementation partners need to confirm an understanding of, community-driven development. In this sense the resettlement-affected households and communities are to be treated as the primary client.

Flexibility for Responsive and Adaptive Implementation

As a matter of good practice, interventions should start as pilots, be small-scale and be supported through short-term contracts to provide the opportunity to verify the relevance of the intervention, the capacity of the implementation partner and their ability to connect with the target households. Decisions for extension and expansion should be performance-based. Ensuring the SOW is focused on outcomes and has in-built flexibility to increase responsiveness, adapt to circumstances and generate quick results is critical. For this reason, large contracts with very detailed scopes of work lock providers, project and intended beneficiaries into approaches and interventions that may not benefit any stakeholder.

Contracting and Procurement (C&P)

- understanding requirements: Contracting and Procurement functions generally are designed to serve the primary needs of the company and as such it is recognised that the requirements of Social Performance/ Resettlement and the associated Health, Safety and Environment (HSE), security, technical and financial criteria applicable to uncontrolled sites are not necessarily known or understood by C&P and HSE staff, i.e., uncontrolled sites may be outside the day-to-day framework of these functions. Further local content criteria can, on some occasions, be unilaterally applied to the Social Performance function without considering the implications of inadequate capacity on livelihood outcomes. For example, managers have been heard to express sentiments that *social development matters should be able to be implemented by local partners*. At the outset of a resettlement program, it is recommended to have an alignment session with C&P and if necessary, management. Key aspects of such alignment include activity profile; need for implementation partners and summary scope including the need for flexibility; timing; expectations regarding capacity; identification of potential providers. The development of a supplier database and engagement with other companies with experience in contracting similar activities may be useful.
- capacity vs cost: typically, C&P processes are driven and decided by HSE, technical and cost criteria, i.e., if potential providers pass the HSE and technical requirement, then the lowest cost bidder is awarded the contract.

Internally, both C&P and relevant management decision-makers are not especially familiar with the concept of capacity building and the importance thereof. As such, it is recommended to ensure broad awareness among C&P and management of the importance of capacity building and define suitably high technical pass marks to enable reviewers to distinguish between those who 'know the language of development' from 'those who can deliver' development. Without a shared understanding of the capacity building requirement, resettlement staff are often drawn into engaging a lower cost and less competent contractor and the intended beneficiaries are the losers. The cost of lack of adequate technical capacity is incompetent implementation; loss of staff time attempting to make the program work; potential termination and replacement of partners; loss of time; intended beneficiaries' loss of development benefits; and loss of trust between project- and resettlement-affected households.

Externally, many potential implementation partners are unfamiliar with the HSE and security requirements of large companies and projects. Projects need to establish clear positions on what HSE and security requirements apply to community-based activities located outside the company and construction contractors' area of operations (i.e., outside controlled areas) and ensure alignment with the office- and site-based HSE and security functions before finalising a SOW.

- ensure flexibility in contracting and procurement: finally, as noted above, there is a need to ensure that contracts are structured to allow responsive adaptation.

Potential Implementation Partners

Besides comprehensive livelihood assessment to inform the development of the program scope of work for re-establishment and development of livelihood activities, the selection of implementation partners to implement these programs is the next most important factor in success. As most implementation partners are likely to have worked with the development/ aid sector with specific language, approach and performance metrics, working with private sector partners and on specific social impact mitigation programs such as resettlement may be a novelty. Further as noted above, knowing the language of development is different from having the capacity to deliver programs. As noted above, it may be useful to develop a database of potential providers highlighting sectoral expertise, project experience, resources, etc. Ultimately following the submission of proposals for specific scopes of work, key considerations in the evaluation, selection and award process include:

- resources – demonstrable expertise; adequate staff
- experience in similar geographical areas; population with similar social, cultural and economic attributes; with similar livelihood strategies and primary production systems
- people vs project – awareness, knowledge and demonstrable practice in using participatory processes that promote ownership, support and active engagement of the resettlement-affected population vs serving the client
- Demonstrable understanding of the importance of outcome indicators (cf. input and output indicators that demonstrate the program is being delivered but not what result it is having)
- track record – demonstrable success that can be shared with the project

Program Management vs Technical Competence

As the operator, the role of the resettlement implementor is to facilitate entry of relevant technical programs and associated expertise, to oversee program implementation by implementation partners and monitor implementation and success/failure. Accordingly, it is important to balance the need for livelihood development and project management expertise with the need for sector-specific technical knowledge. A common shortcoming is engaging a technical individual bringing expertise and experience in one or other primary livelihood activity rather than a livelihood development manager with project management expertise to oversee overall livelihood programming. As a consequence, the ability to monitor component livelihood programs, identify inter-dependencies and linkages and ultimately understand the component programs' contribution to livelihood outcomes may be limited. This capability is essential where there are multiple implementation partners, each bringing relevant community development and technical expertise and delivering a component program but not having overall responsibility for livelihood outcomes. Put differently, component program success cannot and should not be equated with the success of livelihood re-establishment and development.

BOX 8.3 QUALIFICATIONS FOR A RESETTLEMENT LIVELIHOOD DEVELOPMENT MANAGER

A Livelihood Development Manager should demonstrate knowledge expertise and experience in the following areas:

- rural development (economy and people) expertise and experience
- regional and local economic opportunity, market and commodity value chain development
- sectoral development expertise (agriculture, fisheries, livestock, micro- and small enterprise, vocational training)
- understanding of community-driven development processes' participatory learning and action expertise
- socio-cultural appreciation and sensitivity
- stakeholder engagement expertise
- social and environmental awareness
- ability and willingness to work alongside individuals, households and communities

---

Remediation and Legacy Resettlement

Remediation refers to instances of involuntary displacement and resettlement where resettlement commitments are not delivered (successfully) and corrective actions are implemented. This can arise for a number of reasons including where the resettlement-affected population demands redress, where national resettlement committees or Lender Environmental and Social reviews require corrective action or where the implementation of a social audit ahead of further resettlement identifies issues. Issues regarding implementation and delivery of the resettlement plan may concern eligibility and stakeholder engagement; (non-) delivery of agreed benefits; (non-) delivery of livelihood re-establishment and development; and/or shortcomings in resettlement diagnosis, design and delivery as described in other sections in this book. In many circumstances these issues arise through grievances raised by the displaced population or through audits that precede a subsequent phase of resettlement. The redress of such issues may be affected by a breakdown in relations between the implementor and the affected communities and thus there may be a need to reset the relationship.

Legacy resettlement issues refer to situations where the implementation and experience of resettlement in an initial phase establish a (negative) precedent for on-going community aspirations and expectations and further resettlement planning where the project continues to require land access. It may also include retrospective upgrading of initial phases of resettlement where subsequent phase resettlement packages offer different benefits, e.g., solar power, rainwater collection.

Notwithstanding the existence of valid issues, for both remediation and legacy resettlement, there are some practical challenges in addressing these concerns. These include:

- timely completion of resettlement (as per the close-out audit) has led to the closure of the resettlement program.
- the resettlement plan has not successfully re-integrated the resettlement-affected population into the broader project-affected population. Protracted identification of the resettlement-affected population as a distinct and entitled group (rather than integration into a more broadly defined socio-economic development program targeting the project-affected population).
- where the project involves long-life operations with on-going land access requirements, where the resettlement-affected population has the opportunity to directly assess the evolution of entitlement, compensation and benefits and compare and contrast such with their resettlement package.
- where the project involves long-life operations with on-going land access requirements, where the resettlement-affected population has the opportunity to directly assess the success/failure of livelihood re-establishment and development over a protracted period once the formal close-out of resettlement has already taken place.
- opportunistic rent-seeking claiming resettlement benefits, given increasing levels of awareness of the value of land to project operations.

These issues point to the importance of ensuring that the project gives sufficient consideration to the development of land management plans including on-going land access and resettlement; ensuring a common understanding of resettlement; resettlement diagnosis and design; and integration of the displaced households into the broader socio-economic context following resettlement.

The SLF can also be used to evaluate remediation and legacy resettlement. The approach set out in this book – specifically the use of the SLF as described in Chapter 7 and the development and evaluation of a strategy for the re-establishment and development of livelihood activities described in this chapter – can be used to:

- validate the contextual assessment (natural resources, markets and livelihood systems)
- validate the assessment of the project and induced change in resettlement diagnosis and design
- validate the adequacy livelihood assessment
- identify shortcomings in resettlement diagnosis, design and delivery
- understand stakeholder perspectives and stakeholder relations

Issues may be addressed under the rubric of resettlement or more broadly in terms of a commitment to promoting livelihood development.

Conclusion

The re-establishment and development of livelihood activities is a critical aspect of ensuring resettlement-affected households achieve and maintain a positive development trajectory.

RAPs tend to identify traditional natural resource-based livelihood activities across sectors as well as project opportunities and propose programmatic development interventions across all sectors. Consequently, livelihood re-establishment and development may involve a plethora of generic interventions applicable to all resettlement-affected households that have the potential to overload resettlement-affected households, have uncertain livelihood outcomes and are delivered at considerable cost to the proponent. As such, current practice points to the following key shortcomings:

- **delayed start and inadequate duration of programs:** resettlement livelihood programming generally starts too late in the resettlement process and the duration is typically limited to the construction phase of the project. The experience of emergency and development assistance-sponsored livelihood development programs demonstrates the complexity, challenge and time required for the adoption of improved or new practices and/or behaviour change. This experience should inform the design and resourcing of livelihood re-establishment and development programs.

- **failure to engage, consult and ensure ownership and support of the resettlement-affected population:** The project must ensure that the resettlement-affected population and household livelihood categories/groups own and drive livelihood programs. In recognition that development programming often involves medium-to-longterm rewards, it is also useful to identify opportunities for generating 'quick wins' thereby promoting interest and support.

- **failure to develop a strategy for re-establishment and development of livelihood activities.**

- **failure to develop targeted bespoke programs:** resettlement livelihood programming generally delivers generic technical programs to the resettlement-affected households. The ability to categorise households by livelihood strategy and design tailored livelihood re-establishment and development programs promotes ownership, improved design and delivery and livelihood outcomes. Programs should start small and build incrementally based on learning with resettlement-affected households and demonstrable success.

- **conflating re-establishment and development:** assessment of RAP proposed programs and interventions to support livelihood re-establishment and development indicates that most tend towards development programming without adequate assessment verifying potential development outcomes. It is important to recognise the experience of the aid sector in livelihoods programming, especially regarding the relationship between livelihoods and the broader environment; the time required to achieve reasonable adoption/uptake rates, and thus the time required to achieve livelihood development outcomes. In this sense the duration of livelihood re-establishment and development programs – when tied to the project construction phase – is inadequate.

- **Contracting and Procurement processes unsuited to the need for responsive, adaptive program implementation focused on desired results and outcomes.**

As noted in Chapters 6 and 7, the assessment of the rural environment and household livelihoods and the identification of household categories/ groupings is a critical input in the definition of a livelihood re-establishment and development strategy and delivery of targeted component livelihood programs.

The development of bespoke livelihood development strategies for identified household livelihood groups is essential to achieving improved outcomes for the re-establishment and development of livelihood activities. Key considerations for developing component livelihood interventions include design, targeting, screening, timing, sequencing and duration.

Notes

1   Refer Cernea, M. M. (2009) Ch 3 Financing for Development: Benefit Sharing Mechanisms in Population Resettlement) in Oliver-Smith, A., (2009). Development and Dispossession, The Crisis of Forced Displacement and Resettlement. School for Advanced Research Press, New Mexico, USA.
2   The success of training/capacity building depends on many factors including project context, initial capacity, requisite skills and ultimately adoption/ uptake and use. A considerable body of knowledge regarding capacity building and adoption/uptake of new technologies/practices, etc. in rural development is available.
3   See Cernea, M. M., in Oliver-Smith, A., (2009) Development and Dispossession, The Crisis of Forced Displacement and Resettlement.

Bibliography

ADB (1998). A Handbook on Resettlement, A Guide to Good Practice. Asian Development Bank, Manila, Philippines.

Bainton, N. A., Owen, J. R., and Kemp, D. (2018, September 5). Mining, Mobility and Sustainable Development: An Introduction. Special Edition Sustainable Development, 26, 437–440.

Bebbington, A. (1999). Capitals and Capabilities: A Framework for Analyzing Peasant Viability, Rural Livelihoods and Poverty. World Development, 27(2), 2021–2044. https://doi.org/10.1016/S0305-750X(99)00104-7.

BRAC (2021). Graduation Overview. https://bracupgi.org/research-and -resources/economic-inclusion/graduation-overview/.

Catley, A., Lind, J., and Scoones, I. (Eds.). (2013) *Pastoralism and Development in Africa, Dynamic Change at the Margins*. Routledge, London and New York.

Cernea, M. M. (2009) Ch 3 Financing for Development: Benefit Sharing Mechanisms in Population Resettlement). In Oliver-Smith, A. (Ed.). *Development and Dispossession, the Crisis of Forced Displacement and Resettlement*. School for Advanced Research Press, Santa Fe, New Mexico, 49–76.

De Haan, L. J. (2017). *Livelihoods and Development, New Perspectives, Koninkjlijke*. Brill, Leiden, The Netherlands.

Department for International Development (1999). Sustainable Livelihoods Guidance Sheets. https://www.livelihoodscentre.org/documents /114097690/114438878/Sustainable+livelihoods+guidance+sheets.pdf /594e5ea6-99a9-2a4e-f288-cbb4ae4bea8b?t=1569512091877.

Ellis, F., and Allison, E. (2004). *Livelihood Diversification and Natural Resource Access*. Livelihood Support Programme, FAO, Rome.

European Commission (2004). *Aid Delivery Methods, Volume 1*. Project Cycle Management Guidelines, European Commission, Europe Aid Coordination Office, Brussels, Belgium.

FAO & ILO (2009). *The Livelihood Assessment Tool-Kit, Analysing and Responding to the Impact of Disasters on the Livelihoods of People*. FAO, Rome and ILO, Geneva.

https://www.livelihoodscentre.org.

https://www.ted.com/talks/ernesto_sirolli_want_to_help_someone_shut_up _and_listen?language=en.

https://www.ted.com/talks/jacqueline_novogratz_patient_capitalism.

IFC (2002). *Handbook for Preparing a Resettlement Action Plan*. International Finance Corporation, Washington, DC.

IFC (2009). *Projects and People, A Handbook for Addressing Project-Induced in-Migration*. International Finance Corporation, Washington, DC.

IFC (2013). *Addressing Project Impacts on Fishing-Based Livelihoods, A Good Practice Handbook: Baseline Assessment and Development of a Fisheries Livelihood Restoration Plan*. International Finance Corporation, Washington, DC.

IFRC (2010). *IFRC Guidelines for Livelihoods Programming*. International Federation of Red Cross and Red Crescent Societies, Geneva.

Price, S. (2017). Chapter 17, Livelihoods in Development Displacement – A Reality Check from the Evaluation Record in Asia. In van den Berg,

R., Naidoo, I., and Tamondong, S. D. (Eds.), *Evaluation for Agenda 2030, Providing Evidence on Progress and Sustainability.* International Development Evaluation Association (IDEAS), Exeter/UK, 273–289.

Reddy, G., Smyth, E., and Steyn, M. (2015). *Land Access and Resettlement, A Guide to Best Practice.* Greenleaf Publishing, Sheffield/UK.

Rogers, E. (2003). *Diffusion of Innovations,* 4th edition. The Free Press, New York.

Scoones, I. (2015). *Sustainable Livelihoods and Rural Development.* Practical Action Publishing.

Tabares, A., Londoño-Pineda, A., Cano, J. A., and Gómez-Montoya, R. (2022). Rural Entrepreneurship: An Analysis of Current and Emerging Issues from the Sustainable Livelihood Framework. *Economies,* 10(6), 142. https://doi.org/10.3390/ economies10060142.

United Nations High Commissioner for Refugees (UNHCR) (2005). *Handbook for Planning and Implementing Development Assistance for Refugees (DAR) Programmes.* United Nations High Commissioner for Refugees (UNHCR), Geneva.

USAID (2016) Leveraging Economic Opportunities, Final Performance Report, ACDI/VOCA.

Winters, P., Davis, B., Carletto, G., Covarrubias, K., Quiñones, E. J., Zezza, A., Azzarri, C., and Stamoulis, K. (2009). *Assets, Activities and Rural Income Generation: Evidence from a Multi-country Analysis.*

Part V

MONITORING AND EVALUATION OF LIVELIHOOD RE-ESTABLISHMENT AND DEVELOPMENT

9

MONITORING AND EVALUATION

DOI: 10.4324/9781003358725-14

Introduction

Starting with the end in mind, the ultimate success of a resettlement program should be measured by the success of displaced households' livelihood re-establishment and development. Inherent in demonstrating such success is the ability to substantiate that the majority of displaced households have successfully re-established their livelihoods and are on a positive (and sustainable) livelihood (development) trajectory that will allow progression untethered from the resettlement program (and project construction phase opportunities). As such, monitoring and evaluation must be an integral part of the resettlement process and should be addressed systematically from the outset (i.e., from design and planning) through implementation to close-out.

Preceding chapters have argued for the consistent application of a livelihood lens (illustrated in this book through the use of the Sustainable Livelihoods Framework) to the entire resettlement process to ensure that livelihood considerations are integrated into the design of all aspects of resettlement and applied throughout the execution of the resettlement plan. This chapter describes the use and application of the Sustainable Livelihoods Framework to the design of baseline data collection, the monitoring of resettlement and livelihood outcomes throughout the resettlement process and ultimately the evaluation of livelihood re-establishment and development (Figure 9.1).

Figure 9.1 Application of Monitoring and Evaluation throughout the Resettlement Process

Resettlement Design and Planning

Establishing a monitoring and evaluation framework along with key indicators at the outset of the resettlement process, i.e., during resettlement design and planning, will ensure that:

(i)   adequate and relevant data are available for the design of resettlement programs

(ii)   relevant data for monitoring livelihood re-establishment and development are **consistently** collected throughout the resettlement process

(iii)   resettlement and household-level progress can be periodically monitored to better target and improve livelihood interventions for affected
households throughout the resettlement process

(iv)   evidence is collected to support the closure of the resettlement
program

A key component of any resettlement monitoring and evaluation is to collect household-level baseline data as a basis for monitoring change in the
household livelihood and ultimately evaluating the success of livelihood
re-establishment and development. Early establishment of a resettlement
monitoring and evaluation framework requires the project to identify and
select relevant indicators. Typically, household baseline surveys collect
aspects of household demography, livelihood activities and income without considering how monitoring and evaluation will continue throughout
the project life cycle and ultimately be used in the evaluation. As a consequence, a great deal of information goes unused or is not collected again in
a consistent manner, making comparative assessment through the project
life cycle difficult.

Selecting Indicators to Monitor
Livelihood Re-establishment and Development

As Reddy et al. (2015) recommend in their best practice guide for resettlement, it is better to select "fewer indicators of significance, rather than
attempting to track a host of minor indicators."[1] Selecting fewer indicators
will benefit the project by reducing the number of resources required to
collect and analyse the data; will eliminate the "data noise," i.e., the collection of unnecessary or under-used data; and will alleviate participant
survey fatigue.

There are many guides that provide a list of indicators that can be used
to determine the effectiveness of a resettlement program and some debate
about which indicators are the best for determining livelihood re-establishment and development. The key is selecting those indicators best suited for
a specific context, people and project and being consistent with the collection and use of those indicators over time.

Chapter 4 presented aggregate measures of livelihood restoration, describing measures that range from productivity (of natural resource-based livelihood activities) to aggregate indicators of livelihoods (such as income) to broader concepts such as standard of living and welfare. The use of aggregate indicators of livelihood re-establishment and development may be challenged on both a conceptual and a practical basis. From a practical perspective, challenges include:

- households generally are unable to report full production
- households struggle to recall (or choose not to divulge) accurately production and/or income
- units of measurement are irregular and vary from household to household and may not reflect the same base case (unprocessed/processed)
- socio-economic baselines are seldom sufficiently detailed to calculate imputed income from subsistence production activities

Multi-dimensional approaches including measures of household nutrition, standard of housing, ownership of indicator assets, number of productive livelihood activities and income sources (in kind and cash) and income and expenditure may better reflect the entirety of livelihoods.

The remainder of this chapter illustrates the use of the SLF to monitor and evaluate the livelihood re-establishment and development of resettled households. A hypothetical resettlement project involving the displacement and resettlement of rural coastal households[2] is used to inform the example. In general terms, the context and livelihoods of resettlement households may be described as follows:

- accessibility is limited – both by virtue of poor roads and the lack of public transport, the lack of local markets enabling commercialisation of produced commodities and more generally limited integration into the mainstream economy.
- households may be polygamous and maintain families and assets (houses, land) in locations outside areas affected by project land access. Households comprise nuclear families residing in small two- to three-room houses with thatch or corrugated iron roofing and raised clay floors. Generally cooking occurs outside the house on a three-stone open fireplace. Houses are without water and sanitation and electricity

– water is collected from boreholes, shallow wells or surface water, while most households practice open defecation. Access to health facilities is limited. Households have access to primary school education, but completion rates for primary school let alone progress to secondary school are very low.

- households practice diversified livelihoods centred on intertidal collection of marine produce and fishing, low-intensity short-fallow shifting cultivation producing annual crops (maize, beans, peanut) in the first year and cassava for several years as the cultivated field progressively reverts to its natural state and opportunistic cultivation of wetland rice. Households also cultivate perennial cash crops although, with limited market demand, there is limited active management, production and sale. Finally collection of various products from common property and/or fallow land occurs, including fuelwood, fruits, medicinal plants and wildlife. Fishing is the mainstay of resident household livelihoods. Agriculture is adversely affected by low soil fertility and variability of rainfall including unpredictable start and duration of wet seasons, drought or occasional cyclones. However rice production in wetland areas can be very productive. In addition households may practice small-scale house gardening and maintain limited livestock (poultry, goats). Poultry production is adversely affected by the lack of inputs (chicks, feed) and the occurrence of disease. Within the hamlets, a number of households operate small-scale trade stores.

- households may engage as artisans or provide goods and services to the population. With project entry and development, there have been an increasing number of opportunities for employment as general labour and to a lesser extent as semi-skilled and skilled employees. Employment by the project has generally involved a reduction in male participation in fishing activities and increased purchase of dry goods (rice, maize meal, cassava flour) to meet household subsistence requirements.

- overall the resettlement-affected population (and more generally the population in the project area of influence) has a low human development index score. Households secure poverty-line livelihoods with minimal cash incomes. Consideration of the possible categorisation of households suggests the centrality of inter-tidal collecting and fishing and cassava gardening with participation emphasising agriculture at one end of the spectrum and fishing at the other. Greater distance from the coast or access to more fertile lands increases the relative importance of agriculture. However, it is possible to identify households who tend to the one livelihood activity, namely fishing or agriculture. Availability of formal employment reduces participation in daily or weekly fishing activities. The prevalence of male employment pushes the system towards areas operated by women, i.e., house gardening, inter-tidal collection.

Based on the context, the social baseline and an understanding of resettled households' livelihoods, the application of the SLF leads to the selection of specific indicators for each of the household's Five Capitals/Assets (Table 9.1). Those indicators include higher-level community indicators which

Table 9.1 Example of Selection of Indicators for SLF 5 Capitals/Assets

Definition[a]	Household Indicators	Community Indicators (Context)
"**Human capital** represents the **skills, knowledge, ability to labour and good health** that together enable people to pursue different livelihood strategies and achieve their livelihood objectives. At a household level, human capital is a factor of the amount and quality of labour available; this varies according to **household size, skill levels, leadership potential, health status**, etc."	• Number of household members of working age (disaggregated by gender) • Average number of meals per day • Household (HH) members with a disability (age and disability) • HH members who have been ill for longer than 1 month in the past year (age) (note: disability and chronic illness usually take another HH resource to assist in care) • HH members attending or completed: primary school, vocational, literacy, financial management, trade skill, agricultural or fishing programs (age and gender)	• Health services available and accessible • Rates of chronic or long-term illnesses • Access to water and sanitation • School functioning and accessible • School attendance rates

(Continued)

Table 9.1   (Continued)

Definition[a]	Household Indicators	Community Indicators (Context)
"Social capital – ... the social resources upon which people draw in pursuit of their livelihood objectives. These are developed through **networks and connectedness**, ... that **increase people's trust and ability to work together and expand their access to wider institutions,** such as political or civic bodies; **membership of more formalized groups**."	• HH members participating in "social groups": group resource collection, attend spiritual gatherings, savings groups, civic groups or other • HH's perception of being integrated into the community	• Number of CBOs in the community • Mosque/church attendance rates • Crime rates • Formal and informal leadership structures (government)
"**Physical capital** comprises the basic infrastructure and producer goods needed to support livelihoods. Infrastructure consists of changes to the physical environment that help people to meet their basic needs and to be more productive. Producer goods are the tools and equipment that people use to function more productively."	• HH home ownership • HH has access to energy • HH owns productive assets (farming and fishing equipment, transportation, cellphone)	• Community road networks exist • Public transportation is available • Cellphone network functioning • Existence of community radio • Energy is accessible

(Continued)

Table 9.1 (Continued)

Definition[a]	Household Indicators	Community Indicators (Context)
"Financial capital denotes the financial resources that people use to achieve their livelihood objectives. There are two main sources of financial capital … **Available stocks**: Savings … and Financial resources can also be obtained through credit-providing institutions. **Regular inflows of money**: Excluding earned income, the most common types of inflows are pensions, or other transfers from the state, and remittances."	• Type/no. of HH income sources • Estimated HH income by type • HH expenses • HH savings • HH debt • HH participating in a savings group	• Number of small businesses in the community (type) • Number of savings groups in the community • Banking systems and other financial systems (e.g., MPESA) available • Cost of living • Markets available and functioning
"Natural capital is the term used for the natural resource stocks from which resource flows and services useful for livelihoods are derived. There is a wide variation in the resources that make up natural capital, from intangible public goods… to divisible assets used directly for production (trees, land, etc.)."	• HH has access to agricultural land (total ha and location) • HH has access to common property resources disaggregated by type (land and marine – fishing and intertidal collection, bush collection including water)	• Number of conflicts due to competition for, or access to, natural resources • Number and type of open access areas that are closed by the project (e.g., fishing areas)

[a]Department for International Development (1999), *Sustainable Livelihoods Guidance Sheets*, Section 2.3.5.

are intended to provide background/context. A handful of indicators are selected that would accurately reflect a change (positive or negative) to a specific capital/asset. The benefit of a few targeted indicators is that more time can be spent completing detailed interviews with each household to provide an in-depth understanding of the household's assets and, in turn, its livelihood priorities. The intention is to use these indicators to determine the household's capital/asset changes as a result of resettlement interventions, e.g., compensation and livelihood programs.

BOX 9.1 DATA COLLECTION

After the selection of the key indicators, effective and efficient monitoring and evaluation require a systematic approach to the collection and management of data. Whether using focus groups, surveys or interviews, the utility of any framework is lost without discipline in data quality and data management.

In order to best inform planning and decision-making:

- data must be collected by skilled enumerators who are able to develop a fulsome understanding of the household. Where skilled enumerators are not available, having adequate supervision and consistent, timely review of the incoming data is paramount.
- if using surveys, data must be collected consistently with no or very few changes in the survey tool to allow for comparative analysis.
- the project must have an integrated database to manage the data being collected to allow for analysis.

Developing an Integrated Database

During baseline data collection and throughout the project, an immense amount of data will be collected and generated. Examples of various sources of information are illustrated in Figure 9.2. This data is generated by different functions and/or contracted implementation partners delivering different components of the overall resettlement program and is often stored in separate data management systems. Further, because functions and implementation partners are not required to have an overview of resettlement and livelihood re-establishment and development, often, key data points (e.g., household identifier) that would allow integration of the data are not collected systematically. As a consequence, developing an integrated view of resettlement and livelihood re-establishment and development becomes challenging.

Much like developing the monitoring and evaluation framework requires envisioning what is required at the end of the process, database

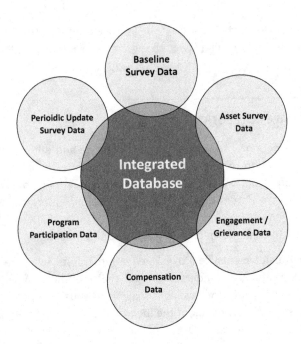

Figure 9.2 Sources of Information Collected for Monitoring and Evaluation of Resettlement

design is the same. The resettlement team needs to engage information management specialist(s) early who can design and develop or assist in the selection of a database management system for all functions and phases of the program. The specialist should work with the team to understand what is required in the short term (during baseline data collection) and what will be required during implementation (monitoring delivery of resettlement entitlements and monitoring and evaluation of livelihoods). The specialist should also develop standardised tools and training for data generators (e.g., implementation partners, internal departments) on the key data requirements.

Using a relational database is good practice as various sources of information can be collated and analysed using a unique identifier, e.g., a reference number. A relational database also allows for the expansion of the database over time. Depending on the size of a resettlement program, a small database (e.g., MS Access) or a larger database (e.g., Oracle) can be customised for the collection of data from various sources. Regardless of

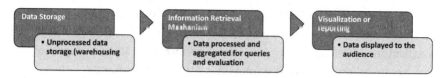

Figure 9.3 Data Management System Considerations

the size of the program, there are three major data management considerations that can guide the development or selection of an appropriate system (Figure 9.3).

(i)   data storage: this stage establishes where the incoming data are stored (e.g., Excel, MS Access, Oracle) in its raw format.

(ii)   information retrieval mechanism: during this stage, data manipulation language is used to aggregate and query the data and to complete cross-functional analyses or evaluations. This can be completed in most database management systems (e.g., Excel, MS Access and Oracle).

(iii)   visualisation or reporting: this stage determines how data are presented in the form of reports or dashboards. There are several software packages commercially available that can be linked to a database to create interactive reports, for example, Microsoft's Power BI was used to create the interactive dashboard presented in Figure 9.5.

All aspects of data management (collection, quality, storage, analysis) are key to an effective and efficient monitoring and evaluation program. If

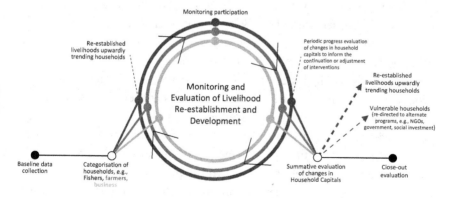

Figure 9.4 M&E of Livelihood Re-establishment and Development

resources are dedicated early in the resettlement planning phases to establishing a data management system, the on-going monitoring and progress evaluations of household livelihood re-establishment and development are less resource intensive during implementation and close-out.

Resettlement Program Implementation – Monitoring and Evaluation

Effective monitoring and evaluation of a resettlement and livelihood re-establishment and development program will:

- monitor household progress in resettlement, i.e., delivery of front-end entitlements, for example, compensation benefits
- monitor participation in livelihood re-establishment and development programs according to household grouping/categorisation
- represent collected household data in an integrated and easily accessible format
- evaluate a household's livelihood trajectory
- inform "graduation" from the resettlement program, i.e., identify those households that have successfully re-established and developed their livelihoods

Figure 9.4 illustrates the monitoring and evaluation process from the collection of baseline data to the eventual close-out. The process begins with the collection of baseline data and its use in categorising the displaced population (e.g., by livelihood groupings) in order to tailor livelihood programs to households. The M&E function then monitors participation in the livelihood re-establishment and development programs and periodically evaluates changes to the household's capitals/assets. Households that have re-established their livelihoods "graduate" from the resettlement process and continue participation in programs at their discretion. Those that have not re-established their livelihoods or who may need further support remain in the resettlement process until they have re-established their livelihoods or are confirmed as being on an upward livelihood re-establishment and development trajectory. At the point where most households have "graduated," the resettlement program will close and those identified as potentially vulnerable will be transferred out of the resettlement process into an alternative support network (e.g., government assistance, NGO support, social investment programs).

Household Livelihood Re-establishment and Development Progress Evaluations

After the initial baseline data collection, the on-going data collected as part of monitoring should be evaluated to determine if there are any changes to the household or its capitals/assets that may require further targeted intervention. Ideally, data on households should be collected every 6 months in order to allow for timely adjustments to interventions; however, annual interviews may be as effective and may ease household fatigue with participation in resettlement activities.

One method for completing this analysis when there are a substantial number of displaced households is to develop a simplified scoring system so that households can be categorised and monitored within the following three categories:

(i)   households that have satisfactorily re-established and developed their livelihoods
(ii)   households on a constant or upward trajectory to re-establishing and developing their livelihoods
(iii) households that have not adequately re-established and developed their livelihoods and are potentially vulnerable

Based on this analysis, adjustments can be made to resettlement programs to "lift" households to the first two categories. For example, adjustments may be targeted interventions for livelihood activities as described in Chapter 8.

Table 9.2 outlines a potential scoring system based on the selected indicators in which to categorise households during the baseline. The scoring system should be designed based on the specific context. Early definition and consistent application are key to effectiveness. Periodic assessments using the same scoring system will alert the project to positive or negative trends and may thus indicate the need for adjustment of livelihood programs and also inform the best timing for resettlement close-out.

Table 9.2 Conceptual Scoring System for Evaluation of Household Status

Indicators	Scoring Criteria (10-Point Scale with 10 Being the Best Scenario and 0 the Worst)
Human Capital Score	
Number of household members of working age/Total number of HH members	10: 91–100%; 9: 81–90%; 8: 71–80%; 7: 61–70%; 6: 51–60%; 5: 41–50%; 4: 31–40%; 3: 21–30%; 2: 11–20%; 1: 1–10%; 0: 0%
Average number of meals per day (in the last month)	10–8: three meals per day 7–4: two meals per day 3–0: one meal or less per day (use range to account for the quality of meals, i.e., better quality, higher score)
HH members with a disability	10: no disabled HH members 9–7: one to two HH members with mild disability 6–4: one to two HH members with severe disability 3–0: multiple HH members with severe disabilities requiring working-age HH members to forego income generation
HH members who have been ill for longer than 1 month in the past year	10: no HH members sick 9–7: HH member(s) mildly ill and recovered 6–4: multiple household members sick with short-term loss of income 3–0: multiple HH members sick with longer-term loss of livelihood
HH members attending or completed: primary school, vocational, literacy, financial management, trade skill, agricultural or fishing programs	10: multiple HH members attending or completed schooling or resettlement livelihood programs 9–6: at least two HH members having completed or participated in the livelihood program 5–2: one HH member completed or attending 1–0: no or one HH member completing primary school but not participating in programs
Social Capital Score	
HH members participating in "social groups": group resource collection, attend spiritual gatherings, savings groups, civic groups or other	2 points for each social network to a maximum of 10
HH's perception of being integrated into the community	10: very integrated 5: somewhat integrated 0: not at all integrated
Natural Capital Score	
HH has access to agricultural land (total ha and location)	10: multiple farming areas 5: one farming area (impacted by the project) 0: no land

(Continued)

Table 9.2 (Continued)

Indicators	Scoring Criteria (10-Point Scale with 10 Being the Best Scenario and 0 the Worst)	
HH has access to common property resources disaggregated by type (land and marine – fishing and intertidal collection, bush collection, water, wood)	2 points for access to each type (water, wood, land, marine areas, bush collection) to a maximum of 10	
Physical Capital Score		
HH owns home	10: owns home	5: rents a home
	3: borrowing home	0: no home
HH has access to energy	10: electricity	8: small solar
	5: wood	0: no electricity
HH owns farming and fishing equipment, transportation, cellphone	1 point for each key asset to a maximum of 10	
Financial Capital Score		
Number and type of HH income sources	10–8: multiple diverse income sources	
	7–5: stable single-income source	
	4–1: unstable single-income source	
HH income	10: greater than average wage in region	
	5: average wage in region	
	0: no income	
HH debt	10: no HH debt	
	5: HH debt is manageable	
	0: debt is problematic for HH	
HH savings	10: has substantially more savings than the average regional savings	
	5: has savings typical of the region	
	0: has no savings	
Household Overall Capital Score (avg. of each capital score)	**10–8: well-established (at baseline)/ re-established (post-baseline)**	
	7–4: transitional	
	3–0: potentially vulnerable	

One of the challenges of using the SLF capital model for on-going monitoring and evaluation is the interpretation of changes in household capitals/assets and overall livelihood score over time. For example: (i) resettlement may lead to an increase (or decrease) in capitals/assets that are not especially relevant to the household livelihood system; (ii) resettlement may lead to increases in one capital/asset and decreases in another capital/asset raising questions about the fungibility of capitals/assets vis-à-vis livelihoods. In partial response to this issue, it must be recognised that the purpose of the exercise is to monitor change over time and facilitate the assessment of the implications of such changes in relation to livelihood re-establishment and development. Therefore the SLF-based scoring system should not be used in isolation. Rather it must be used in association with knowledge regarding (i) identified household livelihood categories and targeted livelihood development strategies;(ii) the evolution of livelihood systems in response to resettlement, project and broad-based area development; and (iii) adequate assessment and contextualisation of short-term, temporary (and unsustainable) contributions to specific capitals/assets (e.g., project construction phase wage employment).

To further illustrate the system, Table 9.3 provides three examples utilising the scoring system.

Development of a Household Dashboard

After the data is entered into an integrated database set-up for the baseline, the project needs to determine how best to represent the status and progress of a household in resettlement and livelihood re-establishment and development. A household dashboard that provides an integrated and holistic picture of household livelihood is useful. Figure 9.5 presents a sample baseline household dashboard.

The key components in the household dashboard are the livelihood analysis (categorisation), the household status (household analysis), key household capital indicators, livelihood activities and the resettlement entitlements:

- The **Livelihood Analysis** is determined at the time of the baseline, the analysis indicates what livelihood strategy and mix of livelihood activities the household is pursuing and sub-divides the resettlement-affected households into groups with similar strategies.
- The **Household Status** evaluation is completed based on a fulsome understanding of the household's capitals/assets at a point in time and repeated periodically. This field indicates if a household is "re-established," "transitional" or "potentially vulnerable." The chart shows the status of the households over time.
- **Household Capital/Asset Indicators** are a selection of the indicators that would be most relevant to visualising the household story, e.g., size of household, asset ownership and participation in social groups.

Table 9.3 Example Case Studies Using the Household Status Scoring System at Baseline

Scenario 1: economically displaced HH

Five household members: female-headed household with one adult daughter and three children under the age of 12. The head of the household is an intertidal collector. The adult daughter assists with childcare and collects when possible.

Two of the three children have a chronic health condition leading to hospitalisation at least twice per year. The household eats two low-quality meals per day.

The household borrows a small home (from an elderly aunt) which needs some improvements and uses wood (when available) as the main source of energy. The household has few physical assets.

The only household income is from the selling of the collected molluscs at the local market which results in less income than the average in the region. The household has a small amount of debt and does not have land or savings.

Given the limited availability of the household head and adult daughter, they have not been able to participate in any social groups within their community.

Scenario 2: physically and economically displaced HH

Seven household members: male-headed household (father), mother, maternal grandmother (blind) and five children. Father is a subsistence farmer; mother works part-time at a local hotel as a cleaner.

The household is generally healthy, but during the past year, the mother has been absent from work for several weeks due to malaria which interrupted the family's income.

The household eats three meals a day, but two of the three meals do not contain protein.

The household owns their home and works almost 1 ha of land and has very few other physical assets. The family uses wood as their main source of energy.

The household attends a mosque and has a close family and friends who live in the community.

Scenario 3: economically displaced HH

Six household members: male-headed household (father), mother, with four children attending school. Father is a farmer/businessman. Mother assists with selling produce to local businesses.

The household has regular, high-quality meals. There has been no prolonged illness in the family or disabilities.

The household owns their home; uses solar energy; and owns farming equipment, a motorcycle and a cellphone. Additionally, the household has very little debt and higher than average savings for the region.

The household owns multiple plots of land within the project footprint but also land that will be unaffected by the project. The land is farmed by family members who receive payment for their service from the household.

The household is well integrated within the community and participates in multiple civic groups and is viewed as influential community members.

(Continued)

Table 9.3 (Continued)

Household status score: 3 (potentially vulnerable)	Household status score: 7 (transitional household)	Household status score: 9 (well-established)
• Human Capital: 4 • Physical Capital: 3 • Financial Capital: 2 • Natural Capital: 4 • Social Capital: 3	• Human Capital: 7 • Physical Capital: 8 • Financial Capital: 6 • Natural Capital: 6 • Social Capital: 7	• Human Capital: 9 • Physical Capital: 9 • Financial Capital: 8 • Natural Capital: 9 • Social Capital: 9
Suggested next steps:	**Suggested next steps:**	**Suggested next steps:**
• Actively monitor household • Enrol household in the project's vulnerable people support network • Implement targeted interventions focused on "lifting" this household's status	• Monitor household • Implement targeted interventions focused on increasing the household's capitals	• Monitor household less frequently • Participation in livelihood programs is at the discretion of the household, but no targeted programs are necessary

M&E LIVELIHOOD RE- ESTABLISHMENT AND DEVELOPMENT STATUS

Household HH Number: 175　　　Recorded Residence: PLACE

John Smith	Displacement type	Livelihood analysis	Household Status
Name of head of household	Economic / Physical	Agricultural / Business	Transitional

Five Capital Indicators

Data Source: Socioeconomic Survey　　Interview Date: 29 November, 2019

Household size	7	#Working age	2

#members with disability: 1

Average # meals per day: 3

Education Levels
- Completed primary 1-7
- Completed secondary 8-10

Electricity — Access to electricity

Owned by the Household — House ownership

#of land parcels owned / cultivated: 1/1

Piped into house — Access to water

Household Status (graph)
8, 6, 4, 2 — Baseline, Period 1, Period 2, Period 3 — HH Status Reference

HH Member Participation
- Civic groups
- Savings groups
- Spiritual gatherings

HH perception of integration: 3

Asset owned by HH　#
Television	1
Solar Panel	2
Small Boat	1
Radio	1
Planked Vessel	2
Motorcycle	1
Machete	1
Hoe	1
Fishing Nets	1
Computer	1
Cellphone	1
Car	1
Bicycle	1

Livelihood Activities
	B	P2	P3	P4
Intertidal collecting	⇄	→	⇄	←
Fishing	∅	←	⇄	⇄
Household Gardening	⇄	←	⇄	←
Short fallow cassava	⇄	∅	∅	∅
Wetland rice	∅	∅	∅	∅
Perennial cash crops	⇄	∅	∅	⇄
Livestock (Poultry, Goats, Other)	∅	←	→	⇄
Collection of produce from common property resources	⇄			
Supply artisanal goods and services	∅	∅	∅	∅
Enterprise		n/a	←	⇄
Employment	⇄	⇄	⇄	⇄

Estimated income per month: 40 $

Estimated expenses per month: 41 $

Financial Reserves: 2000$

Resettlement Entitlements

Housing
	Status	Amount
Received transport allowance	Yes	60$
House #	30$	
Move data	01/06/2022	
Original community	Location A	
Participated in social preparation	Yes	
Received replacement house	Yes	

Land
	Status	Amount
Issued land title for Replacement	No	
Agricultural Land	No	
Received RAL	Yes	
Received replacement trees	No	
Received clearing allowance	Yes	1000$
Received comp for loss of crops and trees	Yes	1250$
Received comp for labour and disturbance	Yes	600$

Business
	Status	Amount
Received replacement stall	Pending	
Received temporary compensation	Pending	
Received transport allowance	Pending	

Fisher / Intertidal Collector
	Status	Amount
Received material assistance	n/a	
Received short term compensation	n/a	

Livelihood Program Participation
	Status	Amount
Animal husbandry	No	
Fisheries - new tools	No	
Fisheries - pilot programs	No	
Literacy training	No	
Trade skill training	No	
Conservation agriculture	Yes	
Financial management training	Yes	

Figure 9.5 Example of a Household Dashboard

Given space limitation, only a selection of the indicators is displayed on the summary dashboard.

- **Livelihood Activities** present a summary of household livelihood activities from baseline and periodically thereafter. For each period, both the practice of the activity and the trend are noted. Households may reduce, maintain or increase activities based on availability and competition for household resources and opportunities.
- The **Resettlement Entitlements** section is a listing of entitlements provided to displaced households and the status of completion of each.

Resettlement Close-Out/Transition to Operations

Towards the end of every resettlement program, the team will decide if closing resettlement is warranted. The timing of this decision should be made based on the final evaluation of the household livelihood (re-establishment and development) status. The final evaluation would be based on the previous progress evaluations that have occurred periodically since the baseline and any field verification data required. When the resettlement entitlements have been completed and the majority of household livelihoods are categorised as "re-established" or are on an upward trajectory, it is beneficial from both a project perspective and for the household, to transition out of the resettlement phase and back into "normal" life with on-going participation in project-sponsored area-wide livelihood programming.

Those households that have re-established their livelihoods or are on a trajectory towards re-establishment of their livelihoods will transition (if they have not already done so) to a post-resettlement life. Those households that are considered vulnerable should be referred to longer-term programs either within social investment projects being implemented by the project or to external party support systems, i.e., government, NGO or religious group support.

After completion of the final or summative evaluation, the project will engage an external assessment team to validate its findings and perform a close-out audit. The audit team utilises the data that the monitoring and evaluation function has collected and field tests desktop findings. The close-out audit typically provides confirmation that the resettlement plan commitments (both outputs and outcomes) have been achieved and provides recommendations for further action if required.

BOX 9.2 NEWMONT AHAFO GOLD COMPLETION AUDIT

The Ahafo South resettlement and livelihood restoration completion audit for Newmont Ghana Gold Limited was completed for the resettlement program of the Phase 1 Ahafo South opencast gold mine. The project's resettlement plan committed to the use of the Sustainable Livelihood Approach and in turn, the close-out audit team used the framework to report its findings. The team used various techniques including both quantitative and qualitative data collection methods and triangulation of informants. The audit defined external factors by examining macro-economic indicators, national food costs, food production and local perceptions of change. The team assessed progress against the SLF Five Capitals and completed an agricultural field study. The evaluation was holistic and broad-based and included the collection and analysis of multiple indicators to determine the success of the resettlement program.[3]

Conclusion

Despite the increasing availability of best practice guidance for resettlement monitoring and evaluation, it is recognised that for many projects achieving best practice is challenging. There are several reasons that, notwithstanding a project's best efforts, there continue to be missteps in execution:

(i) **Failure to Include M&E in Design and Planning Phases:** there is a general lack of awareness and recognition of the need to develop an M&E framework at the outset, and relatedly, there is a failure to recruit appropriate resources to develop and implement it early.

(ii) **Gap Between Design, Plan and Execution:** in some cases, the time between resettlement planning and implementation is years, and during this time, management and key personnel may change, resulting in a change to approach or implementation.

(iii) **Focus on Delivery of Front-End Land Access, Compensation and Relocation:** project managers are usually focused on front-end resettlement deliverables (outputs) as key indicators of progress versus outcome (livelihood) monitoring which is long term. This characterisation also reflects the importance of land access to the project compared with the continuity of resettlement-affected household livelihoods.

In order to follow best practice guidance, the resettlement program team is required to influence senior project managers on the importance of early and meaningful monitoring and evaluation and the necessity of resourcing the function appropriately. Ensuring an understanding and alignment of the monitoring and evaluation framework and associated principles and workplans allows prioritisation of the function along with the other key resettlement planning components.

To conclude, selecting a framework, identifying associated indicators and putting the relevant systems in place in the early stages of resettlement planning are essential for effective monitoring and evaluation. Having fewer but more informative indicators saves resources and helps to reduce household participation fatigue. Periodically, the same indicators must be collected and analysed to identify changes (positive or negative) and to make timely adjustments to interventions. For an automated comparative analysis, a simplified scoring system can be utilised and adapted for the specific project context. This system will assist the project in determining when to close the resettlement program as households "graduate" or no longer require additional resettlement program interventions. Finally, to facilitate the success of this concept, an integrated database is required with the entry of consistent and high-quality data to allow for "telling the household story."

Notes

1 Reddy, G., Smyth, E., and Steyn, M. (2015). *Land Access and Resettlement, A Guide to Best Practice.*
2 The example draws on elements from multiple resettlement projects in Asia-Pacific and Africa.
3 Barclay, R. and Salam, T., *Ahafo South Resettlement and Livelihood Restoration Completion Audit Final Report for Newmont Ghana Gold Limited* (2015).

Bibliography

ADB (2003). *Guidelines on Monitoring and Evaluation of Resettlement* (Draft). Asian Development Bank, Manila, Philippines.

Ashley, C., and Hussein, K. (2000). Developing Methodologies for Livelihood Impact Assessment: Experience of the African Wildlife Foundation in East Africa. Working Paper 129. ODI.

Barclay, R., and Salam, T. (2015). Ahafo South Resettlement and Livelihood Restoration Completion Audit Final Report for Newmont Ghana Gold Limited.   https://s24.q4cdn.com/382246808/files/doc_downloads/ operations_projects/africa/documents/Ahafo-South-Resettlement -Completion-Audit-Full-Report.pdf.

Bebbington, A. (2000). Re-Encountering Development: Livelihood Transitions and Place Transformations in the Andes. *Annals of the Association of American Geographers*, 90(3), 495–520. https://doi.org/10.1111/0004-5608.00206.

BP Tangguh Project (2005). *Land Access and Resettlement Action Plan*. BP Tangguh LARAP. BP Tangguh Project, BP Berau, Ltd.

Bury, J. (2004). Livelihoods in Transition: Transnational Gold Mining Operations and Local Change in Cajamarca, Peru. *The Geographical Journal*, 170(1), 78–91. https://doi.org/10.1111/j.0016-7398.2004.05042.x.

Department for International Development (1999). Sustainable Livelihoods Guidance Sheets. https://www.livelihoodscentre.org/documents /114097690/114438878/Sustainable+livelihoods+guidance+sheets.pdf /594e5ea6-99a9-2a4e-f288-cbb4ae4bea8b?t=1569512091877.

Livelihoods Centre (2016). Livelihoods Indicators Guide. https://www .livelihoodscentre.org/documents/114097690/114438854/LRC. +Livelihoods+Indicators+Guide+vMar2016_EN.pdf/38595574-86cc-10fc -6ab3-a9bfbf204989?t=1569397356722.

Mozambique LNG. (2016). *Resettlement Plan for Mozambique Gas Development Project (Volume 1)*. https://mzlng.totalenergies.co.mz/en/sustainability/ resettlement/resettlement-plan.

Pastuer, K. (2014). Livelihoods Monitoring and Evaluation: A Rapid Desk Based Study. Evidence on Demand. Climate & Environment Infrastructure, Livelihoods.

Price, S. (2017). Chapter 17, Livelihoods in Development Displacement – A Reality Check from the Evaluation Record in Asia. In van den Berg, R., Naidoo, I., and Tamondong, S. D. (Eds.), *Evaluation for Agenda 2030, Providing Evidence on Progress and Sustainability*. International Development Evaluation Association (IDEAS), Exeter/UK, 273–289.

Reddy, G., Smyth, E., and Steyn, M. (2015). *Land Access and Resettlement, A Guide to Best Practice*. Greenleaf Publishing, Sheffield/UK.

Steyn Reddy Associates. *Land Access & Resettlement Insight Series 6: Baseline Data Collection & Analysis*.

Steyn Reddy Associates. *Land Access & Resettlement Insight Series 18: Monitoring and Evaluation*.

Part VI

CONCLUSION

10

TOWARDS AN INTEGRATED VIEW OF LIVELIHOOD RE-ESTABLISHMENT AND DEVELOPMENT

In this chapter

DOI: 10.4324/9781003358725-16

Introduction

For public- and private-sector projects securing land access through a process of involuntary displacement and resettlement, the restoration of the resettlement-affected households' livelihoods is recognised as a persistent failure. More often than not, this failure leads to the impoverishment of the people who (have to) make way for project development.

This book was written to contribute to improved practice in livelihood restoration and hence livelihood outcomes for displaced households and communities. It draws on the experience of resettlement associated with mega-projects that have the potential to be transformational at the landscape-level, applied research in rural (agricultural) development and the promotion of livelihood development in the humanitarian and development assistance fields.

Although many reasons for the failure of livelihood restoration are identified, the book argues that the failure to adequately conceptualise livelihoods and define a framework through which livelihood re-establishment and development will occur drives shortcomings in livelihood assessment, the integration of livelihood considerations into the entire resettlement process and ultimately the re-establishment and development of livelihood activities.

It was proposed that the 'livelihood improvement or at the least, restoration' objective of international standards for land acquisition, involuntary displacement and resettlement be replaced with a 'livelihood re-establishment and development' objective, reflecting changes in both the resettlement-affected households' objectives and aspirations and the context in which livelihoods are secured. Furthermore, recognising that the resettlement-affected population is a subset of the project-affected population defined by the project requirement for land access, and that livelihood development is dependent on a more broadly defined enabling environment, the book argued for the adoption of a *resettlement with development approach*. Practically this means that interventions required to implement resettlement may be delivered outside the immediate resettlement footprint and, consequently, may simultaneously benefit the broader population.

The book draws from humanitarian and development literature, projects and practice to articulate livelihood concepts and definitions and present livelihood models. These models can be used to:

(i)   provide a basis for the conceptualisation of livelihoods
(ii)   inform description and assessment of livelihoods

(iii)   apply the livelihood re-establishment and development objective to the entire resettlement process
(iv)   provide a framework for and inform possible areas of intervention to support the re-establishment and development of livelihoods
(v)   help design and deliver livelihood programs aimed at re-establishment and development of livelihood activities
(vi)   design a livelihood-focused monitoring and evaluation system

Subsequent chapters address these areas in turn. While the Sustainable Livelihoods Framework is used throughout the book, it is important to recognise that the purpose is to elucidate the approach rather than recommend a particular model.

Thus the book sets out the basis for the application of a consistent, systematic and holistic systems approach to livelihood re-establishment and development associated with involuntary displacement and resettlement.

This final chapter elucidates the implications of applying a systems approach for the sponsor/proponent of involuntary displacement and resettlement, setting out operational considerations which are critical to success. These include:

- project management support
- adequacy of human resource commitment to resettlement
- application of a livelihood re-establishment and development perspective in the assessment, design, planning and execution of resettlement
- re-establishment and development of livelihood activities
- monitoring and evaluation

These operational considerations should be read in conjunction with the strategic considerations set out in Chapter 2.

Operational Recommendations Supporting Livelihood Re-establishment and Development

Project Management Support

For project management, securing land access for project development is the primary goal and resettlement is therefore the means to an end. As a consequence, for senior project management leaders resettlement may be deemed 'complete' once compensation has been paid, relocation has occurred and land access is secured and no longer on the critical path for project delivery. The linear resettlement process that illustrates the resettlement process from assessment through design, planning and execution generally reflects this emphasis, with the mechanics and challenges of land access and relocation taking precedence over management of the social impacts of resettlement. However there is no reason why efforts to create an enabling environment for livelihood re-establishment and development could not be started much earlier in the resettlement process.

Accordingly, the importance of project management awareness and understanding of resettlement and particularly the livelihood re-establishment and development objective is fundamental to ensuring commitment, design, scheduling and resources for the entire resettlement process. Key issues include:

- inclusion of resettlement and livelihood specialists in resettlement diagnosis and design focusing on:
  - guiding assessment of the rural environment and rural livelihoods of the resettlement-affected population
  - discussions involving site selection for the project and resettlement and land access (including options for multi-site or dispersed resettlement)
  - design and construction of replacement village and replacement housing including approaches to design, the evaluation of options and the approach to construction
- definition of livelihood development programs focusing on: the creation of an enabling environment for livelihood re-establishment and development (potentially ahead of activities relating to land access and relocation and project construction); the interface between project construction and resettlement; the duration of livelihood development programming and the need to ensure continuity beyond construction as well as commitment to longer-term programs (e.g., education, vocational training) aimed at enabling the resettlement-affected population to manage in an environment that has changed due to project development and induced area development.
- definition of key livelihood targets, the progressive integration of the resettlement-affected population with broader socio-economic

investment/livelihood development programs in the Project Area of Influence, commitment to on-going monitoring and evaluation and, where necessary, support of corrective or additional measures.

In summary the project resettlement team and the resettlement-affected population need project management and leadership to demonstrate their support for achieving livelihood re-establishment and development objectives and outcomes and their understanding of the need for a landscape approach; adequate upfront assessment, design and planning; and livelihood development programming over an extended period of time.

Resettlement Organisation and Human Resource Requirements

This book demonstrates the centrality and importance of livelihood re-establishment and development to the mitigation of impoverishment risks and ultimately the success of resettlement beyond immediate delivery of land access, compensation and relocation. Based on this, it is recommended that the resettlement project create a dual management structure comprising (i) resettlement land access and relocation and (ii) resettlement livelihood re-establishment and development, the latter to be led by a livelihood development specialist from the outset through to the formal closure of the resettlement project (refer to Section 'Applying a Livelihood Re-establishment and Development Perspective in Design') and beyond. The dual structure ensures a focus on the mechanics of land access on the one hand and on livelihood re-establishment and development (including the broader enabling environment) on the other. By ensuring a focus on livelihoods from beginning to end, the project manages the risk of loss of attention as immediate project land access demands necessitate require a greater focus on land access and relocation or once project land access has been secured.

Finally, it is noted that projects often front-load resettlement projects to ensure timely land access. In such circumstances, while the resettlement process identifies livelihood re-establishment and development as a post-relocation activity, it is not uncommon to lose key staff once land access is secured. This means that the most complex and time-consuming aspect of resettlement faces a loss of on-the-ground relationships and networks, knowledge and expertise and on-going management interest. As such, there is a need to ensure recognition that, as the resettlement process is executed, the type of expertise required may evolve, but the resource requirement remains.

Adequacy of Assessment of Rural Environment and Rural Livelihoods and Socio-Economic Baseline

The resettlement-affected communities are a subset of the local population, defined by the project's need for land; impacts on the area, access to and/or use of land and natural resources; or need to mitigate health and safety impacts that make continued in situ residence and use of land and resources impossible.

To properly understand the lives and livelihoods of the resettlement-affected population requires that we locate them within the broader context that helps define how they (and the general population inhabiting the same area) live and secure their livelihoods. In this way, an assessment of the environment, livelihood systems and markets in the broader Project Area of Influence is required. Beyond understanding the pre-project context, an assessment of the broader context is also required to identify opportunities for economic diversification and market-based interventions that may help unlock entry, development and/or expansion of economic activities that have the potential to promote livelihood development opportunities for both the resettlement-affected population and the broader population. In this sense interventions to promote livelihood re-establishment and development may be implemented well beyond the resettlement-affected communities themselves.

A comprehensive assessment of the environment and livelihoods of the resettlement-affected population, a socio-economic baseline and a census of the resettlement-affected population form the backbone for effective and successful resettlement design, planning and implementation. The livelihood assessment, socio-economic baseline and census together inform a comprehensive understanding of the affected households' and communities' livelihood systems and facilitate the assessment of resettlement impacts; allow integration of livelihood considerations into resettlement design; inform analysis of entitlement and compensation; and guide the re-establishment and development of livelihood activities. Furthermore, to the extent possible and useful, categorisation and grouping of households by livelihood systems allow for more targeted and tailored livelihood re-establishment and development interventions.

Applying a Livelihood Re-establishment and Development Perspective in Design

The livelihood re-establishment and development objective must be applied to the entire resettlement process. Such application will pre-empt failure in critical areas, most notably: the identification of replacement land and/or understanding both the practicality and sustainability of mitigations; the design of replacement housing; the capacity and resources of government to assume management and operational responsibility for settlements, infrastructure, services and utilities; and informing improved outcomes in the re-establishment and development of livelihood activities.

The focus on the mechanics of land access (defined by land access and compensation, replacement housing and relocation) together with the characterisation of resettlement as a linear process that places livelihood re-establishment and development occurring as a final step following relocation must be challenged. A new model/process that combines a linear land access, compensation and relocation process with a non-linear process for livelihood re-establishment and development is required (Figure 10.1). This model calls for the simultaneous creation of two teams, the first concerned with entitlement and the 'mechanics' of land access, compensation, replacement housing and relocation and the second with household and community development and the re-establishment and development of livelihoods. In this way the first team creates the basis for departure; the second team creates the foundation for re-establishment and development.

Such a model will allow for the application of a livelihood re-establishment and development lens to the entire resettlement process and must simultaneously allow for the non-linear implementation of livelihood re-establishment and development activities commencing ahead, or at the start, of the resettlement process. This might include a more community-driven development approach to be implemented at the outset as a preparatory step towards more targeted initiatives to improve adult literacy, financial management, traditional livelihood activities, micro- and small enterprise development, training for project-related employment, etc. Put

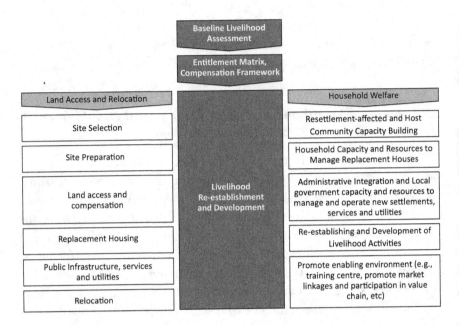

Figure 10.1 Alternative Model for Livelihood Re-establishment and Development in Resettlement

differently, if it is recognised that capacity building and behaviour change only occur over an extended period, the need to start as early as possible is critical.

The recommendation for a dual structure can be taken one step further by the early creation of a separate rural livelihood development function responsible for both the resettlement-affected population and the population in the Project Area of Influence. Such a function would:

- recognise that the early assessment of the rural environment required for resettlement is relevant to the livelihood development of the population in the Project Area of Influence.
- recognise that many of the livelihood interventions relevant to the resettlement-affected population are of relevance to and would therefore also benefit the broader population.
- recognise that some of the proposed interventions should be implemented outside of the 'resettlement footprint' either because the intervention point lies outside the footprint (e.g., commodity value chain and market development) or because some planned resettlement

interventions can be better located so as to simultaneously serve the broader population (e.g., agricultural nursery, training centres), thereby increasing integration and likelihood of on-going use.

- facilitate the continuity of interventions beyond the end of the resettlement and project construction period and where necessary progressive integration with other project socio-economic development programs. Such continuity would demonstrate project commitment to the resettlement-affected population beyond securing land for project development.
- provide a more equal distribution of livelihood benefits to the project-affected population from the start, thereby reducing jealousy from communities not receiving resettlement benefits and improving the social licence.

Finally the adoption of a livelihood re-establishment and development objective must encourage:

(i) greater coordination and collaboration with development practitioners.
(ii) greater innovation in promoting livelihood re-establishment and development by adopting a 'resettlement and development' or 'resettlement as a development opportunity' approach – where resettlement, project development and broader area development occur simultaneously, the project-affected population must be able to avail different and diverse opportunities at different times.

Re-establishment and Development of Livelihood Activities

The context, project characteristics and scope of resettlement should be combined with an understanding of development to define the relevant planning horizon for achieving livelihood re-establishment and development. Time frames of 5–10 years may be appropriate for major resettlement projects involving physical and economic displacement, allowing: (i) completion of project (and resettlement) construction activities and facilitating the demonstration of the sustainability of livelihoods either independent of the project or, in the case of long-life projects, in the project operations phase; and (ii) sufficient time to evaluate the success of livelihood interventions across seasons and attainment of a positive livelihood development trajectory as household livelihood strategies and circumstances (e.g., family structure [and especially labour availability], income requirements, welfare) change. It should be noted that such time frames need not imply that the resettlement program must continue for the entire period. As demonstrated above, structures that allow for transfer and continuity of livelihood development programming may enable the closure of resettlement. Where such structures exist, due consideration of both when and how to transition households from resettlement to area-wide development is critical.

While the project proponent is typically the driver of land access, compensation and relocation, the resettlement-affected population must be empowered to assume ownership and responsibility for the development of livelihood re-establishment and development strategies including identification, evaluation, selection and implementation of agreed re-establishment and development of livelihood activities.

The identification of 'livelihood categories/groups' in the resettlement-affected population allows the project to develop bespoke livelihood re-establishment and development programs tailored to the livelihood strategies of different groups. Decisions to investigate and develop tailored solutions rely on the existence of a critical mass of people.

Proposed strategies for re-establishment and development of livelihood activities need a comprehensive evaluation to assess their fit with the resettlement-affected households, specifically household livelihood categories/groups, their anticipated resettlement recovery and development process and availability of resources (labour, land, capital) vis-à-vis the proposed livelihood re-establishment and development activities. Where the proposed activities involve direct competition for resources (e.g., with labour and opportunities for project employment that may compete with the re-establishment of traditional livelihood activities), the project may need to review the availability of opportunities over time to ensure accessibility to resettlement-affected households on their terms. It may be that different households – at different periods of their family cycle – are able to participate at different times.

Monitoring and Evaluation

Early development and consistent application of a monitoring and evaluation system focused on livelihood re-establishment and development can help drive the delivery of the objective in design, planning and implementation and facilitate the close-out of the resettlement program. Early development and on-going application of the monitoring and evaluation system require dedicated and qualified human resources to be engaged from the outset such that they participate in the livelihood assessment and comprehensive socio-economic baseline survey and understand the basis for individual household re-establishment and development narratives. The addition of resettlement progress and livelihood re-establishment and development indicators to the household story and their consistent tracking throughout the resettlement process can inform continuous improvement, pro-active management of identified challenges and ultimately closure of resettlement programming.

Conclusion

This book has sought to 'put livelihoods first' by re-framing the approach to land access, involuntary displacement and livelihood re-establishment and development.

This book aims to promote livelihood development by:

- bringing together experience from applied research in development, humanitarian and development assistance and resettlement to inform livelihood re-establishment and development
- promoting a landscape-level resettlement and development approach
- recognising project and induced development potential impacts on livelihood re-establishment and development
- promoting the use of a holistic systems-based livelihood model including livelihood assessment, diagnosis and design of resettlement, re-establishment and development of livelihood activities and monitoring and evaluation
- placing greater emphasis on site selection, design of replacement housing and settlements, handover to government administration and re-establishment and development of livelihood activities
- placing greater emphasis on inter-generational and intra-community considerations in the resettlement
- placing greater emphasis on promoting the attainment of positive livelihood trajectories

In any project the combination of context, people and project are unique. While lessons from resettlement livelihood success stories can be identified and shared, it is as well to recognise that success is often specific to circumstance and as such should be interrogated for applicability and subsequently adapted. In this sense this book has sought to focus on strategic issues and processes that, when applied, may lead to improved livelihood outcomes.

This book has placed emphasis on the overall approach to livelihood re-establishment and development, focusing on both strategic and operational dimensions that, when applied, will lead to broad-based general improvement in livelihood outcomes. While lessons from resettlement livelihood success stories can be identified and shared, it is as well to recognise that such success probably derives from a combination of circumstance and approach. As such success stories should be interrogated before being adapted. Finally this book was written to increase general access to livelihood resources, improve awareness and knowledge and promote discourse about livelihood re-establishment and development. It is hoped that these outcomes will lead to improved design, planning and execution of land access and resettlement and in this way, improved livelihood outcomes for those that (have to) make way for project development.

BIBLIOGRAPHY

ADB (1998). *A Handbook on Resettlement, A Guide to Good Practice*. Asian Development Bank, Manila, Philippines.

ADB (2003a). *Gender Checklist Resettlement*. Asian Development Bank, Manila, Philippines.

ADB (2003b). *Guidelines on Monitoring and Evaluation of Resettlement* (Draft). Asian Development Bank, Manila, Philippines.

ADB (2010). *Safeguard Requirements 2: Involuntary Resettlement. Safeguard Policy Statement*. Asian Development Bank, Manila, Philippines.

ADB (2012). *Involuntary Resettlement Safeguards, A Planning and Implementation Good Practice Sourcebook* (Draft Working Document). Asian Development Bank, Manila, Philippines.

Ahearn, A., and Namsrai, B. (2022). Filling a Hole? Compensation for Mining-Induced Losses in the South Gobi. In Sternberg, T., Toktomushev, K., and Ichinkhorloo, B. (Eds.), *The Impact of Mining Lifecycles in Mongolia and Kyrgyzstan, Political, Social, Environmental and Cultural Contexts*. Routledge.

African Development Bank (2013). *Operational Safeguard 2 – Involuntary Resettlement: Land Acquisition, Population Displacement and Compensation, Integrated Safeguards System – Policy Statement and Operational Safeguards.* Abidjan, Cote D'Ivoire.

African Development Bank Group (2015). *The African Development Bank's Involuntary Resettlement Policy; Review of Implementation.* Abidjan, Cote D'Ivoire.

African Union (2009). Convention for the Protection and Assistance of Internally Displaced Persons in Africa (Kampala Convention).

AIIB (2021). ESS2: Land Acquisition and Involuntary Resettlement, Environmental and Social Framework.

Anon (2008). *Sustainable Livelihoods Approaches – What Have We Learnt.* ESRC Research Seminar.

Ashley, C., and Carney, D. (1999). *Sustainable Livelihoods: Lessons from Early Experience.* Department for International Development.

Ashley, C., and Hussein, K. (2000). Developing Methodologies for Livelihood Impact Assessment: Experience of the African Wildlife Foundation in East Africa. Working Paper 129. ODI.

Bainton, N. A., Owen, J. R., and Kemp, D. (2018, September 5). Mining, Mobility and Sustainable Development: An Introduction. *Special Edition Sustainable Development, 26.*

Barclay, R., and Salam, T. (2015). Ahafo South Resettlement and Livelihood Restoration Completion Audit Final Report for Newmont Ghana Gold Limited. https://s24.q4cdn.com/382246808/files/doc_downloads/operations_projects/africa/documents/Ahafo-South-Resettlement-Completion-Audit-Full-Report.pdf.

Bebbington, A. (1999). Capitals and Capabilities: A Framework for Analyzing Peasant Viability, Rural Livelihoods and Poverty. *World Development, 27*(2), 2021–2044. https://doi.org/10.1016/S0305-750X(99)00104-7.

Bebbington, A. (2000). Re-Encountering Development: Livelihood Transitions and Place Transformations in the Andes. *Annals of the Association of American Geographers, 90*(3), 495–520. https://doi.org/10.1111/0004-5608.00206.

Bebbington, A., and Humphreys Bebbington, D. (2018). Mining, Movements and Sustainable Development: Concepts for a Framework. *Sustainable Development, 26*(5), 441–449. https://doi.org/10.1002/sd.1888.

Bennett, O., and McDowell, C. (2012). *Displaced: The Human Cost of Development and Resettlement. Studies in Oral History.* Palgrave MacMillan.

Boudreau, T. (2002). *Practitioners' Guide to Household Economy Approach.* Save the Children.

BP Tangguh Project (2005). *Land Access and Resettlement Action Plan.* BP Tangguh LARAP. BP Tangguh Project, BP Berau, Ltd.

BRAC (2021). Graduation Overview. https://bracupgi.org/research-and -resources/economic-inclusion/graduation-overview/.

Brockleby, M. A., and Fisher, E. (2003). Community Development in Sustainable Livelihoods Approaches – An Introduction. *Community Development Journal,* 38(3), 185–198.

Bury, J. (2004). Livelihoods in Transition: Transnational Gold Mining Operations and Local Change in Cajamarca, Peru. *The Geographical Journal,* 170(1), 78–91. https://doi.org/10.1111/j.0016-7398.2004.05042.x.

Bury, J. (2007). Mining Migrants: Transnational Mining and Migration Patterns in the Peruvian Andes. *The Professional Geographer,* 59(3), 378–389. https://doi.org/10.1111/j.1467-9272.2007.00620.x.

CARE (2002). *Household Livelihood Security Assessments: A Toolkit for Practitioners.* Prepared for the PHLS Unit by: TANGO International Inc., Tucson, AZ.

Carney, D. (2002). *Sustainable Livelihoods Approaches: Progress and Possibilities for Change.* DFID, London.

Carney, D., Drinkwater, M., Rusinow, T., Neefjes, K., Wanmali, S., and Singh, N. (1999). *Sustainable Livelihoods Approaches Compared, A Brief Comparison of the Livelihoods Approaches of the UK Department for International Development (DFID), CARE, Oxfam and the United Nations Development Program (UNDP).* DFID, London.

Castillo, G., and Brereton, D. (2018). Large-Scale Mining, Spatial Mobility, Place-Making and Development in the Peruvian Andes. *Sustainable Development,* 26(5), 461–470.

Catley, A., Lind, J., and Scoones, I. (Eds.). (2013) *Pastoralism and Development in Africa, Dynamic Change at the Margins.* Routledge.

Cernea, M. M. (1988). Involuntary Resettlement in Development Projects, Policy Guidelines in World Bank-Financed Projects, World Bank Technical Paper No 80. The International Bank for Reconstruction and Development, The World Bank, 1818 H Street, N.W., Washington, DC.

Cernea, M. M. (1993). *Anthropological Approaches to Resettlement: Policy, Practice and Theory.* Routledge.

Cernea, M. M. (1997). The Risks and Reconstruction Model for Resettling Displaced Populations. *World Development,* 25(10), 1569–1587.

Cernea, M. M., and Maldonaldo, J. K. (2018). *Challenging the Prevailing Paradigm of Displacement and Resettlement: Risks, Impoverishment, Legacies, Solutions.* Routledge.

Cernea, M. M., and Mathur, H. M. (2008). *Can Compensation Prevent Impoverishment? Reforming Resettlement through Investments and Benefit Sharing.* Oxford University Press.

Cernea, M. M., and McDowell, C. (2000). *Risks and Reconstruction, Experiences of Resettlers and Refugees.* International Bank for Reconstruction and Development/World Bank, Washington, DC.

Chambers, R. (1983). *Rural; Development, Putting the Last First.* Routledge.

Chambers, R. (1999). *Whose Reality Counts? Putting the First Last,* 2nd edition. Intermediate Technology Publications.

Chambers, R., and Conway, G. (1992). Sustainable Rural Livelihoods: Practical Concepts for the 21st Century. IDS Discussion Paper 296. IDS, Brighton.

Cramb, R. A., Gray, G. D., Gummert, M., Haefele, S. M., Lefroy, R. D. B., Newby, J. C., Stür, W., and Warr, P. (2015). Trajectories of Rice-Based Farming Systems in Mainland Southeast Asia. Australian Centre for International Agricultural Research (ACIAR) Monograph No. 177.

Cramb, R. A., Purcell, T., and Ho, T. C. S. (2004). Participatory Assessment of Rural Livelihoods in the Central Highlands of Vietnam. *Agricultural Systems,* 81(3), 255–272.

De Haan, L. J. (2012). The Livelihood Approach: A Critical Exploration. *Erdkunde,* 66(4), 345–357.

De Haan, L. J. (2017). *Livelihoods and Development, New Perspectives, Koninkjlijke.* Brill, Leiden, The Netherlands.

De Wet, C. (2005). *Development-Induced Displacement: Problems, Policies and People* (Studies in Forced Migration, Vol. 18). 1st edition.

Department for International Development (1999). Sustainable Livelihoods Guidance Sheets. https://www.livelihoodscentre.org/documents/114097690/114438878/Sustainable+livelihoods+guidance+sheets.pdf/594e5ea6-99a9-2a4e-f288-cbb4ae4bea8b?t=1569512091877.

Doloi, H., and Donovan, S. (2020). *Affordable Housing for Smart Villages.* Routledge, New York.

Doloi, H., Green, R., and Donovan, S. (2019). *Housing, Planning and Infrastructure for Smart Villages.* Routledge, New York.

EBRD (2014). *Performance Requirement 5, Land Acquisition, Involuntary Resettlement and Economic Displacement.*

EBRD (2017). *Resettlement Guidance and Good Practice.*

EIB (2013). *Environmental and Social Handbook.*

EIB (2022). *Environmental and Social Standards, 6. Involuntary Resettlement.*

Ellis, F., and Allison, E. (2004). *Livelihood Diversification and Natural Resource Access.* Livelihood Support Programme, FAO, Rome.

Emery, M., Gutierrez-Montes, I., and Fernandez-Baca, E. (2013). *Sustainable Rural Development, Sustainable Livelihoods, and the Community Capitals Framework.* Routledge, New York.

Equator Principles (2020). *Equator Principles EP4.*

European Commission (2004). *Aid Delivery Methods, Volume 1.* Project Cycle Management Guidelines.

FAO (2015). Environmental and Social Management Guidelines. ESS 6 Involuntary Resettlement and Displacement.

FAO & ILO (2009). *The Livelihood Assessment Tool-Kit, Analysing and Responding to the Impact of Disasters on the Livelihoods of People.* FAO, Rome and ILO, Geneva.

Frankenburger, T. (1996). *Measuring Household Livelihood Security: An Approach for Reducing Absolute Poverty.* Paper prepared for the Applied Anthropology Meetings, March 27–30, 1996. Baltimore, MD.

Giovanetti, F. (2009). Guidance Note on Urban Resettlement, Report No. 49000-IN. World Bank.

Global Protection Cluster Working Group (2010). *Handbook for the Protection of Internally Displaced Persons.* Global Protection Cluster (GPC).

Haidar, M. (2009). *Sustainable Livelihood Approaches, the Framework, Lessons Learnt from Practice and Policy Recommendations.* UNDP.

Holling, C. S. (1973). Resilience and Stability of Ecological Systems. *Annual Review of Ecological Systems,* 4(1), 1–23.

Holzmann, P., Boudreau, T., Holt, J., Lawrence, M., and O'Donnell, M. (2008). *The Household Economy Approach, A Guide for Programme Planners and Policy-Makers.* Save the Children.

HRC (2019). *Guidelines for the Implementation of the Right to Adequate Housing.* Report of the Special Rapporteur on Adequate Housing as a Component of the Right to an Adequate Standard of Living, and on the Right to Non-Discrimination in This Context. United Nations.

IBRD/World Bank (2004). *Involuntary Resettlement Sourcebook, Planning and Implementation in Development Projects.* The World Bank, Washington, DC.

ICMM (2015). *Land Acquisition and Resettlement: Lessons Learned.* ICMM, London.

IDB (2019). *Involuntary Resettlement in IDB Projects. Principles and Guidelines.*

IDB (2021). *Guidelines for Environmental and Social Performance Standard 5: Land Acquisition and Involuntary Resettlement.*

IFC (2002). *Handbook for Preparing a Resettlement Action Plan.* International Finance Corporation, Washington, DC.

IFC (2009). *Projects and People, A Handbook for Addressing Project-Induced in-Migration.* International Finance Corporation, Washington, DC.

IFC (2012). *IFC Performance Standards on Environmental and Social Sustainability.* International Finance Corporation, Washington, DC.

IFC (2013). *Addressing Project Impacts on Fishing-Based Livelihoods, A Good Practice Handbook.* International Finance Corporation, Washington, DC.

IFRC (2010). *IFRC Guidelines for Livelihoods Programming.* International Federation of Red Cross and Red Crescent Societies, Geneva.

Inspection Panel/World Bank Group (2016). *Involuntary Resettlement, Emerging Lessons Series No. 1.* International Bank for Reconstruction and Development/The World Bank, Washington, DC.

Intersocial Consulting (2013). *Land Acquisition and Resettlement Benchmarking Report.* Intersocial Consulting.

Krantz, L. (2001). *The Sustainable Livelihoods Approach to Poverty Reduction, an Introduction.* SIDA.

Levine, S. (2014). How to Study Livelihoods: Bringing a Sustainable Livelihoods Framework to Life. Working Paper No 22 Secure Livelihoods Research Consortium Overseas Development Institute, London.

Lillywhite, S., Kemp, D., and Sturman, K. (2015). *Mining, Resettlement and Lost Livelihoods: Listening to the Voices of Resettled Communities in Mualadzi, Mozambique.* Oxfam, Melbourne.

Livelihoods Centre (2016). Livelihoods Indicators Guide. https://www .livelihoodscentre.org/documents/114097690/114438854/LRC. +Livelihoods+Indicators+Guide+vMar2016_EN.pdf/38595574-86cc-10fc -6ab3-a9bfbf204989?t=1569397356722.

Loison, S. A. (2015). Rural Livelihood Diversification in Sub-Saharan Africa: A Literature Review. *The Journal of Development Studies*, 51(9), 1125–1138. https://doi.org/10.1080/00220388.2015.1046445.

OCHA (2001). *Guiding Principles on Internal Displacement*. United Nations. https://www.unhcr.org/en-us/protection/idps/43ce1cff2/guiding-principles-internal-displacement.html.

OCHCR (2011). *Guiding Principles on Business and Human Rights*.

OHCHR and UN-Habitat (2005). Indigenous Peoples' Right to Adequate Housing, A Global Overview. United Nations Housing Rights Programme Report No. 7.

UHCHR (2009). Basic Principles and Guidelines on Development-Based Evictions and Displacement, Annex 1 of the Report of the Special Rapporteur on Adequate Housing as a Component of the Right to an Adequate Standard of Living. A/HRC/4/18. United Nations.

UNHCR (2011). *UNHCR Resettlement Handbook*. UNHCR, Switzerland.

McCabe, J. T. (2004). *Cattle Bring Us to Our Enemies: Turkana Ecology, Politics and Raiding in a Disequilibrium Environment*. University of Michigan Press, Ann Arbor, MI.

McDowell, C. (1996). *Understanding Impoverishment: The Consequences of Development-Induced Development* (Refugee and Forced Migration Studies, Vol. 2). 1st edition.

McDowell, C. (2002). Involuntary Resettlement, Impoverishment Risks and Sustainable Livelihoods. *Australian Journal of Disaster and Trauma Studies*, 6(2).

Mphande, F. A. (2016). *Infectious Diseases and Rural Livelihood in Developing Countries*. Springer Science+Business Media, Singapore.

Moser, C. (2005). Assets, Livelihoods and Social Policy. Arusha Conference, "New Frontiers of Social Policy"– December 12–15, 2005.

Mozambique LNG. (2016). *Resettlement Plan for Mozambique Gas Development Project (Volume 1)*. https://mzlng.totalenergies.co.mz/en/sustainability/resettlement/resettlement-plan.

Nakayama, M., and Fujikura, R. (2014). *Restoring Communities Resettled After Dam Construction in Asia*. Routledge.

Oliver-Smith, A. (2009). *Development and Dispossession, the Crisis of Forced Displacement and Resettlement*. School for Advanced Research Press.

Partridge, W. L., and Halmo, D. B. (2021). *Resettling Displaced Communities: Applying the International Standard for Involuntary Resettlement*. Lexington, MD.

Pastuer, K. (2014). Livelihoods Monitoring and Evaluation: A Rapid Desk Based Study. Evidence on Demand. Climate & Environment Infrastructure, Livelihoods.

Price, S. (2017). Chapter 17, Livelihoods in Development Displacement – A Reality Check from the Evaluation Record in Asia. In van den Berg, R., Naidoo, I., and Tamondong, S. D. (Eds.), *Evaluation for Agenda 2030, Providing Evidence on Progress and Sustainability*. International Development Evaluation Association (IDEAS).

Reddy, G., Smyth, E., and Steyn, M. (2015). *Land Access and Resettlement, A Guide to Best Practice*. Greenleaf Publishing.

Robinson, W. C. (2003). *Risks and Rights: The Causes, Consequences, and Challenges of Development-Induced Displacement*. The Brookings Institution-SAIS Project on Internal Displacement.

Rogers, E. (2003). *Diffusion of Innovations*, 4th edition. The Free Press, New York.

Satiroglu, I., and Choi, N. (2017). Development-Induced Displacement and Resettlement. In *New Perspectives on Persisting Problems*. Routledge.

Scoones, I. (1998). Sustainable Rural Livelihoods; A Framework for Analysis. IDS Working Paper 72.

Scoones, I. (2015). *Sustainable Livelihoods and Rural Development*. Practical Action Publishing.

Scudder, T. (2011). Development-Induced Community Resettlement. In Vanclay, F., and Esteves, A. M. (Eds.), *New Directions in Social Impact Assessment, Conceptual and Methodological Advances*. Edward Elgar.

Seaman, J., Boudreau, T., Clarke, P., and Holt, J. (2000). *The Household Economy Approach: A Resource Manual for Practitioners*. Save the Children.

Slater, R., Holmes, R., and Bhuvanendra, D. (2013). *Social Protection and Resilient Food Systems: The Role of Integrated Livelihoods Approaches*. ODI.

Smyth, E., Steyn, M., Esteves, A., Franks, D. M., and Vaz, K. (2015). Five 'Big' Issues for Land Access, Resettlement and Livelihood Restoration Practice: Findings of an International Symposium. *Impact Assessment and Project Appraisal*, 33(3), 220–225. https://doi.org/10.1080/14615517.2015.1037665.

Smyth, E., and Vanclay, F. (2017). The Social Framework for Projects: A Conceptual but Practical Model to Assist in Assessing, Planning and Managing the

Social Impacts of Big Projects. *Impact Assessment and Project Appraisal*, 35(1), 65–80. http://doi.org/10.1080/14615517.2016.1271539.

Sonneburg, D., and Munster, F. (2001). *Involuntary Resettlement, Research Topic 3: Mining and Society. Mining Minerals Sustainable Development Southern Africa*. African Institute of Corporate Citizenship, South Africa.

Steyn Reddy Associates. *Land Access & Resettlement Insight Series 6: Baseline Data Collection & Analysis.*

Steyn Reddy Associates. *Land Access & Resettlement Insight Series 18: Monitoring and Evaluation.*

Tabares, A., Londoño-Pineda, A., Cano, J. A., and Gómez-Montoya, R. (2022). Rural Entrepreneurship: An Analysis of Current and Emerging Issues from the Sustainable Livelihood Framework. *Economies*, 10(6), 142. https://doi.org/10.3390/ economies10060142.

Tangguh LNG Project. *Land Acquisition and Resettlement Action Plan, Tangguh Project, Papua/Indonesia.*

Tefera, T. L., Perret, S., and Kirsten, J. F. (2004). Diversity in Livelihoods and Farmers' Strategies in the Hararghe Highlands, Eastern Ethiopia. *International Journal of Agricultural Sustainability*, 2(2), 133–146. https://doi.org/10.1080/14735903.2004.9684573.

UNDP (2013). *Promoting Sustainable Livelihoods, Reducing Vulnerability and Building Resilience in the Drylands, Lessons from the UNDP Integrated Drylands Development Programme*. United Nations.

United Nations High Commissioner for Refugees (UNHCR) (2005). *Handbook for Planning and Implementing Development Assistance for Refugees (DAR) Programmes*. United Nations High Commissioner for Refugees (UNHCR).

UNHCR (2011). *UNHCR Resettlement Handbook*. UNHCR, Switzerland.

USAID (2016) Leveraging Economic Opportunities, Final Performance Report, ACDI/VOCA.

Vanclay, F. (2017). Project Induced Displacement and Resettlement: From Impoverishment Risks to an Opportunity for Development? *Impact Assessment and Project Appraisal*, 35(1), 2–21. http://doi.org/10.1080/14615517.2017.1278671.

Vanclay, F., Esteves, A. M., Aucamp, I., and Franks, D. M. (2015). *Social Impact Assessment: Guidance for Assessing and Managing the Social Impacts of Projects*. International Association for Impact Assessment.

Vivoda, V., Owen, J., and Kemp, D. (2017). Applying the Impoverishment Risks and Reconstruction Model to Involuntary Resettlement in the Global; Mining Sector/Mining, Resettlement and Livelihoods: Research and Practice Consortium, Centre for Social Responsibility in Mining (CSRM), Which is Part of the Sustainable Minerals Institute (SMI). University of Queensland, Australia.

Winters, P., Davis, B., Carletto, G., Covarrubias, K., Quiñones, E. J., Zezza, A., Azzarri, C., and Stamoulis, K. (2009). *Assets, Activities and Rural Income Generation: Evidence from a Multi-country Analysis.*

World Bank (2004). *Involuntary Resettlement Sourcebook, Planning and Implementation in Development Projects.* The World Bank, Washington, DC.

World Bank (2017). *ESS5 Land Acquisition, Restrictions on Land Use and Involuntary Resettlement, Environmental and Social Framework.* The World Bank, Washington, DC.

Yumiko, K., Joffre, O., Laplante, B., and Sengvilaykham, B. (2017). Coping with Resettlement: A Livelihood Adaptation Analysis in the Mekong River Basin. *Land Use Policy*, 60, 139–149.

Online Resources

https://www.livelihoodscentre.org.
https://www.ted.com/talks/ernesto_sirolli_want_to_help_someone_shut_up_and_listen?language=en.
https://www.ted.com/talks/jacqueline_novogratz_patient_capitalism.
IFRC. https://www.livelihoodscentre.org.

APPENDIX 1

A CRITIQUE OF RAP APPROACHES TO RESTORATION OF LIVELIHOODS AND LIVELIHOOD ACTIVITIES

In this chapter

Livelihood restoration is a consistent weakness in the majority of resettlement projects. The focus on the development and implementation of Resettlement Action Plans (RAPs) has promoted a focus on process over outcome. Many RAPs lack a comprehensive baseline livelihood assessment. Where RAPs include livelihood assessment, they typically include 'point-in-time' descriptions of livelihood activities without adequate description of household capabilities, assets and activities and analysis of how households combine these to pursue household livelihood strategies with intended outcomes. Further where RAPs have addressed livelihood restoration, it has generally been equated with the restoration of livelihood activities and it has too often become the final step of a resettlement action plan implemented as a linear process. Restoration of livelihood activities has been evaluated first and foremost through the delivery of inputs and consequent outputs (rather than intended outcomes) and secondly through aggregate measures (primarily household income). Taken together these observations confirm why success in meeting the livelihood restoration objective remains elusive.

Review of the Use of Livelihood Restoration Approaches in RAPs

A review of current practice in the development and implementation of Resettlement Action Plans (RAPs) demonstrates:

- RAPs neither define nor utilise a framework for livelihood restoration. Consequently it is not known whether and to what extent the livelihood restoration criterion has been used to guide the design of component resettlement and livelihood restoration activities and requisite monitoring and evaluation.
- livelihood assessment is inadequate. RAPs provide relatively generic, aggregate descriptive approaches to livelihood assessment, often only considering livelihood activities.
- generally RAPs equate livelihood restoration with the restoration of livelihood activities. This interpretation has led to livelihood restoration often being considered as a final activity that follows land acquisition and, where physical displacement occurs, relocation. While a project may characterise successful land acquisition and resettlement as the primary objective, for those (having to) make way for a project, positive livelihood trajectories are the key objective. This objective should inform and guide all aspects of land acquisition and resettlement planning, design and implementation.
- projects have relied on the expertise and experience of external consultants and NGOs (as opposed to in-house capacity) to develop plans for the restoration of livelihood activities. The lack of in-house capacity together with inadequately defined programs constrains the ability of the project to sustain a livelihood restoration and development focus, this being further exacerbated by the tendency for project interest to wane following successful land acquisition and physical relocation (see below).

- project commitment to livelihood restoration diminishes after the project has secured the site, people have been relocated (and the site is vacated) and, most importantly, the project has been developed. By the time a project becomes operational, resettlement and specifically livelihood restoration are often no longer an active project concern. Nonetheless it is typically at this time, when construction-phase employment declines and the associated cash injections into local communities diminish, that particular attention should be given to the success of livelihood restoration (particularly livelihood activities).
- in-house project capacity to oversee livelihood restoration is often limited, and typically monitoring and evaluation are poor.

RAPs and Livelihood Activities

While recognising that the livelihood restoration requirements of RAPs are context- and project-specific, a review of project Resettlement Action Plans (RAPs) description of interventions aimed at restoring livelihood activities demonstrates that:

- plans do not have a comprehensive analysis of pre-project household livelihood objectives and strategies (i.e., the ways in which households combine their capacity, assets and activities to achieve their objectives). For example, the operation of diversified livelihoods to manage food security and reduce risk/vulnerability; the rationale for household allocation of labour and resources to competing objectives and activities; life cycle analysis assessing how household livelihood strategies might change through family household life cycle. Such analysis might lead to the identification of household livelihood categories or groups comprising households with similar livelihood objectives and strategies within the resettlement-affected population. Without thorough assessment and analysis of the pre-project livelihoods and application of a diagnosis and design process, key questions regarding the livelihood restoration program are difficult to define.
- specifically these questions include the rationale for the selection of sectoral livelihood interventions – in summary, why are these interventions selected, who is the target of the interventions, what are their anticipated outcomes in relation to household and community

livelihood objectives (i.e., what is deemed to be success?), and in what time frame will these anticipated outcomes be observed. All too often projects point to the implementation of livelihood programs as an indicator of success rather than citing the programs' outcomes relative to people's livelihoods.

- plans do not conduct a vulnerability analysis for individual livelihood activities and the livelihood strategy as a whole – what are the threats to the targeted livelihood activity and thus the risks to the livelihood activity and the overall livelihood strategy. Analyses should be applied to every livelihood activity and to the whole livelihood strategy, the latter identifying potential red flags for aggregate competitive and non-viable use of resources (e.g., land, labour, income).

- plans do not explicitly consider the sustainability of every selected livelihood activity (in terms of productivity; stability (of production); vulnerability/resilience (of production); human, physical and financial resource requirements; viability, and relative contribution to overall livelihood (i.e., able to meet needs)).

- plans do not articulate the requisite conditions for the success of the intervention as well as the assumptions regarding the resettlement-affected population's participation and uptake/adoption rates in liveli-hood activities and their relative contribution to household income/ welfare.

- restoration of livelihoods has tended to be evaluated in terms of liveli-hood activities and income restoration. The use of a single measure (i.e., income) as an indicator of livelihood restoration has:

  ○ led to the minimisation of the real-life complexity of livelihoods and thereby reduced our ability to analyse factors contributing to the viability and sustainability of individual livelihood activities and overall livelihoods

  ○ implied that income streams from different activities can be treated equally and that trade-offs between such streams are deemed acceptable

  ○ encouraged on-going monitoring and evaluation and successful completion of resettlement to be defined in terms of income levels rather than livelihoods (e.g., monitoring and evaluation demon-strate that average gross incomes are above pre-project levels so one can conclude livelihood restoration has been successful).

o   plans do not adequately define what success is and fail to define and
implement an M&E framework suited to evaluating whether the
selected livelihood restoration activities are achieving the desired and
necessary outcomes. The success of livelihood activities has typically
been reported (if not evaluated) in terms of inputs delivered and activities implemented (including participation rates) rather than livelihood
outcomes. Where outcomes have been considered, the focus has been
on income generation, often reported as an 'average' figure, thereby
discounting those people who fall below the average.

APPLICATION OF THE IRR FRAMEWORK TO RESETTLEMENT ASSOCIATED WITH THE TANGGUH PROJECT, PAPUA, INDONESIA

Table A2.1 Impoverishment Risk, Assets/Resources Foregone and Restoration and Development Strategies for Tanah Merah Households Moving to Tanah Merah Baru

Risk Type/Intensity	Foregone Assets/Resources	Restoration/Development Package
1. Homelessness and Loss of Access to Village Property and Assets	Village Housing, Infrastructure, and Public Facilities	Physical Village Reconstruction
Risk Assessment: High	68 houses	• 101 new houses with land certificates
	Reduced access to land adjacent to village as a result of village expansion through either splitting of existing households or residents returning from outside the village	• 54 additional house plots for expansion
	Two wells, one spring, and tap from the Calmarine Camp	• Reticulated clean water system providing water to each house
	Meeting hall	• Replace community building • Addition of village office
	Elementary school	• Replace elementary school • Addition of kindergarten • Addition of junior high school and dormitory
	Headmasters'/teachers' quarters	• Housing facilities for teachers
	Places of worship (two churches and one mosque)	• Replace places of worship • Addition of houses for the Imam, Pastor and Priest
	Christian and Muslim cemeteries	• Provision of cemetery areas in new village • Fencing of cemeteries in Tanah Merah and agreement for ongoing maintenance during plant construction and operations, as well as for provision of periodic visitation rights for Tanah Merah Baru and Onar Baru households • Possible future relocation of cemeteries depending on requirement to expand LNG plant

(Continued)

Table A2.1 (Continued)

Risk Type/Intensity	Foregone Assets/Resources	Restoration/Development Package
	Sacred sites	• Re-design of Plant Dock to avoid disrupting the Sowai Batu Kumapa (sacred sites) • Protection of other sacred sites to extent allowed by requirements for development of LNG plant • Relocation of sacred sites where necessary • Renovation and protection of sacred site in Tanah Merah Baru
	Volleyball courts (2x)/soccer field	• Replacement and addition of sporting facilities (one soccer field, one basketball court, and three volleyball courts)
	One dirt road system	• Compacted gravel roads throughout new village
	Beach access to the Bay at high tide	• Jetty and boat dock on the Saengga river providing 24-hour access to the Bay • Two boat landings providing high tide access to the Bay

Additional assets provided:

• House for village babinsa (security official)
• Village head visitor's residence
• Cooperative office and gallery
• Health clinic
• Market shelter
• Solar and electrical power generation and distribution system
• Night street lights and dock lights
• Sewage, drainage and waste management facilities
• Prepared lots for future post office/bank/phone booth; teachers' housing; customary building

(Continued)

Table A2.1 (Continued)

Risk Type/Intensity	Foregone Assets/Resources	Restoration/Development Package
2. Homelessness and Loss of Access to Village Property and Assets	Access to Natural Resources and Income-Generating Activities	Natural Resource Use-Based Income Restoration
Risk Assessment: Moderate	• Access and use of existing gardens including area required for rotation of gardens in swidden agriculture • Access, ownership and development of gardens in new location	• Payment for productive trees cultivated on land released to theTangguh Project (completed in 1999) • Compensation for sago on land released toTangguh Project (completed in 1999) • Replacement gardens (-0.2 ha) on new village land • Technical and material assistance supporting establishment of agroforestry systems in Tanah Merah Baru and on lands to the east of the LNG plant • Facilitation of overland access to land resources (agriculture, forest, sago swamp) east of the LNG plant • Facilitation of *adat* negotiations to ensure Tanah Merah Baru households have access and use rights to Simuna forests south of new village
	• Loss of access to shoreline marine resources and artisanal fishing grounds by development of LNG plant and imposition of marine safety exclusion zone • Fishing grounds in front of Tanah Merah Baru overlap with current fishing grounds of Saengga	• Support for improved boats allowing fishermen to bypass marine safety exclusion zone and access other fishing grounds in the Bay beyond the area in front of Tanah Merah Baru • Development of overland access to areas east of the LNG plant • Facilitation of *adat* negotiations to ensure Tanah Merah Baru households have access and use rights to Simuna fishing grounds

(Continued)

Table A2.1 (Continued)

Risk Type/Intensity	Foregone Assets/Resources	Restoration/Development Package
		• Artisanal fisheries development program to increase and diversify marine produce and promote value-adding initiatives • Facilitation of entry of commercial marine produce buyers (especially prawn buyers) to the resettlement-affected communities, including buyers willing to invest in processing and storage facilities
3. Joblessness Risk Assessment: Short term: Low Long term: High	Employment Limited pre-Project employment Competition from influx (migrant) population	Employment-Related Income Restoration • Skills training and employment in village reconstruction, LNG plant construction, and plant operations • Vocational training • Project workforce recruitment and management policy and procedure providing positive discrimination for locals
4. Marginalization or 'Downward Mobility' Risk Assessment: Moderate	Small Business Business assets (7 kiosks/ businesses) Competition from influx (migrant) population	Business-related Income Restoration • Market shelter • Cooperative office • Savings/Loan program promoting improved money management • Small enterprise development programs • Savings/Loan program promoting improved money management • Small enterprise development programs

(Continued)

Table A2.1 (Continued)

Risk Type/Intensity	Foregone Assets/Resources	Restoration/Development Package
5. Risk of Increased Morbidity	Health Facilities	Health Support
Risk Assessment: Moderate	One health outpost (*posyandu*)	• Medical clinic to be shared with Saengga • Two multi-function health posts (*posyandu*) • Housing for doctor and nurses • Clean water, sewage, drainage and waste management system • Benefit from Bay-wide health program implemented by Project • Health practices mandated at Project construction sites
	Risk of migrant workforce introducing new disease	• Basic immunity of resettlement-affected communities due to coastal dwelling and regular contact with outside people • Policies and procedures for workforce management and recruitment limiting contact between workforce and local population • Health programs for Project workforce • Community health programs including malaria prevention. HIV/AIDS awareness and prevention, TB control mother ard child health, water and sanitation and improved health service delivery • Mosquito control programs around construction camps and work areas to reduce risk of outbrea<s of mosqjito-borne diseases (malaria, dengue)

(Continued)

Table A2.1 (Continued)

Risk Type/Intensity	Foregone Assets/Resources	Restoration/Development Package
6. Risk of Food Insecurity	Food Production Resources	Food Production Restoration
Risk Assessment: Moderate	Loss of standing crop at relocation and temporary loss ol access to productive gardens (until new gardens established in new sites)	• Provision of weekly and nonthly food packages for each household throughout the 12-month period following relocation • Technical and material support for the establishment and sustainable cultivation of vegetable and field crop gardens
	Loss of perennial crop harvest and temporary loss of access tc productive gardens (until replaced)	• Technical and material support for the re-establishment of perennial estate, fruit and timber crops
7. Risk of Community Disarticulation	Social Assets	Social Restoration
Risk Assessment: Moderate	Disruption and/or loss of established social systems and networks	• Establishment of and capacity-building for the Tanah Merah Resettlement Committee • Village participation in new village design • Village participation in the construction of new village and homes • Support ceremonies for riove from Tanah Merah and arrival in new locations • Provide community development training, capacity-building, and the opportunity for community participation in all development activities
	Inter-tribal jealousy and conflict regarding distribution of Project benefits	• Outreach promoting Bay-wide awareness and understanding of rationale and content of Project Resettlement Program
	Influx (migrant) population introduces new customs, culture, etc	• Projcct workforce rccruitmcnt and manogement policy ond procedure preempting in-migration to bay • Outreach promoting Bay-wide awarenftss of potfintial disruptive effects of influx (migrant) population and promoting community and government management of these issues (refer to Project Indigenous People's Development Plan)

APPENDIX 3

RESETTLEMENT ISSUES BY PROJECT FOOTPRINT

Table A3.1 Resettlement Issues by Project Footprint

Type/Location	Examples	Characteristics	Key LA and Resettlement Issues
1 **Discrete consolidated rural and/ or coastal footprint**	• Intensive Agribusiness • Infrastructure (including bridges, ports, jetties) • Power plants • Manufacturing (e.g., cement, steel) • Mining • Oil and gas (LNG facilities, storage, terminals) • Renewable energy – windfarms, solar	• Competition for limited resources including land, water • Reliance on extended input supply chain may be associated with multiple land acquisition and resettlement impacts • Land take may also be associated with the development of energy supply routes (e.g., transmission lines) and transportation routes including roads, rail and ports	• Potentially significant land take affecting household and community land and resource holdings • Potential competitive use for scarce agricultural resources – land, water • Reduced area and/or reduced access to/use of common property resources • Potential direct and indirect impacts on agriculture, grazing, inter-tidal collection and fishing • Disruption of formal and informal enterprise and business by affecting market access, causing displacement and/or creating alternative and/ or new enterprise and business opportunities in other locations, thereby affecting market share, competitiveness, etc. • Construction-phase risk of influx together with need to manage induced area development may be addressed by regional development interventions • Induced impacts (workforce, inputs, trucking, etc.) • Larger projects catalyse on-going local and regional development; concerns with elite capture; exclusion of local population from benefit sharing (i.e., capture and distribution) • Opportunities to provide employment and supply goods and services

(Continued)

Table A3.1 (Continued)

Type/Location	Examples	Characteristics	Key LA and Resettlement Issues
2 Linear Footprint			
Linear footprint	• Transport – road, rail • Transmission – canals, power • Pipelines – water, oil, gas, etc.	• Projects may be either or both urban and rural, often traverse multiple ecological zones, thereby presenting significant challenges to E&S management; urban Right-of-Way (ROW) may involve significant levels of displacement • Land take (both temporary and permanent) varies from limited (e.g., oil and gas) to significant (e.g., road, rail, transmission line) • Land take involves both partial and entire acquisition of household landholdings; partial acquisition may render remaining landholding unviable • Establishment of camps at regular intervals associated with land take and specific project impacts (direct and indirect) • Specific impacts determined by ROW requirements for safety and security, e.g., exclusion of residence and cultivation within transmission line ROW	• Public knowledge of routing creates incentives for significant opportunistic behaviour (e.g., cultivation, construction within intended ROW) • Access to and use of resources within ROW may be restricted including restrictions on occupation, deep soil cultivation, crop type and tree planting • ROW may result in the division of property and difficulties regarding household access to entire landholding; severance within and between communities and from markets, employment, etc.; reduced access to common property resources • Disruption of formal and informal enterprise and business by affecting market access, causing displacement and/or creating alternative and/or new enterprise and business opportunities in other locations, thereby affecting market share, competitiveness, etc. • Construction-phase risk of influx • For transportation infrastructure projects risk of on-going roadside (ribbon development); progressive re-configuration of rural settlements to road-side settlements; entry of migrants; entry of disease; facilitation of resource use/extraction

(Continued)

Table A3.1. (Continued)

Type/Location	Examples	Characteristics	Key LA and Resettlement Issues
3 Extensive Rural Land Take			
A Extensive rural land take	• Agriculture – food, plantations • Forestry	• Significant land take • Potentially significant conversion of land use (increased mono-culture, reduction in smallholder agriculture, reduction in natural vegetative cover) • Utilisation of (potentially scarce) resources, i.e., fertile lands, water • Landscape-level conversion of access, land use, common property resources fundamentally changes the basis of livelihoods of the affected population	• Significant land take – often characterised as involving state lands – absorbing traditional landholdings leading to loss of integrity of territorially defined ethnic groups • Significant conversion of land use associated with fundamental changes to potential livelihood strategies and activities • Reduction in common property resource base and access leading to reduced access to and use of lands for grazing, timber and non-timber forest products, etc. • Utilisation of (potentially scarce) resources, i.e., water, reducing household access to water and reducing productivity whilst increasing vulnerability • Project benefits largely associated with the development phase (e.g., rubber, palm oil) and operations-phase labour-intensive activities (e.g., weeding, harvesting) unless a smallholder component is included. Increased dependency on employment and reduced dependence on smallholder agricultural systems for subsistence and income generation • Where the activity is highly mechanised, a significant increase in scope for rural unemployment unless a smallholder component is included

(Continued)

Table A3.1 (Continued)

Type/Location	Examples	Characteristics	Key LA and Resettlement Issues
B Dams	• Hydroelectricity • Water storage • Irrigation • Flood protection	• Medium- and large-scale irrigation projects utilising potentially limited water resources • Hydroelectricity projects requiring inundation of extensive areas, loss of productive lands and potential physical displacement	• Displacement impacts households and communities located both upstream and downstream from dam • Upstream inundation of land associated with loss of highly productive resources, i.e., fertile, irrigable lands that generally cannot be replaced with equivalent resources • Potential change in aquatic resources (e.g., fish) and resource use opportunities and patterns • Potential change in livelihood strategy from one reliant on private land ownership to one reliant on access to and use of a common property resource (i.e., fishing) • Downstream changes in water regime (quantity, availability for irrigation, seasonality, flooding) associated with the potential loss of production, changes in crop selection, rejuvenation of soil fertility, etc. • Lack of direct project benefits to the land-based activities of resettlement-affected communities displaced from fertile lands

(Continued)

Table A3.1 (Continued)

Type/Location	Examples	Characteristics	Key LA and Resettlement Issues
C Resource protection	• Protected areas and conservation projects	Various types of projects that involve land take and/or reduce area and/or affected population's use of common property resources. Types of projects include: • Projects associated with the creation of large contiguous restricted-use buffer zones and exclusion zones (both land and marine) • Projects needing to establish offsets (biodiversity, forest, etc.) • Projects involving the implementation of protection/conservation areas including national parks, forests, etc.	• Utilisation of land and natural resources (often common property resources; categorised as provisioning and protective ecosystem services in IFC PS6) upon which displaced populations have historically relied upon • Low likelihood that resources within exclusion zones can be adequately assessed, replaced and compensated • At a minimum allow resettlement-affected communities to participate in regulated integrated resource management and use systems, co-management and benefit sharing that provide scope for continuous benefit stream but recognise this is likely to be inadequate and investment in alternatives will be required to reduce people–resource use conflicts

(Continued)

Table A3.1 (Continued)

Type/Location	Examples	Characteristics	Key LA and Resettlement Issues
4 Aquatic (Riverine, Lacustrine and Marine)			
• Lacustrine (lake) • Riverine • Marine – estuarine, coastal oceanic	• Near-shore and on-shore development including oil and gas, agribusiness, windfarms, etc. • Ports • Offshore facilities, e.g., oil and gas platforms, windfarms	• Projects associated with off-shore, near-shore and on-shore developments that may adversely impact fish resources, fisheries and fishing-based livelihoods through the development of infrastructure, creation of safety exclusion zones and/or operational impacts	• Significant challenges in characterising fishing-based livelihoods including participation, seasonality, role in resilience/vulnerability • Correlating fisheries productivity with project impact is difficult and should be approached scientifically and rigorously so as to avoid increased public perception that projects are fully responsible for on-going changes in fisheries, i.e., the need to define boundaries of project impact and responsibility • Difficulties in determining affected population participation rates (i.e., occasional, part-time, full-time fishermen) and impacts associated with loss of fishing ground, declining fish stock, loss of access to fishing grounds and overall loss of productivity (harvest/unit effort) • Investments in interventions that may benefit the livelihoods of all impacted households. Such investments may include access; services (ice, cold storage); markets; etc. • Mitigation measures generally aim to increase catch/unit effort and may be associated with increased resource use intensity of a smaller resource base raising concerns regarding medium-to-long-term sustainability

Appendix 4

LIVELIHOOD RE-ESTABLISHMENT AND DEVELOPMENT ISSUES AND APPROACHES BY PRIMARY LIVELIHOOD SYSTEMS

This appendix describes approaches for assessing and mitigating project impacts on primary livelihood systems, considering projects impacting sedentary agricultural systems; artisanal fisheries-based livelihood systems; and pastoral systems in turn.

Table A4.1 Displacement and Re-establishment and Development of Livelihood Activities for Projects Impacting Sedentary Agricultural Systems

Project Characteristics	Issues Associated with Displacement and Livelihood Re-establishment and Development	Approaches

• Projects occurring in the rural and coastal environment with land acquisition and/ or reduction of area and/or disruption of access to and/or use of common property resources	• Challenge in the assessment of:
	
	  ○ customary land and natural resource ownership and use patterns and identification of appropriate compensation options, i.e., have multi-layered land ownership and land/resource use rights
	
	  ○ within diversified livelihood system, failure to adequately explore livelihood strategies and objectives and identify household livelihood groups/categories
	
	  ○ the extent to which land acquisition results in the division of household property, thereby disrupting farm operations; constraining household access to entire landholding; and, the viability of remnant landholding
	
	  ○ different land owner–cultivator relationships, i.e., tenants, share-croppers, farm labourers
	
	  ○ severance within and between communities and from markets, employment, etc.
	
	• Need to distinguish between extensive and intensive agricultural systems (i.e., shifting cultivation, short fallow rotations, annual cropping, commercial agriculture). Different systems rely on different enabling environments and have very different characteristics (land and labour-use intensity, input requirements, outputs and markets)
	
	• Challenge of finding replacement land – combination of issues regarding location (access), tenure security and site characteristics (quality, quantity) as well as broader political economy of development – and often failure to adequately assess replacement land and provide adequate mitigation of shortcomings
	
	• Agricultural intensification promoted as a basis for livelihood re-establishment and development. However agricultural intensification requires the development of capacity and is associated with higher land- and labour-use intensity. As such and is neither cost-free nor does it necessarily address issues such as stability, vulnerability, risk minimisation
		• Interventions need to include raising awareness and building the capacity of resettled affected people to manage broader landscape-level change
		
		• Adequate assessment – particularly of land tenure (i.e., ownership and use rights); users; vulnerable groups
		
		• Importance of identifying and assessing land owner–cultivator relationships and providing appropriate compensation for the different groups
		
		• For land owners' identification of replacement land with suitable favourable physical and social characteristics and where limitations are identified, ensure mitigation of those limitations
		
		• Importance of tenure security although needs to recognise multiple vehicles through which this can be achieved, i.e., formal, customary
		
		• Compensation – replacement costs including productive crops (both cultivated subsistence and cash crops as well as naturally occurring)
		
		• Importance of adequate economic analysis, particularly in relation to input costs and existence of markets
		
		• Adequate assessment of impacts of project development on existing livelihood strategy, new opportunities and threats. Often restoration is neither the preferred option (of affected households) nor feasible
		
		• Relevance of livelihood re-establishment and development approaches that consider near-term re-establishment of traditional activities and medium-to-long-term transition of livelihood strategies to employment, goods and services and markets. Accordingly need to invest in enabling environment (i.e., infrastructure and market development) and education, and vocational training, to compete for semi-skilled and skilled employment opportunities as well as participate in the broader mainstream economy

(Continued)

Table A4.1 (Continued)

Project Characteristics	Issues Associated with Displacement and Livelihood Re-establishment and Development	Approaches
	• Resettlement often fails to adequately address transitional costs associated with the loss of productive crops and the time taken for their replacement, especially with perennial crops (cash crops and fruit trees) that only become substantially productive over 5–10 year period	• Ensure livelihood re-establishment and development activities are started early, i.e., resettlement not implemented as a linear process
	• Resettlement often associated with reduced access to/loss of common property resources (forest, pasture). Offset through diversification and employment fail to address the utility of common property resources to livelihoods, i.e., diversity and number of household benefits derived from such resources are under-recognised. Hence the potential for such impacts to contribute significantly to impoverishment	Interventions may include:
		○ Introduction of crop type and improved cultivars addressing subsistence or commercial agriculture and more adapted to local conditions (climate, soil)
	• Project development and operation generates an insulated economy with which traditional livelihoods cannot compete. Accordingly identify a change of livelihood strategy from a subsistence and cash crop economy to one reliant on a project-driven economy (i.e., employment, provision of goods and services to project and households with employment and greater disposable income). Local communities' livelihood strategies change to include the objective of participation in (and benefit from) the project; progressive loss of traditional knowledge and traditional production systems; increased dependency on the project	○ Improved agronomic practices – soil fertility, weed and pest management; crop rotations; multi-cropping; intercropping; etc.
		○ Improved harvest, processing and storage
		○ Interventions requiring intensification in land or labour use, i.e., a change in the agricultural system, likely to experience slow adoption
	• Project -driven and induced changes imply competition with the mainstream population better equipped to take advantage of such opportunities	○ Use of safety nets to address vulnerability associated with primary production
	• Project-induced changes leading to in-migration lead to substantial changes in the social, economic and physical environment and may also adversely affect resettlement	• Given the unpredictable nature of development catalysed by project development, ensure resettlement re-establishes base (i.e., tenure security, landholding) and provide a platform for on-going development. Importance of creating vehicles through which resettlement-affected households can seek participation in the project through employment, finance for micro- and small businesses, etc.

Table A4.2 Displacement and Re-establishment and Development of Livelihood Activities for Projects Impacting Upon Fishing-Based Livelihoods[a]

Project Characteristics	Key Issues Associated with Displacement and Livelihood Re-establishment and Development	Approaches
• Projects affecting lakes (lacustrine), rivers (riverine) and marine (estuarine, near-shore and oceanic) environments. Includes both near-shore (on land and near land) and offshore projects. • Both near-shore and offshore project activities may impact fishing-based livelihoods. • Near-shore includes mangrove conversion, changing access to fisheries, etc. • Short-term offshore impacts include disruption of household fishing activities, e.g., through dredging, seismic activities. • Long-term near-shore and offshore projects may impact access to fisheries (e.g. offshore infrastructure and exclusion zones) or productivity of fisheries	• Key challenges associated with open access/common property nature of fisheries; mobility of the resource and determination of household participation rates which vary over time and space as well as in intensity and productivity. • Correlating project activity and impact on fisheries productivity is difficult and should be approached scientifically and rigorously so as to avoid increased public perception that projects are fully responsible for on-going changes in fisheries, i.e., need to define boundaries of project impact and responsibility. • Difficulty estimating impacts associated with loss of fishing ground, declining fish stock, loss of access to fishing grounds and overall loss of productivity (harvest/ unit effort). • 'Fishing communities' often combine multiple livelihood systems in livelihood strategy including fishing, employment, business, etc. and participation may vary according to opportunity, season, etc. As such, determination of participation, eligibility and compensation are dependent on the nature of the project impact.	• On-going studies on resource use intensity, productivity, etc. critical to protecting the project from criticism • Factor in adequate lead times and resource commitment to develop an adequate understanding and assessment of fishing-based livelihoods including shoreline, near-shore and offshore activities. Different products, e.g., intertidal collection of molluscs, fish; crustaceans; seaweed; sea cucumber. Different roles and activities of men, women and children. • Baseline livelihoods and fisheries assessment including a focus on participation rates and eligibility. Factor in the nature of project impact (temporary, permanent) in defining participation and eligibility. • Impact mitigation approaches commensurate with impact and exclusive to the affected groups. • Interventions may target individual, household, group or community. ◦ Individual, household or group interventions may include – facilitating access to alternative fishing grounds (access roads; fishing camps; motorised boats); improving access to key inputs; improved hardware – boats, motors, nets; improved fishing techniques; improved post-harvest processing and storage; diversification of produce

(Continued)

Table A4.2 (Continued)

Project Characteristics	Key Issues Associated with Displacement and Livelihood Re-establishment and Development	Approaches
	• Difficulties in determining affected population participation rates (i.e., occasional, part-time, full-time fishermen) and productivity. • For group activities (e.g., beach seine fishing; offshore multi-day fishing activities involving larger vessels), the ownership of vessels, composition of crew and distribution of benefits can be complex. • Typically mitigation measures aim to increase catch/unit effort and may be associated with increased resource use intensity of a smaller resource base raising concerns regarding medium-to-long-term sustainability.	○ Where impacts affect a majority of the population consider (i) development interventions that improve the underlying constraints to fisheries and their contribution to livelihoods (e.g., supply of water and ice; supply of inputs (cool boxes, nets, outboard motors); cold storage; marketing); (ii) assessment of commodity value chains and promoting the entry of market players; (iii) promoting improved natural resource management through awareness building, establishment and operation of fisheries resource management groups, etc. • Introduction of new activities, e.g., seaweed, sea cucumber need consideration of commodity value chains including inputs and outputs, requisite volumes; required community-level organisation and management. These initiatives are often experimental and implemented on a pilot basis. Further such interventions typically have long lead times for proof of concept, participation and returns and as such are better considered as development initiatives. • Increasing access and productivity of fishing activities may threaten sustainability. Where households practice diversified livelihoods, promoting entry into alternative activities may be strategic. • Alternatively, engaging fisherfolk to assist in project activities – patrolling exclusion zones; participation in security; etc. – may provide for employment and income diversification.

ᵃIFC (2013) Addressing Project Impacts on Fishing Based Livelihoods, A Good Practice Handbook International Finance Corporation, Washington DC, USA.

Table A4.3 Displacement and Re-establishment and Development of Livelihood Activities for Project Impacting Pastoralist Systems[a]

Characteristics	Issues Associated with Displacement and Livelihood Re-establishment and Development	Approaches

• Project construction and operation in areas where pastoral activities are the primary livelihood activity, e.g., arid and semi-arid areas in Africa and Asia	• Need to recognise the complexity of the environment and the population's understanding and utilisation thereof. This complexity exists in terms of:
	
	  ○ rainfall and groundwater availability
	  ○ pasture resources (type – grass, trees, etc., including geographical location, ecosystem specificity, seasonality of growth and stock)
	  ○ species-specific pasture/water/husbandry requirements
	  ○ institutions governing (seasonal) access and use of resources
	  ○ community social structure and organisation and implications for resource access, migration and safeguards
	  ○ migration patterns to access seasonally available resources (including relation to other pastoralist groups)
	  ○ landscape-level impacts of discrete project footprints – both direct such as access to and continued existence of water sources, salt pans, seasonal pasture resources and indirect impacts that may be associated with displacing one group of pastoralists to what are traditional territories of other pastoralists
	  ○ the extreme variability of rainfall – occurrence of drought – make issues associated with vulnerability/resilience critical
	  ○ marketing
	
	• Adverse centre–periphery relations: historical and current relations between state and pastoralist societies in semi-arid and arid lands are often contested with the state: being challenged in exercising control; perceiving pastoralism as backward and thus undesirable; and potentially being a locus for and through which illegal activity (e.g., arms, drugs) occurs. Pastoral societies – by virtue of migration and mobility – challenge mainstream aspects of development and law and order (e.g., delivery of and participation in health and education services; high value of livestock resources being subject to raiding).
		Given the nature of pastoralist production systems and their resources, most interventions will have broad-based development outcomes for pastoralist communities:
		
		• On-going studies of the relationship between resource, resource use and user including spatial, temporal and relational dimensions thereof
		• On-going studies of stock and vegetation and water resources
		• Improvements in pasture and/or pasture management
		• Improvements in breeding and animal husbandry
		• Improved availability of veterinary services
		• Development and/or improvement of water sources/watering points and management thereof
		• Development and/or improvements in market linkages; processing and marketing
		• Diversification of livelihood activities and income sources – alternative produce from natural resources

(Continued)

Table A4.3 (Continued)

Characteristics	Issues Associated with Displacement and Livelihood Re-establishment and Development	Approaches
	• Recognise that pastoralist societies are increasingly heterogeneous. Progressive integration with mainstream society, associated with impacts on continuity of traditional systems; patterns of migration and settlement, with impacts on livestock management; competitive and often conflicting leadership, governance systems reflecting change within society; mixing of tenure systems and mechanisms for managing land use including how land may be allocated for project activity	
	• Assessing the impacts of land access and economic displacement extremely challenging without awareness of the nature of resources and their use thereof. Given the geographical extent of resources, land take and economic displacement impacts may be limited, but impacts on seasonality/resilience, water resources, disruption of migration pathways, etc. may be locally significant	
	• Project entry and impact (land, water, migration, employment) may exacerbate inherent conflicts within the pastoralist population and between pastoralists and the state	
	• The introduction of alternative livelihood activities – employment, enterprise – may allow diversification, but this may occur without a reduction in traditional pastoralist activities. In fact increases in modern sedentary lives may also involve the maintenance of larger herds managed by contracted herdsmen, reduced mobility and seasonal migration increasing resource pressures in a smaller area, etc. Changing patterns of settlement, migration and stock are important in terms of the sustainability of natural resources	

[a] Ahearn, A., and Namsrai, B., Filling a hole? Compensation for mining-induced losses in the South Gobi, in Sternberg, T., Toktomushev, K., and Ichinkhorloo, B., (2022) (eds). The Impact of Mining Lifecycles in Mongolia and Kyrgyzstan, Political, Social, Environmental and Cultural Contexts. Routledge; Catley, A., Lind, J., and Scoones, I., (2013) (eds). Pastoralism and Development in Africa, Dynamic Change at the Margins. Routledge UK; McCabe, J.T., (2004). Cattle Bring Us to Our Enemies: Turkana Ecology, Politics and Raiding in a Disequilibrium Environment. University of Michigan Press. Ann Arbor; Tullow Oil Kenya (2013) Stakeholder Engagement Framework, South Lokichar Basin, Turkana, Kenya. Unpublished.

INDEX

Page numbers in *italics* represent figures or photographs while page numbers in **bold** represent tables.

Printed in the United States
by Baker & Taylor Publisher Services